UNDAUNTED

A Life in Training

Hugh O'Brien

EBURY

An Ebury Press book
Published by Random House Australia Pty Ltd
Level 3, 100 Pacific Highway, North Sydney NSW 2060
www.randomhouse.com.au

First published by Ebury Press in 2014

Addresses for companies within the Random House Group can be found at
www.randomhouse.com.au/offices

National Library of Australia
Cataloguing-in-Publication Entry

O'Brien, Hugh, author.
Undaunted / Hugh O'Brien.

ISBN 978 0 85798 348 0 (paperback)

O'Brien, Hugh.
Australia. Royal Australian Navy. Clearance Diving Branch.
Divers – Australia – Biography.
Navies – Australia – Amphibious operations.
Special forces (Military science) – Australia.
Mercenary troops.

359.9840994

Cover design by Luke Causby, Blue Cork
Typeset in Adobe Caslon Pro by Midland Typesetters, Australia
Printed in Australia by Griffin Press, an accredited ISO AS/NZS 14001:2004
Environmental Management System printer

Random House Australia uses papers that are natural, renewable and recyclable
products and made from wood grown in sustainable forests. The logging and
manufacturing processes are expected to conform to the environmental regulations
of the country of origin.

For my father,
who is *as tough as I wish I was*

FOREWORD

Having personally worked as an Australian Navy clearance diver with Hugh, I knew that his book would be an honest and open-hearted depiction of a life spent where few can claim to have been. Only those of us who have served deep in the ocean's embrace will ever fully comprehend the self-doubt that it can instil. Within seconds the ocean can snuff out your flame, but to be at one with the dark blue can also provide a great sense of achievement and honour.

Hugh's story defines the adversities that all clearance divers face when challenging themselves to become a member of a brotherhood that many hope to join but few do. It made me reflect on my own career with pride that I could pass the gruelling selection processes and made me wish I could go through it all over again.

Paul de Gelder
Former paratrooper, clearance diver and author of
No Time for Fear
Director, Big Bite Enterprises
www.pauldegelder.com

CONTENTS

AUTHOR'S NOTE

To all the lads and NCOs I served with: these are my memories; it's the story as I saw it. I apologise for any inaccuracies. Any faults are my own, though I'm sure they'll be in your favour!

Prologue

ABYSS

'Fairytales don't tell children that monsters exist,
they already know they do; fairytales tell children
monsters can be killed ...'

— GK Chesterton

The waves gave me no comfort as they lapped the ever-receding shoreline. Whipped by the afternoon wind, sweat stung my eyes, and the chill of my cheeks intensified with the fading warmth of the setting sun. The page of the calendar hadn't yet turned since my last day in the military. I'd been running for hours along a Byron Bay beach, no doubt appearing to passers-by like a man training for a defining event or forthcoming goal. They were gone now, the goals, the daily need to test myself.

Mid-stride I stopped and crumpled to the ground, well short of my usual endpoint further down the beach. Quitting was something I hadn't done in over seven years. It was as if the flame that had driven me flickered and faded as suddenly as it had been ignited all those years ago.

I sat hunched on the sand. The ocean, formerly a friend, was an aquatic wasteland. The first tears I'd shed since infancy now added to its infinite volume. It was as though a crushing black cloud took up residence around my form. Why would my consciousness betray me so? I sat and pondered, trying to understand why I felt so low when I should have been feeling free.

My thoughts on having just left the military were mixed at best. I'd spent six years at a fever pitch of operational readiness, perpetually crouched at the starting line waiting for the deafening crack of the starter's gun. But the tempo had weakened me, and the last couple of weeks – on a post defence-force separation program – had been solemn and pensive.

I'd left the military with no concrete plans. All I knew was that I'd had enough and I was utterly spent. What would I do now? Who was I, if not a staunch, unwavering member of the military establishment? It seemed I had come to define myself by my military success. What was I without it, if anything? I needed to know.

Straining to look forward seemed only to crystallise the past. What had been behind my burning desire to join up? There was that George Mallory adage – in answer to the question of why he had climbed Everest – 'Because it was there.' As well, there had been a quest for a sense of self-knowledge. Some people pay a psychiatrist for it, some people jump out of a plane for it, some jab a vein for it, but all I'd had to do was join the Australian Defence Force for answers to be forthcoming. It had been my home, my teacher and my guardian. Serving had given me so much: broadened my horizons, emboldened my spirit and given me a life I would not otherwise have had. But it had also taken.

When I'd joined up, I'd put all thoughts of leading a normal life on hold: friends, family, the possibility of marriage and kids were all stowed away in a place I now found hard to access.

One of the things I'd always tried to avoid was living a life that is small. But in chasing a larger one, was I doomed to miss out on the things that make a life matter? I've never wanted or cared for what most of those around me valued: safety, security, hope that their endeavours would result in success. What interested me was the uncertain, the unattainable, the impossible. Achieving goals within the scope of my ability seemed worthless. I strived for something more; I wanted that which I could not have, that which I was told wasn't for me.

I saw a movie once where the lead character was asked by his physically stronger brother how he'd managed to win a dare to see how far they could swim out to sea. The protagonist looked at his brother and said, 'I never saved anything for the swim back.' And that sums up my way; it's as simple as that. Call it lateral thinking or plain madness. Many would claim the latter, and I wouldn't disagree. If I had started life with that tendency, it was in the military that I developed it as my approach to living. It was a conscious decision to jump first and think about the net second.

To be frank, I'm not what you'd call a remarkable person; it's just that I've done and witnessed some remarkable things. I've spotted pirates off the coast of Africa, I've spoken to Afghan gangstas in their shimmering Mercedes Benz, stood watch on rooftops in the drafty Kabul night. I've watched mortars and rockets sail over my head while drinking cool beer in the blazing Baghdad sun. I've always sought *more*, and tried to reconcile that drive with the debilitating self-doubt and loneliness that sometimes wash over me like the proverbial ocean spray – less so as time goes on.

I believe I have found my way and it was the army and navy that laid the path to that self-knowledge. They gave me a lighthouse by which to navigate a turbulent youth, and it's with those experiences I continue to move forwards. If ever I feel doubt about what is to come, I can look back to that day on Byron Bay beach and know that it was a blip in an otherwise worthwhile journey, one I have come through, scarred maybe, but satisfied and proud.

As I start to write, I think of all the other military books out there, of which there are many. None of them conveys the reality of the struggle and effort it requires to achieve your goals – especially, as in my case, when the narrator has little to no ability, minimal physical prowess and no fucking idea of what he is doing! Okay, not every writer of a military memoir fits that description, but that's me. I can't remember powering through training, performing Arnold Schwarzenegger-like feats – doing a spinning backflip and killing ten terrorists with a single blow. For me, it wasn't like that at all. The road to becoming one of the military elite, if you want to call it that – and some do – was an incredibly long and hard, albeit rewarding, one that allowed me to learn a lot about myself and others. Only within the military have I ever witnessed the incredible heights the human spirit can soar to when confronted with adversity.

By way of introduction, my name is Hugh 'Obi' O'Brien, a bloke who grew up on a farm and had an ordinary upbringing, and this is the account of my time in one of the best military forces in the world and the path I have since followed. It's not an ordinary path.

I've written what I believe to be true; take from it what you will. To be fair, I never went to war while still serving in the military, but that's not what this book is about. There are plenty of lads who have written those books and, frankly, I don't hold a candle to them and probably never will. I have never and would never claim anything else. What I'm endeavouring to do is to tell the story of how I, and a few lucky others, earnt a place with Special Forces, the military elite. And we did get there.

Hopefully, if there is a nagging doubt inside you, a sense that you demand something more from life – to journey on a path less travelled – then maybe, just maybe, this will give you a nudge in the right direction. Or inspire you to stand when all else falls.

One

INCEPTION

'You go down to the bottom of the sea, where the
water isn't even blue anymore, where the sky is only
a memory, and you float there, in the silence. And you
stay there, and you decide that you'll die for them.'

– The Big Blue

'How are you travelling, mate?' I enquired of the guy next
to me. I'd come to know him as 'Salty' – his last name was
actually Pepper.

'I'd rather be drinking Cascade,' was his muffled reply.

Salty, me and twenty-seven or so other hapless souls were
swimming across Hanns Inlet, a vast black stretch of water
off the Mornington Peninsula, near Melbourne. Swallowed
whole by a nasty Victorian winter, we'd been at it for the best
part of four hours in eight-degree-Celsius water, clothed in
nothing but mechanics' overalls.

Why the fuck would anybody want to engage in what
basically amounts to torture? Well, each of us had it in our

heads that we wanted to be Royal Australian Navy clearance divers, one of the hardest jobs in the Australian military. We were six weeks into Recruit School, the eleven-week starting point for life in the navy. At that moment we were competing for an invitation to Dive School – an invitation each of us would have sold our soul for. This opportunity, an honour in itself, was only available to the clearance diving candidates in our Recruit School intake. Few of us were destined to make it, and we were all struggling, despite what any of those candidates might tell you now. Barely twenty-one, I felt as though I was ageing a year for every agonising set of push-ups completed, but I gritted my teeth and reminded myself how rare and privileged this experience was.

During that godforsaken swim at Hanns Inlet, four of our brothers fell by the wayside; in the course of the day's mind-bending evolutions several others had put their hand up in resignation. As we got changed for the next evolution, it struck me that it was the biggest and strongest – or those who claimed as much – who were being ruled out.

Only days before I had sworn allegiance to the group; we'd all pledged that we'd stick together through thick and thin, having already been through so much in Recruit School, though thrown together for no other reason than the shared date of our joining orders. But now I was in so much physical pain I didn't care. I was a quivering, blubbering mess, struggling to do up my runners with hands so cold they wouldn't work properly. The only thing that I could think was, 'Fuck bro, don't quit; don't you fucking quit.' I wanted in to Diving School more than anything on Earth. I wanted that black salt-encrusted beret and to wear that badge high on my right arm. I would have walked through fire to get it.

Those of us who remained ran towards the gym at a pace far in excess of our current physiological capacity. Purely by reflex I jumped aside as one of my fellow candidates collapsed in front of me. My spark of concern was as fleeting as the barrage of abuse from the surrounding instructors. My impulse to stop and help was, I'm ashamed to admit, superseded by the instructions that were barked out. I later learnt that it would not have mattered much as the guy was unconscious before he hit the ground. He recovered, but I don't remember seeing him again – his battle for selection was over.

There is a certain clarity that comes with pain. You focus on what you need to do to survive. Scoff if you will, but this was the old-school navy. There were no medics hovering around us, no OH&S standards, only a bunch of blokes saying in no uncertain terms, *If you want to be in our club, well, you play by our rules. Keep going, don't give up, don't lie down and never ever bloody stop . . . Complete the mission for the mission's sake, not because you're being told to do it.*

The toll on our initial numbers was obvious, and it kept growing. What wasn't so obvious was the change already occurring within me – and, I presume, the others who were still going. The qualities that I'd previously believed to matter, and the confidence displayed by the arrogant, were now painfully passé, irrelevant. We'd been on the go for three days straight, with barely an hour or two of sleep a night, and those who remained for the final hours of that selection process seemed only to possess a solitariness, a quality that outlasted fitness, strength and downright good sense. All else dropped away except refusal to concede, repudiation of defeat.

On arrival at the gym, we were unceremoniously thrown into the pool to commence unrecorded hours of swimming, poolside push-ups and a bewildering practice of jumping in and out of the water at the pool's edge; I experienced my fifth regurgitation of the day.

There was method in this madness. In order to obtain the right people to become divers, the instructors must push you past your natural ability; they must overcome your skill, your speed, your strength; they must see the real you, the you that's cold, tired and hungry. No pretensions, no bravado, no lies; they want to strip away all your armour and judge the man inside, the man at his most honest, shivering and bedraggled – ideally unbeaten and defiant.

One of their techniques – the bane of our existence – was to make each of us carry at all times, without a moment's break, a fifty-metre Hauser rope, a burden that grew heavier as it soaked up the blood, sweat and tears of the beaten and only magnified the absence of those who quit. Over marathon-distance runs under a barrage of belittling abuse and carrying that crushing weight, dudes were folding faster than Superman on laundry day. The list for acceptance grew shorter as more and more pressure was brought to bear: obstacle course, fitness tests aplenty.

The end of the process, although near, was unknown to the six candidates still standing, and we were all running on empty. My motivation roared back the moment one of the instructors walked in front of me and my eyes settled on the clearance diver badge on his right shoulder. Though I'd never been into symbolism, that almost innocuous image of an old dive helmet, with the small 'C' below it, was the emblem of everything I had recently come to believe in; the attainment of it was my obsession.

Back now at the freezing dock by the navy's Seamanship School near Frankston, the next test began. Tossed once again into Hanns Inlet, I began sinking and quickly. The bone-chilling ocean encapsulated my form, coating me in a fluid darkness. It started rushing into the poorly fitting wetsuit, jolting me from my exhausted semi-coma. Strong hands gripped the shoulder straps of my dive gear and I was shaken violently back and forth like a rag doll. Surely only an animal could have that much power beneath the surface? This delusion vanished when I clasped my shoulders and felt the anvil-sized fists of a human; someone was controlling my verticality, my every movement. I was finding it hard to get my bearings – it was like being in a plane or car crash; all my senses were overloaded and being underwater made everything happen in slow motion, like a memory of a long-forgotten nightmare.

One of the hands came towards me out of the darkness, seeking my attention, then tapped the thin perspex layer of my mask that separated my eyes from the salty liquid all around: 'Tap, tap, tap, tap.' Momentarily I focused – as was the desired response – with just enough clarity to register the black outline of a neoprene-clad behemoth in front of me. He was signalling for me to give the okay. I put my thumb up. Never has such a lie been communicated by a simple hand gesture. I wasn't okay, but I'd be fucked if I'd let him know that.

Then fists gripped me again and drove me into the muddy seabed. It was like I'd been tackled in rugby; the force and violence were unbelievable. Not a second later I was being lifted out of the mud and shaken again.

What the fuck was happening! I'd never felt so out of place in my life; my world had ceased to exist and I was in some watery hell! A rope tightened swiftly around my upper body and dive gear, like a giant spider web.

My choices were limited: I could panic and wriggle like an insect or I could remain calm, think, and systematically work to improve my situation. I not so much chose the latter as something inside chose it for me. I grabbed the offending rope from around my neck and torso, righted myself, cleared my mask and gave a begrudging thumbs-up to my tormentor.

Next I was grabbed by the scruff of the neck like a baby kitten and reefed to the surface, my legs flailing beneath me; my head broke the surface into pitch-black darkness. A dot of light from a single lamp high above the wharf was the only indication I had ascended from the murky depths; my head and mind were so frozen by cold, I could still be submerged for all I knew.

'How'd he do?' A naval diving officer was standing above us in what seemed like mocking comfort.

My head gave an involuntary slump to my right in time to see a large, tattooed arm in front of a sleek black body give a rudimentary thumbs-up.

'That's generous,' I thought, and concentrated enough to hear the instruction to exit the freezing water and make way for the next sucker. Thus ended my first scuba dive with the navy.

From that moment, I was on a path that the warm and dry self of an hour earlier could not have foreseen. For the next five years, give or take, I would battle to achieve my goal of getting into Special Forces.

Yes, it's a long bloody time, but bear in mind I did most of the selection trials twice because of my lack of ability. Even if I had been a natural, it would still have taken ages – not through any fault of the system or mythological conspiracy to keep me out, despite what most failed candidates might claim. And I wasn't involved in designated selection that entire time, either. But as anybody who's been a clearance diver can tell you, every day is a test and, as the saying goes, 'The only easy day was yesterday.'

The price of admission to Special Forces was high. Little did I know that as well as working towards that goal, I was cultivating the audacity to rise above my abilities, a trait that would reshape my world.

Two

BEGINNINGS

'The woods are lovely, dark and deep,
But I have promises to keep,
And miles to go before I sleep,
And miles to go before I sleep.'

– Robert Frost

Fear and trepidation consumed me. Could I do it, could I make the leap? The scale of it was becoming insurmountable in my mind and I felt my gut tense up. Then it dawned on me: the mind, it was all in my mind. *Just let go; be not afraid.* The thing I feared most was the fear itself. And so I jumped . . .

I was eight years old and I had successfully jumped off the roof of my house onto the lawn, a drop of at least seven metres. No one was around to watch; there was nobody to impress. I'd needed to see if I could do it, to know if I could face things that scared me. It wasn't about being tough or cool, and I don't think I was reckless. I just had an innate desire to test myself.

Living on a farm was like growing up in a nursery of adventure. For a while, every afternoon after school I would grab my .22 calibre Sportsco rifle and go hunting in the bush, moving as silently as a twelve-year-old is able to manage. I felt at home in the bush, its enforced solitude a soothing comfort and beguiling companion. I could walk for hours across our farm, lost in my own world of pretend mission objectives and fictional orders given to my platoon of one. In saying that, I wasn't especially enamoured with the military, unlike my younger brothers, the twins, Matt and Phil, who used to pop up from anywhere dressed in full camouflage, ready to ambush any passer-by. Theirs was a world of whimsical battles against an unseen enemy in a neverending war, waged with extreme prejudice against the forces of illusory evil.

To say that sibling rivalry existed in our family of four boys would be an understatement. You had to fight tooth and nail every day. We were forever wrestling with each other, mostly in good fun but at times it did get out of hand. It was a continuous epic of battles fought, side-taking and uneasy alliances formed that could last as long as a week or as little as an afternoon. My elder brother, Andrew, and I would rally our respective troops – usually one twin apiece – into pitched battles. But the balance of power could swiftly change, especially as the twins swapped sides with the ease of a Frenchman. In the more memorable battles, such as 'The King's Thistle Campaign', 'The Chookyard Trenches', 'The Fig Tree War', we were allies against an unseen foe.

All my brothers are strong in their own way – Andrew with his hulking strength and Matt and Phil with their guile and determination – and all three are physically bigger than me. The only real advantage I had over them was an under-developed sense of self-preservation, meaning I cared not for my own safety. Though acquiring survival instincts was one of the most important developments in the homo sapiens evolutionary chain, for me its *absence* was an asset: I could only hope to ever win any of our daily contests by simply being unafraid to lose. It's a principle I still try to live by: worry not about an adverse outcome; 'Fear not, if ye are to be feared.'

My family were farmers and graziers; they grew crops and raised sheep near Young in the southern highlands of New South Wales. The farm, 'Marree', near the tiny hamlet of Greenethorpe, had been handed down from my grandfather. I say handed down, but that would imply a gift of some kind: no such gratuity. Gerard O'Brien, my father, worked his fingers to the bone to pay off every square centimetre to the old man.

Dad would regularly put me and my three brothers to work in the shearing shed, out on the tractor or generally get us helping out wherever else we were needed. My father was a strong man, but kind and unwavering in his love for his children. We were his world and everything he did was coloured with a magnified sense of family. He would knock off work at a moment's notice to play football with us in the backyard, and all it took to drag him away from his tractor was for us to ambush him at lunch, tackling him to the ground, and the fun would begin.

Amanda, my mother, was a nurse by trade but a closet academic who completed university degrees for fun. She was a pacifist, and with those convictions I'm sure she struggled daily with her four rambunctious boys. Her ability to make each of us feel like we were her only child was rivalled only by her capacity for unconditional love. If you needed a problem solved, you went to Mum.

It was an invaluable upbringing, based on a sense of responsibility and hard, selfless work. What it ingrained in me was the belief that some things hold an intrinsic value far outweighing any fiduciary remuneration.

Life on the farm wasn't always rosy. We experienced the early 1990s recession with the best of them, which was hard on my parents. Thanks to Dad's farming ability and general inventiveness, we always seemed to keep our heads above water. I remember an especially tough time when we couldn't afford to keep our sheep anymore; there was no food for them and they were suffering. One day I went with Dad to the lower paddock, where he had them penned, and I noticed a large hole in the ground. Even though I was a young kid, I knew the gig was up. Most farmers in the region were experiencing similar difficulties and could ill afford the bullets to put down their livestock as each round cost more than the sheep it was destroying. Not my father though; he refused to knock the animals on the head with a blunt instrument; he paid for the ammunition. It was about the only time I can remember seeing him beaten; he cared deeply for every living thing under his charge. The calamity of that day's events still resonates with me. Dad was in a position he couldn't have foreseen. The weather, the environment and circumstance were things he couldn't control. The only thing he could control was his reaction to them, a strength I've yet to master and a fear I carry daily.

*

I feel my school years had a lot to do with the exquisite punishment I would later inflict upon myself in order to achieve certain things. Growing up, I was not a high achiever, unless you count 'Everybody gets a ribbon day' at my primary school, a small Catholic educational institute in the local township of Young. It was my high school years in Sydney that were the most formative. Boarding school is no place for the faint of heart, and St Joseph's College Hunters Hill, aka Joeys, proved to be an education in survival as much as in academia.

Arriving at this massive boarding school was daunting for a country kid who'd been to a small primary school. It wasn't unlike turning up for military selection: there were standards to meet, relationships to be formed and people to fear. Buzzing with adrenaline and excitement, I was thrust into this prestigious, big-city high school and a living environment rivalling that of the novel *Lord of the Flies*. 'Fit in or fuck off' appeared to be the general motto. I guess I didn't do too badly in that regard, mostly because I never had much trouble making friends.

Not a moment was left unaccounted for. It was study and sport, sport and study, and once you got up to the dormitory at night, it was like being in a prison movie: you had to watch your back, remain aware and never back down. Remaining on high alert was a virtue at Joeys. So I learnt to be a survivor, to think quickly and critically. It was a bit of a jungle; good training really.

The early years were hard. I wasn't as mature as many of the other kids; I was far too sensitive and carefree, and the realities of the human race were a shock to my system. Joeys

is a great school with many fine attributes but I did witness
some terrible bullying there. I managed to avoid the worst of
it, for I was spry and quick-witted and I had my mates, but it
left its impression on me. I hated injustice, and witnessing the
suffering of those who couldn't defend themselves has stuck
with me.

Out the back of the school one evening, I saw a large lad
grab one of the junior kids – an Asian – and slam him up
against the wall, uttering a racist taunt. Call me naïve but
I had never seen anything like it before and it shocked me.
As I moved closer, against my better judgement, I recognised
the older boy; I knew the guy from before I started at Joeys!
Never had I observed this side of him; nor had I suspected he
would even contemplate such rottenness.

I rushed up and separated the two. As I pushed my
acquaintance aside, I could see a fire in his eyes. He was in
the year above me and more than a little bigger than me.
I just looked at him with a questioning gape, silently asking
why. It's doubtful he even knew himself. It was almost as if
he was picking on a weaker individual just because he could.
He raised his fist to strike me, expecting me to cower or run.
I just stood there, not breaking our gridlocked gaze. Then he
lowered his fist and walked away. I could only imagine he fed
on the fear of the Asian kid, and seeing none in me had the
opposite effect on him.

It was time to grow up. Prior to that experience, evil had
been only a comic-book ideology. But I knew now what it was
and I hated it with an intensity, an intensity I would cultivate.

Rugby was Joeys' real religion – it was our school's bread and
butter, our heart and soul and, from my limited perspective,

the path to manhood and glory. But I never excelled at rugby union as much as I would have liked to, and it seemed to be the only measure of success in that world.

Unlike most of the other lads, with their strapping country frames, a stiff breeze could have blown me over. My footy skills were limited at best, this self-assessment worsened by the fact that my brother Andrew was, and still is, a stunningly gifted rugby player who starred in the First XV. The highest level I reached was selection in the Fourth XV in Year Twelve, which by any other school's yardstick was probably quite good. But that fact didn't comfort me. I craved the adulation that the First XV received; those guys were like walking gods at Joeys.

Although I was acutely aware I was not good enough to get there, it didn't stop me wanting it. I managed to keep myself from sliding too far down the rankings through fitness and a terrier-like tenacity to throw my body into the game without fear of injury. But that only gets you so far.

Most of my sporting endeavours required a level of skill that I didn't have, which put me in a difficult position. No matter what people tell you, some things do require a form of natural ability. I don't want to take anything away from those who did achieve success, far from it. They all worked very hard to develop their gifts. It's just that I felt I had nothing to develop! The only thing I possessed was an unwavering ability to keep fear and emotion at bay in order to achieve an end result, regardless of the consequences.

My limited rise in the ranks troubled me terribly. It was nobody's fault; I didn't have overbearing parents or mocking teachers. Mine was a self-imposed suffering, albeit a double-edged one. The short-term angst and self-loathing I bore, although momentarily harmful in those formative years, would grow into an unwavering drive for excellence and bottomless tolerance for physical and mental pain.

Boarding school wasn't where my risk-taking and sense of justice started, but it's certainly where those things were nurtured. My lack of sporting success and need to prove myself led to some harrowing scenarios in my senior year. Though I wasn't big or tough or gifted, I was fearless; often, terrified friends would watch as I jumped off bridges, ran through traffic and walked along the eight-centimetre-wide ledge of our boarding house, towering fifty metres above the pavement. Working out that fear, or lack of it, was a currency I could deal in was a revelation. It was almost like I'd discovered a superpower that others didn't possess.

The thing I took most from my Joeys years was the importance of mateship. Although falling squarely in the chunky part of the bell curve academically and on the sporting field, I don't mind bragging here that I excelled at friendships. My ability to form close bonds has come to define my life, and that process started at Joeys.

Joeys also taught me self-reliance and tenacity. It was a breeding ground for success and ingrained in you a sense that striving for excellence was a worthwhile endeavour. There were also the unofficial lessons to be learnt: toughness, don't leave a mate hanging, personal responsibility – all traits to be valued in the military.

In spite of a propensity towards mischief, I did okay at school and graduated with good marks and half-decent sporting achievements, but nothing that would push me in any one direction. Consequently I found myself drifting. My friends all seemed to know what they wanted to do, and their choices seemed to marry with their personalities and attributes. What I had on offer was a more eclectic mix of stubbornness and appetite for danger, tinged with a self-deprecating sense of humour . . . not very employable really.

My mother's desire for me to go to university didn't get me far. I enrolled in an education degree at the University of Technology Sydney, but my heart wasn't in it and soon I left.

Within a short time of finishing school, I had become lost and disillusioned. Despite the innumerable opportunities my private education had given me, I didn't feel I had that much worth. I worked on the farm for a bit and in bars in Sydney. I even tried to make it again on the club football circuit, playing for the Gordon Rugby Club. Although I like to think I gained a reputation for tenacity, my skill level wasn't that high and the Wallabies weren't coming knocking on my door any time soon. I lacked any real motivation for the normal employment pursuits; nothing I tried seemed to fit.

I travelled and worked in meaningless jobs; I tried to find myself in any number of adventures. But what I didn't realise was that you'll never find the truth when looking for a lie. I had such a myopic view of what was worthy, who was coura-geous and what was honourable. All the basic building blocks were there but they were scattered like driftwood, broken and rotting in the sun, just waiting for the inevitable tide.

While watching one of my favourite movies, *Unbreak-able*, I heard a statement about a person discovering their true calling that stirred up feelings deep in my core:

That little bit of sadness in the morning you spoke of,
I think I know what that is. Maybe you're not doing what
you're supposed to be doing . . .

– M Night Shyamalan

I experienced this same sense of longing when, quite by accident, I saw a documentary called *Silent Warriors*. The values of the military world seemed to mirror my own but despite the appeal, I lacked the will to act on this discovery.

Eventually, a chance encounter with an old school friend led to me making a big change of direction. Haphazardly arriving at the twenty-first birthday party of one Andrew 'Fordy' Ford was a fortuitous event. He is a giant of a man with a heart of gold. As usual I was drunk and probably waxing lyrical about the lack of meaning in my life, as I was wont to do. In passing, I mentioned that I'd seen on TV a documentary about navy clearance divers. I thought they were awesome and said something like, 'Wouldn't it be great to meet one of these subaquatic supermen!'

Fordy, who is quite softly spoken, stopped me short and whispered, 'My dad's one. He's over there in the corner if you want a chat. But Obi, enough with the Superman crap; you sound like a wanker.'

'Are you serious?' I slurred.

'Yea bro, he's a CD.' The abbreviation for clearance diver is CD, and even that sounded cool.

So I plucked up some courage, which wasn't hard considering the amount of grog I'd imbibed, and that's when I met 'Dixie' Ford. Later I discovered he was a legend in the clearance diving fraternity.

It didn't take long for Dixie to conclude that, despite my youthful exuberance and naïveté, I might have the heart required to at least attempt selection. I dismissed his gracious assessment as merely a mate's dad being kind to a drunken kid. However, at 0-dark-hundred the next morning I woke at the sound of my phone and, despite being hung over, I took the call. 'Helloooo,' I croaked.

'Yes, yes, hello, this is Dixie Ford, Andrew's dad. Remember? Okay, yes, now listen up. Now I've arranged for you to go to Dive School this morning for work experience and a fitness assessment. Yes, okay, here's the address . . . and don't be late . . . yes, yes, okay, goodbye.' He hung up.

What the fuck! Who was that? I'm going where? At what time this morning? What's happening? Though he caught me stunned and unprepared, I'll never be able to thank Dixie enough for what he did for me.

After a cup of elephant-killing coffee I thought, 'Shit! I can't not go; it's a mate's dad. I've got to show some respect. I'll just fucking go. How hard can it be?'

The Royal Australian Navy Dive School occupies a reasonably small but important piece of land within the suburban Sydney naval base HMAS *Penguin*, which is located close to Middle Head. Even approaching it is awe-inspiring. No bullshit. I'm telling you that as you walk down the hill, you feel it in your whole body, like a chill of excitement. It's like the first time your dad shook your hand instead of patting you on the head. You feel like those who came before you are watching you, as if to say, 'This thing is more than the many, it belongs to the few. Watch your step down here, son.'

When I arrived there was no ceremony or grand tour – no such luxury. The Chief Diver looked at me after my meek introduction and growled, 'So you're the kid Dixie sent, are you? What the fuck was he thinking? Get in line.' I jumped in with a bunch of blokes who looked like a rugby team but a bit more apprehensive.

We began by running down to a park just outside the back gate, adjacent to beautiful Balmoral Beach. Here we began the fitness test. It consisted of a 2.4-kilometre run to be completed in less than nine and a half minutes, fifty push-ups, one hundred sit-ups, twelve chin-ups and an 800-metre fin (swimming on your back with the aid of diver's fins) in the ocean in under nine and a half minutes. This was merely the basic, bottom-of-the-line, beginner, don't-bother-showing-up-if-you-can't, run-of-the-mill entry-level test! You were expected to improve exponentially as you progressed to the next level of testing. The fact that I was playing club rugby and had been doing plenty of training put me in good stead for that day, but only just.

For the run I finished in about the middle of the group, which pleasantly surprised me. The sit-ups and that stuff were no big deal. The fin, however, was a totally foreign experience. We had to don a pair of overalls – the chosen uniform for CDs – and lie on our backs, hands across chest, wearing a pair of fins (not *flippers* – you'll only make that mistake once around CDs; and while I'm at it, a mask is a mask not *goggles* and a cylinder is not a *tank*!). Then we had to kick like hell and maintain momentum through the surging waves.

There I was at six in the morning, out in the ocean, fighting against the elements with a bunch of blokes who must have been as crazy as me, trying to be the last man standing. And something clicked.

From what I could see, it didn't require any specific skill other than a single-minded desire to not give up: just keep going; if you have to, then hurt yourself to cross the line and let the authorities assess your commitment to the cause . . . Simple, right? Well, I thought so. And that's exactly what I did.

I walked away from that experience with a hunger in me. I fucking wanted to be one of these blokes. I wanted to wear that badge and have a thousand-yard stare. It hurt my head to think about it.

As I headed for home after this brief but eye-opening introduction, the parting words of the Chief Diver rang in my ears: 'If you think you've got it, join up. This was nothing.'

That was nothing! Fuck!

But he was right; there's no use talking about it. At some point I would have to jump – jump like I had off my farmhouse roof – show myself I wasn't afraid, even if I was.

There was only one problem: I didn't think I was good enough to make it. I'd never seen a Hollywood movie about these men; I'd read no books about their exploits. Somehow, though, I knew that they didn't seek nor did they desire the adulation of others – and it was a big stretch for me to visualise myself being one of them. It was clear to me they did what they did because it was necessary; they punished themselves and faced danger for the protection of people they would never know. It wasn't a sport, it wasn't a job, it was a life – a life of sacrifice dedicated to an unnamed cause, existing for that day when the mission's urgency trumped their right to personal safety.

Did I want to stand with these guys? You fucking know I did. Somewhere deep inside, I sensed that this could be the defining cause of my life.

In case you're thinking that having had that lightbulb moment I was instantly wise, I wasn't; my civilian life of mediocrity continued unabated.

Searing pain is the best way to describe it. That and stupidity. I was putting a cigar out on my hand in a pub in North Sydney to win a bet. Yes, I know; bloody idiot, right? Geez, I had a long way to go.

Yet I did get one thing right. Not long after that cigar incident, I snapped out of self-doubt and procrastination and signed up. Actually, it was Dad who convinced me to 'stop talking about it and just do it'. It was that and my brother Phil, who had already joined the army, basically daring me to do it.

It was to be a long time before I would stop craving the shallow public acknowledgement of my feats and be happy with anonymity.

Three

RECRUIT SCHOOL

'There's no such thing as sharks, cold or can't.'

– Diver saying

Apart from Phil and Dad, my family and friends were a little shocked to hear that I had gone through with it and signed up. No one expressed any view other than the likelihood of a polarised outcome: stunning success or dismal failure.

There was a wait of about a month before I was to report to the recruitment centre in Sydney so I took the time to train on my parents' farm. I would run for hours along the dusty country tracks, lift tractor tyres, do chin-ups in the shed and laps in our eight-metre pool – a pale comparison to the ocean I sought to conquer.

Signing the stack of government forms for my intake, one phrase stood out among the inky storm of official rhetoric: 'six-year commitment'. It was usually four years in other areas of the forces. Obviously, if you wanted in to this club, it was for keeps.

The sun came up on my first day of Recruit School in early 2000. My instructions were to turn up at Defence Plaza, the Australian Defence Force's multi-storey administrative base in Sydney's CBD, from where a defence force bus would take me to the airport. The ultimate destination was HMAS *Cerberus*, the navy's recruit training establishment, seventy kilometres southeast of Melbourne.

As I waited for the bus, I looked around at the others in the room and thought, 'Holy shit, have I just made the biggest mistake of my life? Who are these clowns?' It may seem an overly negative opinion of the calibre of recruits, but you should have seen this lot.

The rabble I was surveying was the New South Wales intake for the navy for that month. They had all preselected which branch they wished to join, be it as a clearance diver, marine engineer, electrical technician or a boswain's mate. There were all these groups of men and women – well, girls and boys really – and, to me, they looked and acted like they were going to summer camp.

In my defence, my younger brother Phil had told me horror stories about the army's Recruit School in Kapooka. Phil is a tough guy and one hell of a soldier, and for him to think it was hard . . . Well, I had been expecting to rock up to a kill-bot factory.

Then I reminded myself how whenever I get arrogant I get brought back to Earth with a thud. Swallowing my initial disappointment, I studied the group more carefully and started to notice some steely-eyed, large, triathlon-looking types. These had to be the diving hopefuls. It occurred to me that I might have been a tad hasty in my appraisal. At least if

I was up against the others, I might have a chance of making it through, whereas looking at the obvious CD candidates and listening to their boasts, I'd be on my way home before the ink dried on my intake papers.

Soon enough it was time to move off. I stood in the corner of the elevator, wondering what to expect. As we headed towards the waiting coaches, I quite unintentionally expressed my internal monologue externally: 'This'll be fucking interesting!' I whispered.

The bloke next to me burst out laughing, as if he had been thinking the exact same thing. He then introduced himself in a strange accent, not quite Irish, not quite American; turns out it was Canadian.

'G'day, bro. My name's Whitey, ay.'

'Hey,' I said. 'What you going for?'

'Trying for clearance divin', ay.'

'Yer, me too,' I said.

I noticed he was of a similar build and demeanour to me. Although we spoke little after that, I had this feeling that, unlike the rest of the CD hopefuls, this guy was definitely going to make it.

Recruit School proved to be a mixed bag. For my money, too many of the instructors exhibited an ethos of instilling averageness in candidates. This is a harsh indictment I'll admit, but the place seemed to me to be run by people who had lost their passion for the job – and yes, in some cases, even for life. At almost every turn, we diving hopefuls encountered opposition – and not the constructive kind but snideness – from naysayers. I've never been able to abide bullying and to me toughness is what you can endure yourself, not what you can inflict on others.

There was plenty of good stuff about Recruit School. In particular, one of the physical training instructors was a great bloke, who helped us diving wannabes prepare for our upcoming Week Six 'Hell Weekend' by smashing the shit out of us every chance he got. Some of us even volunteered to stay back on our only weekend off so he could run us through a mini Hell Weekend of his own. We were put through our paces, with over forty kilometres of running a day, along with a neverending barrage of push-ups, sit-ups and lap swimming. It was invaluable in preparing us for what was about to come – well, as prepared as one can be for a cyclone of pain.

All in all, Recruit School came and went without much fanfare. That is, except for Week Six – 'Hell Weekend' – which, as described in Chapter One, only six CD hopefuls survived.

The line-up of the six broke down like this: the stoic Canadian, whom the rest of us imaginatively called Canada (his dad was Australian but he grew up over there); the irrepressible Salty from Tasmania; the Gold Coast surfie Strongy; a tall good-looking lad named J. Houston; and the quiet giant we affectionately called Stealth because of his uncanny ability to be standing right behind you without you knowing it. Oh yeah, and me, Obi: a seventy-five-kilogram, 1.65 metre-tall ball of nerves with a growing ability to hold my breath.

The six of us became inseparable; friendships formed over such hot coals always seem to elicit a tighter bond. We'd been flash-fired and moulded in a furnace of adversity, and the high rate of failure only amplified the effect, hardened the seams and cemented the connection to each other. As far as we were concerned, we were in a life raft together and fuck the storm.

Five weeks after 'Hell Weekend', the six of us left Recruit School and moved across the road to the navy's Seamanship School, where we had a few weeks of instruction before receiving our orders to depart for Dive School in Sydney. We filled the time with endless training, moving as a pack to the Olympic-sized swimming pool every morning and night to conduct our own regimen of punishing aquatic circuits. For the drill we made up, we'd each put on a set of overalls and fin 100 metres, then do fifty push-ups on the pool's edge, repeating this without break for a solid two hours. Canada and I were often the last out of the pool. We'd regularly run late for dinner because neither Canada nor I wanted to get out of the pool first for fear of ridicule from the other.

Running also become an obsession with us: we would regularly run to the coast and back through the bushland surrounding the base, barely getting back in time for the nightly roll call. We'd had a glimpse of what was in store for us when we got to Dive School and had made up our minds that if we were going in, we were going in packing.

Shortly before the six of us left for Dive School, we went out on the town for a couple of quiet beers, maybe a stroll through the park and a trip to the opera . . . You get the idea. We were at the wrong end of a big drinking session and about to call it a night when one of the boys bumped into a rather large gentleman, who took exception to his forward momentum being hampered.

He spun around, 'bravely' selected the smallest member of our group – me – and threw a king hit! I was half-turned away when a fist the size of a Buick collected me on the cheek, shattering my eye socket. I staggered forward, not completely aware of what happened, but I didn't go down as the big fella had expected. I turned and went at him for all I was worth. A crowd formed and broke the fight up, then sirens could be heard and the bloke ran away, leaving me standing in the street daring him to return, secretly wishing he wouldn't. Thank fuck he didn't because he probably would have killed me.

The lads helped me limp back to barracks, an agonising hour's journey up the coast and, despite protesting treatment, I was checked out and admitted to the base hospital. Although benched for a week from the Basic Seamanship School we were attending, my fractured eye socket would need more time to heal and I was supposed to make it to Dive School the following week. My stress levels ran high.

Among the routine requirements for anyone about to head to Dive School was an eye exam: I had to pass it before the navy would allow me to continue with the program. When the day came to take the eye exam, I still couldn't see a bloody thing and it hurt like a bastard when I looked in any direction but forward. Going into the appointment, I was thinking, 'Fuck! Fuck! What am I going to do here? They're not going to let me go through with my mates!'

Out of the blue, the doctor had to leave the room to take a phone call. At that stage, I don't mind saying, I was so wound up I was on the verge of tears. Then suddenly it struck me. I could go up and memorise the eye chart with the good eye while the doctor was out of the room.

The doc came back and I listed the letters in quick succession before I forgot them, then lied my ass off when he conducted the exam, covering the limitations of my sight considerably. Luckily, he passed me!

It would be weeks before my sight returned to normal so I spent a lot of time kicking around with only one functioning eye. Frankly, I don't know how pirates do it.

But there is another side to the story: the upshot of the injury was that I started to think outside the box; my bung eye forced me to apply the diver adage of 'Improvise, adapt and overcome'. Soon it would become a principle to live by.

It had to be if you were to succeed in the more specialised areas of the military. You know, it's not always the obedient guy with the polished boots who wins. Selection often favoured 'the greater fool', the guy who took chances, rolled the dice and ignored the odds. Try, if you will, to understand the mindset required to embark on the journey in question, and the perspective one must adhere to in order to not only survive but flourish in the waters of adversity.

Looking back on Recruit School, I realise that I had already absorbed an important lesson in this principle: in Week Five, a small but significant event occurred that revealed, in a nutshell, what it would take to succeed in the CD Branch. This particular training session had progressed steadily in the dying sun of a wintry afternoon, and saving the rope climb (a fifteen-metre vertical barometer of unhappiness) for last now seemed like a foolish decision.

Salty gathered the clearance diving candidates from our intake and spoke eloquently of the need to master this heinous activity, for it had been rumoured that the coming selection weekend contained this ill-conceived path to nowhere. As we lined up, ready to ascend the beast, someone – it might have been Stealth – suggested that we make a competition of it: the winner would be the first to touch the ground again.

Claiming bragging rights at breakfast the morning after an exercise had quickly become the pattern in our group, so that was all the encouragement we needed. Now the task had an element of competition it had lacked minutes earlier. Shouts started to ring out.

Looking to gain some perspective on technique and style, I positioned myself at the back. Canada stood next to me and it seemed we were the only two silent participants.

Salty, clearly in front, touched the roof and commenced his descent, with Houston trailing by some two metres.

Canada, a true stoic, never talked much, least of all about his upbringing or his past. But he carried himself with rigid pride, and on the odd occasion he spoke, the words were worth listening to. Having for the last several minutes appeared to be lost in thought, he raised his head and made the observation: 'Just drop and you'll win.'

Even among the resounding cheers, there was a kind of stillness about his words. 'Just drop and you'll win'; there it was again: a way of looking at the problem that none of us could have come up with.

For no other reason than a desire to achieve the outcome of victory, in thinking on the rules of the competition, the lateral-minded Canada had homed in on an oversight on our part; perhaps it was plain semantics. Simply put, the instructions for our challenge were: 'Climb the rope, touch the ceiling, and first back to touch the ground wins.' He'd identified that there was no prerequisite to remain in physical contact with the rope on your descent.

To Canada, the predicament of being behind in the race could be overcome with one simple action, letting go of the rope! You would plunge to the hardwood floor, but you would touch the ground first – the velocity of that contact mattered not; well, not as far as Canada was concerned – and you would succeed.

I stood slack-jawed. This philosophy was uttered not out of vanity or stupidity, but came from a place much deeper than that. It was the unassailable truth: to complete the mission at any cost, to possess the desire for victory, even in the face of adversity, was our governing purpose.

It was Canada, Troy White, who stumbled upon this wisdom in his idiosyncratic way and it is as real to me today as it was then: 'Just drop and you'll win.'

Salty walked away with the victory but that's not what we all remember from that day. We remember the Canadian and his words, words that started us thinking, much like in George Orwell's *Animal Farm*, that 'we may all be equal, but some of us are more equal than others'.

Four

DIVE SCHOOL

'Here be dragons.'

– Maritime adage

Starting Dive School was what the six of us had all been waiting for. Recruit School had been a necessary speed bump on our road to that Promised Land. Arriving at HMAS *Penguin*, Mosman, late on a Saturday night, we just found our racks – a naval term for beds – and turned in. As we had the day off on Sunday, I was planning to show the lads round my old town of Sydney; Dive School began on Monday.

Before heading out to see the sights, we decided to eat breakfast on base, so chuffed as roosters we headed down to the mess.

'Jesus, boys, how good's this?' remarked Salty, as we sat down on the balcony to a superbly set table overlooking Balmoral Bay. It was great! We all stacked our plates high with bacon, eggs and hash browns, a hearty navy feast. As we took our seats out on the deck, we noticed there was no one

36

else around. This was a little odd for a junior sailors' mess; in our limited experience, there was always someone on duty or you'd see junior sailors who lived on base.

Next thing, one of the civilian wait staff approached us and asked rather gingerly, 'Are you guys officers?'

Fuckkkkkkkkkkk!!!!!! We had strolled into the Clearance Diving Officers' Mess, helped ourselves to their grub and best seats . . . Shit, shit, shit! We looked at each other like stunned mullets, aware that if anybody were to see us, the consequences at Dive School for us all would be horrendous.

Faster than greased Scotsmen, we packed up and got the fuck out of there, and to this day I don't think anybody found out. So thank you to that gentle civilian who warned us: whoever you are, you probably saved a bunch of careers, mine included.

Day One, Week One: Dive School, baby! The anticipation was palpable. Before we left Melbourne we had received our joining instructions, so we knew to rock up to Dive School at 06:30 dressed in physical training (PT) attire – the standard naval white T-shirt and blue running shorts. The six of us got ready and headed down into what felt to me in that moment like Dante's inferno, except with more water.

We were starting with a fortnight-long ship's diver's course, focused on elementary scuba (self-contained underwater breathing apparatus) diving skills, basic hull searches and repairs. For us it was the entry-level qualification for the Clearance Diving Branch but the course was not exclusive to CD candidates; a navy entrant who completed it could return to their ship with the sub-rate of ship's diver. On our course, there were six fleet candidates, or fleeties. They were easily recognisable in their grey navy overalls.

All of us milled around outside the Dive School office quarters, a parcel of buildings, including the instructors' offices, some admin offices and two classrooms. The office section was partway down the hill and overlooked the wharf and warehouse areas of Dive School proper; we were about to line up in front of those buildings – and would do every subsequent morning on course – for roll call and orders for the day, immediately followed by PT.

Was I up to this? I turned to Canada and expressed my anxiety in the best way I knew, by quoting from a movie, this time *Top Gun*: 'Hey, do you have the number of that truck-driving school we saw on TV? Truck Master, I think it is.'

Like Goose and Maverick at the beginning of their training, I felt we might need alternative employment plans, just in case. Such was my nervousness, I even had a plan to hitchhike to Cairns to be a pearl diver if I failed.

Canada, perhaps slightly amused – you could never tell – muttered in his typically monosyllabic way, 'She'll be right bro, ay.'

It may not seem like much, but the effect was calming: the simplest comment from a mate you respect can really buoy your spirits.

Other guys started arriving. At any one time, there were always two or three different courses of clearance divers at various stages of their training at the School; there was a definite pecking order that you had better work out quick, lest you step on the wrong toes.

All CD courses are allowed to have their own course T-shirt made up, featuring an image – a caricature – a one-line platitude like 'Pain is just weakness leaving the body', plus their specific course number on the left breast. Alongside the experienced guys – standing there in their sun-faded, salt-stained PT gear and their briny blue caps – with our brilliant white T-shirts and relatively unblemished appearance, we looked more like choirboys.

We lined up ready for inspection by the Chief Diver, one Chief Hanrahan. How can I convey to you the respect I have for this individual who was to have such a profound influence on my diving career? Hanrahan was of medium build but wiry like a Tour de France winner, and had an air of confidence about him that was not arrogance, just . . . well, the closest thing I can think of is what the ancient Romans called gravitas: strength, wisdom and integrity. This bloke only had to look at you with his cold, shark-like eyes and you felt like a kid in the principal's office. In his presence, you felt equal parts fear and admiration.

Later, I found out Hanrahan had a forty-centimetre scar down the side of his upper thigh from when he had been knocked off his road bike and broken his femur. The bone had snapped and been driven out the side of his leg, yet he had ridden to the hospital unaided and been stalwart and uncomplaining in his long recovery.

Once I asked him, after I'd known him a while and we were on more familiar terms, 'What keeps you going, what makes you train so hard?'

'It's about the question.'

'What question?' I asked.

'Well, every time you go out to train, whether you know it or not, everyone's asking each other a question. You're silently asking the other guy if he can go that bit further in order to push yourself to obtain maximum benefit from whatever it is you're undertaking. Because heaven forbid, on the day you're asked to activate those skills for real . . . you'll have an answer.'

That has stayed with me; it is the most eloquent description of the CD mindset I have ever heard.

Hanrahan would fast become our group's mentor. He was harsh but fair. He knew we wanted to be tested, that we would welcome any advance on the CD training in our immediate future. On a daily basis he would issue us challenges and mini missions, constantly keeping us in competition with each other. His knowledge of clearance diving was unparalleled; even at that initial encounter, we could tell he was someone to learn from. Addressing us on that first day he spelt out in no uncertain terms that the life of a clearance diver required 100 per cent commitment and a steely determination not to fail.

As soon as roll call finished, we were instructed to head down behind the base to the park on Balmoral Beach for a PT test, to be followed by kit issue at the stores room, and then our first classroom lessons in scuba equipment.

The first day passed in a bit of a whirlwind; we were trying to find our feet and work out who's who in the zoo. It was already clear that the treatment we six CD candidates were going to receive, and the standard we were being held to, was a tad higher and harsher than the fleeties on course with us. Mind you, they were about to cop a fair amount of indirect fire as innocent bystanders, having been 'lucky' enough to be posted to a course containing baby CDs.

Dive School, we rapidly discovered, existed in its own bubble of tradition, ritual and routine. Its rules differed from those of the rest of the military, and it took a while to figure them out. For one thing there was no saluting or even much ceremony. Operational requirements meant that rank and position didn't always determine day-to-day working structure. On a dive site, for example, everyone rotates around different positions, of which there are many. Once you'd graduated you could find yourself diving with an officer, an NCO (non-commissioned officer) or a seaman diver, and the senior rank wasn't always in charge of the dive.

Uniforms were almost a thing of the past: you could get around wearing a wetsuit, overalls or even Speedos! The job was what was important, not the institution; the mission, not the individual. Everything was practical and any extraneous military pretensions were done away with.

The School was a hive of activity. There was an invisible line in the sand that marked the boundary to Dive School. Once you crossed it you had to switch on and *run* everywhere, no matter how far or close. Urgency was a desirable trait, and a trait we were expected to adopt almost straight away.

Our introduction to Dive School was a baptism of fire. With units like this, any outsider is treated with suspicion and contempt until they prove themself under duress. It's because there are lives at stake. The military, and diving in particular, is an inherently dangerous business. If an instructor turns out an inferior product then that person is not only a danger to himself, but they could kill someone else with their mistakes. So training must be the hardest thing you ever go through, in order to prepare you for real events where everything turns to shit!

For us CD trainees, as our first hurdle of many, the ship's diver's course was designed to be physically and mentally testing. It was where the instructors got to know you and your capabilities. If you didn't measure up, you were gone. Not back to the safety net of the 'grey' navy, like the fleeties, but back out on the street where you came from, sunshine!

Ship's diver's also introduced us to the basic formula of diving course instruction. The days were broken down into different sessions. In the early morning, there was roll call, then PT, followed by classroom instruction, some practical diving instruction or task demonstration. For the rest of the day and night you would put into practice what you had learnt, mirroring the morning's lessons and hopefully assimilating the information efficiently enough to avoid punishment, which you hardly ever could. Punishments were accrued on an hourly basis: you could never do anything up to the standard required and were regularly kept back till two or three in the morning completing push-ups or duck diving for mud in order to pay for the day's mistakes.

Across the board, the military takes PT seriously, so whether you are army, air force or navy, all sessions are run by highly qualified staff – they even have their own branch. But Dive School had a different idea: our PT was run by divers. Often we'd be put through our paces by the Leading Seaman Diver – the 'Second Dicky' – who was assigned to help the NCOs run the course. This was a feared man indeed; he pretty much possessed the power of life and death over our frail mortal frames.

'Fins and overalls! End of the wharf!' You'd hear those words and your heart would sink and your stomach churn in anticipation of the pain to come. 'Run jump' was the name given to these little excursions.

Sounds fun, doesn't it, kind of like a kids' game or a sport? I can say with absolute certainty – and I'm sure I speak for most divers – that they were the most feared words on the course. They meant you were about to suffer hours of physical torment. Most likely your course was not performing up to standard: staff tended to reserve this punishment for when they'd had enough of mounting mistakes and wanted to shake you up a bit or generally rally you to sort out your shit. Small mistakes could lead to larger ones and the ocean forgives no man.

On our course, a guy lost a compass board, which resulted in a horrendous run jump that had us climbing an eight-metre rope at the end of a boom stretched out over the water. After three hours of this, followed by sprints along the wharf, we did a 500-metre fin back to start the circuit again. What made the circuit especially difficult was that we were wearing our diving fins the whole time.

Run jumps always consisted of a barrage of activity in and out of the water – push-ups, sit-ups, sprints, off the wharf, up the rope, under the boat and so on – the particulars were only limited by the imagination of the instructor. Continuous instructions, each seemingly more impossible than the last, would be given. Carrying a Zodiac over your head yelling 'ho-ya' may seem cool in the movies, but after an hour or so you feel like curling up into a little ball and requesting a saucer of milk.

I must confess that I found a kind of perverse enjoyment in all of this; it was a challenge, yes, but I found it exhilarating. No matter how bad things got, it only seemed to make me want it more.

One of the most challenging components of the run jump, and my personal favourite, was an exercise called 'Get mud'. When these words were uttered – which could be at any time, and it happened frequently – you had to stop whatever you were doing and free dive – holding your breath – to the seabed and retrieve a fistful of sediment in order to prove you had been there. This exercise had a quite practical application: in the Branch you never knew when you would be required to manage tasks where dive gear was not immediately available. Thanks to my self-imposed routine of practice most afternoons in the pool, I began to gain some prowess in this area. Quite regularly I would discreetly hand over some of my mud on return to the surface: any course member returning without their 'treasure' would be sent down again.

Blackness, blackness, all-consuming blackness. That was the spectre of night diving. Holy shit, was it freaky! All your senses were simultaneously lost and found during your immersion in that alien environment. It felt terrifying, exhilarating and new, kind of like the first time you kissed a girl.

Terrifying or not, I was keen to get in the water and test out my recently learnt skill of lifeline signals. These are a series of pulls (long tugs) and bells (short tugs) received on a rope tied around your waist. It's a communication system as old as the navy itself and operates between the diver and the person on the surface, known as the attendant. The combination of tugs could give a diver directions for searching or important information on decompression procedure.

There are about four A4 pages of signals to learn – covering diver to attendant and attendant to diver. The signal has to be sent down the line and the recipient then sends it back up as confirmation. And depending who sends the signal first, it can mean different things.

Confused yet? Well, I was. I spent weeks learning this cryptic system and tonight was to be the first real test of those skills for all of us on the ship's diver's course: the six CD hopefuls – we were known as swinging dicks, by the way – and the six fleeties who were trying to obtain their diving cuff rate. The cuff rate was so named because if they passed, they were entitled to sew a small dive helmet badge on the cuff of their navy uniform.

As we prepared to enter the water, I heard a noise behind me. The sound, I realised, was coming from one of the six fleeties, a massive Kiwi fellow – over two metres tall and nearly as wide. Even though he looked like an American wrestler, he was wigging out!

'I'm not going in there,' he protested. He was literally shaking.

The instructor was like, 'What the fuck! Get the fuck in the water!' But the big fella was having none of it and strolled back down the wharf and out of the course.

Now I don't tell this story to sledge this poor bloke; quite the opposite. For sure it took courage just to sign up to undertake selection, and he was probably a red hot operator in his own area of military expertise. But it neatly illustrates two things: firstly, diving is not for everyone. Regardless of your task in the water, simply jumping in can take tremendous strength of character. Secondly, it shows that size, attitude and appearance are not an indicator of your inner worth. It's what's in your heart that makes you the person you are, not how you look or who you profess to be.

'Everybody wants to be a diver', or so it is said at every navy base in the Southern Hemisphere, and for good reason. Diving was a boys' own adventure, a jump into the unknown, full of devil-may-care attitudes. It welcomed you with one hand and cast you asunder with the other. It was a hideous bitch goddess and it drank the blood of the unprepared.

Having completed our first couple of days and nights learning the dive set and the basics of diving physics, at the end of the first week we started to learn the more intricate techniques and procedures of a ship's diver. One of a ship's diver's main tasks, be they fleet or clearance diver, is to sweep the ship's hull for limpet mines. These are small magnetically attached explosive devices used to disable or even scuttle a ship while in harbour. The first Italian frogmen used this method to great effect against the British in the First World War. Subsequently, the British Navy captured some of the Italians' equipment and turned the tables. This spawned a long line of Australian and English tactical and underwater demolition teams (UDT) within diving units.

As ship's divers, we were taught the 'half necklace' and 'full necklace' search techniques. Basically, your divers (usually in scuba gear) spread out in a line, connected via a thin nylon rope. For a half necklace, they move across the underside surface of the hull dragging the nylon, like an inverted skipping rope, down one side of the ship from the keel to the waterline. A full necklace requires two sets of divers, one on each side of the hull, and you sweep the entire underside of the vessel in one go. Communicating with a series of pulls and bells, the divers search the ship forward and aft, performing a detailed inspection of the hull.

When we began learning these drills, it was made considerably easier for me if my mate Salty did his practice first. As I descended at his exit point, all I would have to do was look for a large handwritten sign, finger-painted into the mud-soaked hull, saying something like 'MINE, THIS WAY —>' with an arrow and everything! From then on location of the little bugger was academic.

As time went on, the boys and I were growing even closer, if that were possible. We were a tight-knit unit within a unit; we watched each other's backs and helped one another through the long cold nights and sunburnt manic days. Even on the weekends we stuck together: we would go fishing, free diving and generally hang out, not to mention we had some big nights out on the cans!

It truly was like having five new brothers: we loved each other but we were competitive as hell, and we had our fair share of arguments along the way. Salty was the most sensible member of the group and was always trying to rein in Canada and me. Houston often did his own thing and on occasion we had to hassle and berate him to get him into the group activities, though once he got started, he was fine. Stealth tended to do his own thing as well but it was easy to put a guilt trip on him and get him coming along; he was such a nice guy and gentle giant that all it really took was a look from Canada, Salty and me and he would be up for any adventure. Strongy was terrific value but because of his passion for surfing, he was forever on the Gold Coast in our holiday periods, whereas the others and I stayed in Sydney together. The formation of our small unit came about quite by accident but it would serve us well in the trials ahead; whether consciously or subconsciously, we knew it was imperative that we close ranks and form a phalanx if we were to continue on the road to the Promised Land.

Barely a flicker of light could be seen through the cardboard that covered the small portholes in the forward deck. Not that I could make out much anyway as, like my ten trembling mates, I had been blindfolded and crammed in the forward storage area of a Steber dive vessel which now ferried us to an unknown destination.

The statement that baby divers were like mushrooms (fed shit and kept in the dark) seemed more apt than ever, and I couldn't help but smile.

A couple of hours went past and, despite the growing anticipation, silence prevailed within the group. We were on what was termed an 'initiative run', but unofficially, the purpose of this experiment was to see what stuff we participants were made of. Unlike in some areas of the military, we CDs were encouraged to be creative and develop the skills of 'improvise, adapt and overcome'. It was entirely conceivable – and I have since experienced it time and time again – that as a clearance diver you would find yourself in a situation, be it underwater or not, where you had no specific orders to follow and no officer to direct you. It was imperative that you learnt to think for yourself and problem-solve.

Eventually, when we were hauled onto the deck, it was evident that night had fallen, and the unfamiliar surroundings hinted that we were far from home. Blindfolds were removed, then the instructors lined us up and unceremoniously pushed us off the back of the boat. I was the last to go and shortly before receiving the shove I felt a piece of paper being stuffed down the back of my wetsuit, and heard the words 'Read that.' I flew face-first into the cold ocean and was pushed back by the wake as the boat sped off.

Our group huddled together in the water, surrounded by blackness; our previous uncertainty was replaced with confusion. Then, just visible on the far shoreline, we spotted a Zodiac with a small light on it. It was like a beacon of hope radiating from the adjacent bank. We swam over to it and clambered aboard, grateful at least for this floating miracle.

Houston retrieved the note from my wetsuit and read it out. It contained a list of instructions, stating that we were to assemble the following items:

1) Four witches' hats
2) Two cases of beer
3) A street sign
4) One item of women's clothing each.

Lastly, we were to return to Dive School by no later than 2 am.

'Holy shit!' was the collective sentiment. How the hell were we going to achieve all that? We were dressed in wetsuits, had no idea where we were and, apart from the boat, had no equipment whatsoever.

Recognising that indecision in these circumstances can be worse than making the wrong decision, we picked a direction and got moving. After an hour or so we reached an arm of the main harbour in Sydney and, following a brief discussion, we headed to Darling Harbour, tied up the boat and split up to achieve the individual tasks.

Running around Darling Harbour clad in soaking wet neoprene, we must have looked a sight, but the mission was our focus. We had been asked to achieve something and, to us, it was as important as any wartime directive. With dogged determination we went about the task.

Three of the boys ran up the road to source the witches' hats, while me and Canada approached a local bar and penitently explained the situation to the bouncer. To our amazement and relief, he jogged off to the cellar and returned with two cases of beer. He handed them over with the words, 'Good luck, boys. I always wanted to be a clearance diver.' *Score!*

Now for the women's clothing. Luckily for us, it was the time of year high school graduates get dressed to the nines and converge on Darling Harbour's large venues for their formal celebrations so there was no shortage of busty beauties to plead our case to. After a few minor wins, amounting to hairnets, scrunchies and a stocking or two, time was running out and we could see that the rest of the guys were waiting for us back at the boat, keen to return with the booty. Spotting our last hope – three lovely young lasses – and with all the shyness of a schoolboy, I explained the situation and asked could they spare a garment or two. Without hesitation they looked at each other, and as one, with skill and dignity, removed their bras and handed them to me. Thank you, ladies!

I turned tail and sprinted towards the water and the waiting Zodiac, the ladies' laughter echoing in my ears.

When we arrived back at Dive School, we were tired but cautiously optimistic. The instructors inspected the haul and said, 'Nice, boys, nice; well done. Now crack those beers and let's get on it!' Unexpectedly, these men were inviting us to sit with them and share a cold beer and a warm story or two.

I sat back in my chair on the deck of the instructors' office, overlooking the Balmoral coastline and thought, 'This is the shit. This is where I want to be. This is who I am. Everybody wants to be a diver.'

Five

CLEARANCE DIVER ACCEPTANCE TEST

'I can sleep when the wind blows.'

– *Anon.*

To the uninitiated, the Clearance Diver Acceptance Test (CDAT) sounds quite innocent – even the acronym rolls off the tongue – but I can assure you that test hung like the sword of Damocles over our salt-encrusted hopes and dreams.

CDAT was a series of mental and physical challenges conducted over two weeks in order to induce maximum stress and fatigue; the aim: to determine who, if any of the attendees, had the right stuff to attempt clearance diver course.

In truth, there are many things I could fear and simply don't. But I don't say this to be tough – as a character in the movie *Man on Fire* says, 'There's no such thing as tough; there's trained and untrained.' Aside from the physical preparation for CDAT, I had to get my head in the right place. To do this, I revisited a scene from boyhood.

When I was a kid, my brother Andrew had this special folder where he kept all the information, football moves and inspirational material issued to the Joeys' First XV players. Knowing I would never receive such an honour and therefore that this near-mythic information would never be viewed by the likes of me, I started wondering what was in there: 'What could be given to them on pieces of A4 paper to help them perform Herculean feats?'

I had to know, and even though I respect the sanctity of that which is given to those who earn it, I snuck a peek at this 'Dead Sea Scrolls' of football.

The first page I picked up was a story about a farmhand, entitled *I Can Sleep when the Wind Blows*. Intrigued, I devoured every word. It went something like this:

A farmer needed some help on his allotment, so let it be known that he would employ a suitable candidate from the local area. He was inundated with applicants but could not choose until, late in the piece, an outsider approached him, a boy of slight appearance and little to no experience.

The farmer inquired what was it the boy could bring to a job that seemed outside his ability.

'I can sleep when the wind blows,' the boy replied cryptically.

Though more than a little puzzled by this, the farmer thought he saw promise in the lad and decided to take a chance and hire him.

A day or two went by and the boy carried out his duties with nary a word of complaint. Late one night, a terrible storm rolled in and created a horrendous stir. The farmer awoke, sat bolt upright in bed and then went to check the barn door: it was closed tight. Next he checked the animals: they too were secure and protected; the same was the case for the machinery shed and the feedlot.

Amazed, the farmer went to the boy's quarters to thank him for his good work. He found the boy sound asleep. It was then that the farmer remembered the phrase the boy had uttered when they first met: 'I can sleep when the wind blows . . .' The boy had done everything he was supposed to do, when he was supposed to do it, and had prepared to the full extent of his ability. There was nothing more he could have done, and therefore he could sleep soundly, regardless of the conditions.

That was enough; I read nothing else from the folder, merely replaced the sheet, put the folder back, and went on my way with those words – 'I can sleep when the wind blows' – ringing in my ears. The power of the fable stayed with me: in the lead-up to testing situations, if I do all I can to prepare, then I can rest easy in the knowledge that I have left nothing to chance.

Recalling this story, and with unwavering desire, I approached CDAT. It loomed, like the mythical Grendel, over eighteen of us, and I for one intended to slay this most heinous of monsters. Or else they would have to drag my lifeless body from the field of selection . . . Well, probably not lifeless, but at least unconscious.

Standing to at Dive School on the day of the test, drenched with sweat, I felt calm and confident. Our course had fallen in summer and the heat was oppressive. Though some divers will tell you that this is the best time to do CDAT, as your chances of passing are better in the warmer water, I strongly disagree:

1) It gets fucking hot! This increases the chances of your being removed because some overly cautious medic thinks you have heatstroke;
2) Running around in the sweltering heat carrying untold kilos on your back or atop a stretcher is way more annoying than taking a bracing swim (for me anyway); and
3) If you had a summer CDAT and passed, you were then likely to receive a nine-month winter course. Meaning you then spent infinitely more time in a frozen wetsuit wishing for the relative warmth of death!

My mates and I had trained hard and picked up one or two pointers from the less hostile among the graduates that we ran into on daily duties. Mostly we were unsure what to expect; among the victorious and failed alike, CDAT was spoken of in hushed tones. Details of what the test contained were shadowy at best. From what we could gather it was a mixture of wet and dry physical 'events', psychological tests and mind games, with a sprinkling of good old-fashioned abuse.

I use the term abuse loosely. I thought then, as I do now, that the less orthodox methods of selection were an absolute must in order to end up with the right type of person. Who would want to serve alongside some fair-weather-racehorse-type athlete who would ace all the sporting obstacles, but when things got tough or 'unfair', and they were cold and hungry, would throw their hands up in the air and cry foul.

The true test of a man does not come when he expects it and is prepared; it is thrust upon him when times are at their worst, and that's exactly what the instructors tried to simulate. The idea was to pre-fatigue candidates, so that when the real test started you were already fucked. That was what I was expecting in CDAT.

That's what we got, in excruciating detail, with the first trial, the aptly named 'gate-to-gate'. It was practically a rite of passage, along with many others, that gave the Branch its reputation. Beforehand, we'd completed a speedy PT test consisting of the usual push-ups, sit-ups, chin-ups, 2.4-kilometre run and 500-metre fin, then there was a small briefing outlining the rules and overall conduct of the selection prior to the next evolution. The gate-to-gate was a run from the gates of HMAS *Penguin* around the foreshore of Mosman and back to Dive School, a distance of around fifteen kilometres. The kicker in the run was a set of stairs with the gradients from hell. Once completed, the gate-to-gate would be repeated, in order to break the faint of heart who mistakenly thought they'd finished.

Several factors made this run difficult. Because it was the first real CDAT event, it was used to thin the ranks and get rid of any pretenders. People from all over the defence force were allowed to apply; this open casting call always attracted a few misguided souls who interpreted this generous offer as a chance to prove themselves. But typically, they were woefully underprepared; on my CDAT, a bloke fainted after the first brief and was swiftly removed. By the same token, it allowed naturals to be plucked from obscurity and go on to brilliant careers. CDAT was a giant sorting bin that quickly and efficiently separated the wheat from the chaff; if you didn't possess the qualities required you would be found out.

Duration of the gate-to-gate was open-ended: the run could go for six minutes, six hours or until the instructors ruled out whoever they viewed as unsuitable. Mind games were never far away in any physical test. With this run, the instructors would usually goad you into sprinting the start, knowing they could simply drop back, take a break, and then come at you again. They took it in turns to sprint next to each participant, pre-fatiguing you, and you wouldn't know how to pace yourself as the duration of the run was undesignated.

Finally, we got underway, and I managed to position myself somewhere in the middle of the pack. The sprints did hurt me at the start but I had some running ability and settled into a rhythm, despite the shouts and taunts of the surrounding CDs – the support staff, numbering around fifteen, had convinced all the Dive School instructors to come along. It was an unofficial tradition to invite any idle CD to run, too, even if they weren't on the selection panel, as most divers felt it their personal responsibility to remove from the course any so-called 'weak cunts', a term most feared in the Branch. The reason was that, in a little over nine months, that bloke could very well be in charge of your life.

Houston, bloody Houston. The bloke was a racehorse, and no matter how hard I tried I couldn't for the life of me keep up with, let alone overtake, this guy in a run. Sometimes I'd get close in training, but then I'd catch a glimpse of his face, see him grin and stroll ahead, leaving me in his dusty wake. He was a freak, gliding along without a care in the world, utterly convinced he would beat all comers and then some.

Jon Houston was from South Australia, or SA as he would constantly refer to it; you've never heard someone so in love with their own state! A painter by trade and a bit of a party boy, man, was he fit.

In training, my motto has long been, always train against someone better than you. It's a terrible way to build self-esteem but an excellent way to develop in areas you are lacking and will teach you humility and tenacity. Sticking next to Houston on our long morning runs up to this point was now paying dividends, and I knew if I could stick with him through the gate-to-gate I would be in the upper bracket of selectees.

I can't tell you how long the run went for; it was all a blur. At some stage I registered that it was night-time and we were at least two guys down. Fluoro vests emblazoned with their candidate numbers hung like scalps on the course boat that was tied alongside the wharf, acting as a makeshift finishing line. They reminded us that the grim spectre of failure was ever present, waiting, in the dark, to steal away all aspirations of membership into what was turning out to be a very exclusive club.

Rumour had been swirling through our group that the run would be followed by a nine-hour night fin from Mosman to Manly, and sure enough it was. I had a bit of trepidation about embarking on this journey as finning still wasn't my strongest skill, even though I had worked on it a bit with the lads. In the evenings after mess, we would sneak back down to Dive School, grab our fins, and head out unaccompanied into the bay and around the point.

Stealth would always come with me, even if the others went to the gym to work on their 'guns'. He was good like that: silent, staunch, always ready to help a mate. Nobody ever said a bad word about Stealth, and I never once saw the guy waver in skill or kindness.

Hitting the water was a relief. So often, the stress you put yourself through worrying about something prior to it happening is worse than the event itself. I was next to Salty, which was fortuitous as his humorous mumblings and backward observations kept me buoyant throughout the nine-hour ordeal; the guy was unequivocally the most positive individual you could ever meet. In a way I quite enjoyed the fin; it was a welcome break from the instructors' sledging and it gave me a chance to think.

My thoughts turned to the farm where I grew up, the long runs I would take out the back gate towards the old white tank that stood atop the hill overlooking our land. They were long and silent times, much like the swim I was doing now. Running had always been a cathartic experience, albeit a painful one. When I ran for any length of time the pain would rise through my aching feet and join the excoriating stabbing that would well up in my shins due to shin splints. I would calm my thoughts and tell myself: *focus, breathe, breathe, fucking breathe* – chest thumping, eyes stinging with sweat – *harden up; for fuck's sake don't stop; just a little further, just a little further . . .*

This mantra once again consumed my waterlogged brain as I stared into the night sky and tried to maintain the imposs-ible cadence of leg power my comrades were now setting. Nine long hours of battling the tide, cold water and the punishing tempo of what is a clearance diver's primary mode of transportation. If we were going somewhere on CDAT, then we were finning there, and we'd better get used to it. In the previous week, the water had become our world, the sea our friend, the ocean our mistress, and if we wanted that badge we would swear allegiance to her and welcome her dark embrace. It would simultaneously be our greatest ally and our most feared enemy.

The fin drew to a close, and with it some of my doubts in my ability. If I could do this, then what else was I capable of?

Upon returning to dry land we undertook another traditional naval test, the kit muster. The idea was that despite your depleted physical and mental state, you were still expected to 'keep your shit in one sock'. You would be issued with a list, then on the cement pavement next to the wharf you would lay out all your kit for inspection, to see whether you could maintain mission-essential equipment under duress.

The main items usually posed no dramas but you never could tell what would be useful or when. I found myself being asked to present the three rubber bands I had been issued with at the start of the course. 'Holy shit,' I thought, 'are they kidding?'

I quickly looked around and against all odds was able to find two. A glance to my left and right showed some other blokes in the same quandary. It wasn't till later in my career that I would realise the importance of a seemingly pointless task like holding on to those three rubber bands. It comes down to being 'squared away' and maintaining the integrity of the task.

There was no sign of the third band; I'd lost it. Then I remembered I had put an ordinary rubber band on my notebook to hold it together. I ripped it off and held it up, hoping they wouldn't notice the significant size difference between the issued variety and my shoddy replacement.

The instructor looked at me and muttered, 'Improvise, adapt and overcome, eh?' He knew full well what I was attempting.

'Roger that,' I replied, my heart pounding, and he moved on.

There's a saying, 'It's only cheating if you get caught.' I don't really subscribe to this, but we were always being encouraged to improvise to get the task done, a fact the instructor had acknowledged.

By halfway through CDAT, the lack of sleep and food, combined with extreme physical exertion, was starting to take its toll. The smiles and confident swagger of most, if not all, of the lads had disappeared and been replaced by a downward zombie-like gaze and a Cliffy Young shuffle.

The next phase of CDAT took place up in Pittwater, a large estuary about thirty kilometres north of our Balmoral base. We were ferried up to Pittwater via the ubiquitous 22-seater bus used on all military selections. I can't prove it but I have an inkling they turned the heater up and played that classical music just to screw with us. Our destination was Pittwater Annexe, an old navy warehouse that had been used for munitions during the war and now acted as kind of a training base for clearance divers undertaking selection. Few were privileged enough to even lay eyes on it; setting foot on the ancient wooden floorboards and chipped concrete floor was an entrance onto hallowed ground indeed.

In this warehouse were displayed banners – usually stolen then modified – large tarplike posters made by each course and individually decorated with their motto, which consisted of a cartoon symbol and the names of each participant. The banners stood as a testament to what could be achieved if you stuck around long enough. Yet in a stark reminder that we guppies were still at the beginning of a long journey, some names had been crossed out, indicating where an individual, despite having passed CDAT, subsequently failed to pass course.

Just off a small beach somewhere in the Pittwater Reserve, we stood goggle-eyed and gazed at the thirty-five kilograms of lead in the form of gym lifting plates that we had been ordered to deliver to the instructors' dive launch, some forty-five metres off the shore. The ship was anchored and, we were told, 'unable to move' – the reason as unknowable as the solution to our now poignant problem of cargo haulage. A test it was, the goal of which was to determine if our group of candidates could problem-solve and work together, despite being cold, wet and hungry in the extreme.

Yes, yes, we tried a raft. We tried every bloody thing, and nothing was getting the job done until my sleep-deprived brain came up with a solution that wasn't quite, well, sane . . . 'Why don't I just walk the fucking thing out there!'

The others looked at me, and I think a few Jesus remarks were even bantered about, but I clarified in quick order. 'Lads, I'll breath-hold and just start walking. The weight will hold me to the deck. You guys swim above me and, when I get tired, someone dive down and carry on.'

The boys looked at each other and, with apparently no better ideas on offer, nodded their assent.

We guided the weights into the shallows, stacking them firmly in a cradle grasp, like I was carrying groceries home from the shops. I took an almighty breath and started my descending stroll. It wasn't all that bad. The weight held me fast to the seabed and I felt good, really good. Sometimes on a free dive you hit your stride and oxygen feels like an afterthought. A few of the lads dove down to see if I needed any assistance but I had fixed my eyes at the sand and was pushing my legs on, driving forwards, oblivious to the gradient and what would soon be an issue – the distance to the surface.

You see, I'd accounted for running out of breath at the relatively tame distance of five metres. But the linear distance of my push towards the boat had placed me under about fifteen metres of seawater by the time I was ready to ascend. Oops.

When I was shit out of luck and squarely out of breath, I dropped the weights like a bad habit and shot to the surface, hoping for the best. As I came up, I had to avoid a massive obstacle. Fuck me, it was the bloody dive boat! I'd walked the weights practically the whole distance, so awaiting me at the surface were a bunch of puzzled diving candidates. 'What the fucking hell are you doing, Obi!'

At this stage, the job was only half-done; we still had to get the burdensome load from the seabed to the tailboard of the vessel, a not too shabby manoeuvre in fifteen metres of salty deep. Shifting weight along the sea floor is no drama, really; the trick is getting it to the surface. With no mechanical devices available, it was going to have to be 'hand-drolic' all the way. After a brief discussion and a hasty plan to 'just grab the fucken thing', we took a collective breath and dove hard for the bottom.

Getting it up was straightforward, but as we neared the

surface, the awkwardness of the weight made it a chore to flip it onto the boat to complete the task.

The instructors just looked at us and one of them remarked, 'Jeez, boys, you did that the hard way.'

Oh well, too bad. It was job done as far as I was concerned.

It was time to get into the large, heavy two-man canoes. By now there was an uneven ratio of personnel to boats, which meant that one unlucky bastard had to paddle one by himself, a task that was difficult enough with two people.

At first nobody leapt forward to carry this weighty cross; a foolish decision at this stage could mean the end of you; no one wanted to see their numbered vest hanging up on the instructor's boat with the other scalps. True to form, Canada raised his hand and said, 'I'll paddle da bitch, ay', in his broad highlander-like accent.

'Fuck you,' I said. 'You're not taking all the glory. I'll have a crack.'

Canada and I both laughed and agreed we would share the individual canoe between us for the duration.

The rest of the course just looked at us and no doubt thought, 'You mad bastards! Fighting over who gets the short straw.' But that was just us: Canada and I were always trying to outdo each other, though not in a bad way. It's difficult to explain but the way we saw it – like old Chief Hanrahan said – one of us was 'asking the question' and the other would always answer.

Jumping into the bulky canoe I was optimistic, even though my legs were throbbing and my feet resembled the face of a long-entombed Egyptian pharaoh, such was the level of wrapping and tape. But I thought that the paddle around to Pittwater would give me a bit of a break and allow me to rest up for things to come. Boy, was I wrong! The canoe portion, or 'paddle ex', proved to be demanding to say the least.

My lower back ached, and trying to manoeuvre that green beast through the water was like pushing shit uphill.

Sudden blinding pain!

'Fuck, fuck and double fuck!' I yelled. Reaching for whatever alien was glued to my already swollen face, I realised the paddle in front of me had flicked up a bluebottle jellyfish right into my left cheek. Minutes passed and I was going mental with the pain but thankfully the instructor's boat was a long way behind us: I didn't want to call for assistance as that might result in removal from course. So I continued on in abject misery, with Canada laughing hysterically all the bloody way.

This was the first in what would be a lifelong feud with these goblins of the sea; I fucking hate jellyfish! What bloody purpose do they serve? I don't give a damn about the subtle balance of the ecosystem! Kill the lot of them, I say; dispatch them back to hell, where they belong, and tell 'em Obi sent ya!

Our 'excursion' finally brought us to the Basin, an area of national park on the western side of the Palm Beach peninsula. Pulling our canoes ashore, we discovered we were at the foot of a giant hill covered in bush so thick bugs bounced off it.

The task before us was to simulate carrying an injured person up the hill on a stretcher, to be evacuated by chopper; to my mind, it was the hardest thing on CDAT. Old Second World War stretchers were loaded with five sandbags, each weighing in excess of twenty-five kilograms. That's one obese casualty, if you ask me, but it was a worst case scenario. Four to a stretcher was the norm but, as we had uneven numbers, one team would have to consist of three. Canada and I were to make up the bulk of this unlucky triumvirate. The third was a stocky lad called Huck. Until recently, he had been one course behind us but when a spot opened up, his work ethic around Dive School was rewarded with a place on our CDAT.

Ahead of us, the other groups progressed painfully up the mountain and we struggled along in their wake, the wooden handles digging into our shoulders as if the whole of creation rested on them. It was ridiculously dangerous trying to guide these stretchers up the steep, narrow incline, through the undergrowth and over rocks. Guys were running on empty and cracks were starting to appear in the façades of some of the previously unflappable. And this is exactly what the instructors wanted to see; this is what it meant to be a clearance diver – to be faced with a seemingly unachievable task, stare it in the face, make a joke and carry on.

I once heard a CD say that you needed to have a sense of humour like Monty Python if you were to pass CDAT, and how right he was. If you were told the sky was purple, then it was! Carry on regardless. This nugget of wisdom got a real workout when we faced Day Eight of CDAT. The day went down in history as Groundhog Day, a reference to the Bill Murray movie of that name where the main character is doomed to live the same day over and over. The Seventh CDAT day – that contained, among other things, the stretcher carry, forced march, hill climb and long fin – had been tough, to put it mildly. The following daybreak, after getting little to no sleep, imagine our reactions to the news that we were about to repeat the whole sequence. This could – and did – break the spirit of certain individuals. We began the weights session on the beach, and knowing that the previous day it had lasted three hours played on your mind. Thirty minutes in, after receiving a drubbing by the staff, one of the candidates started crying. Groundhog Day had got him. The thought of what was to come was too much; he would have been better off not knowing . . . Oh well, another scalp.

During a short break, I slipped into the bush off to the side and was hanging a piss when I thought I glimpsed a shadowy green figure in the undergrowth. 'Jesus!' I exclaimed. It was the Warrant Officer (WO) of Dive School, the head honcho, and he was up here hiding in the bloody woods watching us!

I think I was the only one to see him. He raised his right index finger up to his lips indicating, 'Shussh.'

'No dramas,' I thought, as it couldn't help anybody knowing he was watching us, though to be honest it didn't fill me with a sense of confidence either. It was fairly unusual for a WO to be out on a CDAT; that job was normally left to the Petty Officers (POs) and chiefs. But the WO was new at the School and he obviously wanted to know what clay he was to be handed, the men he would later mould as he saw fit.

The environment of selection is quite unlike anything else. You stand alone. It's like you're in a fishbowl; your every move is magnified. All your faults, foibles and failures are ready to be recorded and read back to you in mind-numbing detail.

The navy took the step of hiring three or four psychologists to tag along for these fun-filled weeks. It was rumoured that between them and the instructors, some four hundred observations per day were noted down on each student. Can you imagine that? Think about it for a second. You're closely watched over the course of a typical day at work, except that you are physically and mentally exhausted before you start. Then incorporate hunger, rain, extreme cold and emotional distress. Now throw in abnormally complex tasks and imagine what four hundred things would be written about you that day! A sobering thought, no?

As CDAT continued unabated, taunts about the many opportunities we had to fail were lobbed at us relentlessly:

Number 11, do you want to be here? Number 11, is it worth it? Number 11, all you have to do is hand me your vest and it will all be over: the pain will stop, you can have a warm meal, a shower, get some sleep and no one will think less of you. *Stop, stop, stop.*

It was becoming hard to differentiate the instructors' voices from the ones in my head, the ones expressing that inner uncertainty, that rotten core of weakness and failure that wanted to envelop me, take me with it and sleep in a pit of mediocrity.

I was entering the third hour of a four-hour PT session on Avalon Beach and all I could think was, 'Air, air, I need more air.' The steel bar I was carrying, which had seemed manageable only hours ago, now weighed a tonne and fatigue was taking hold. Then a funny thing happened: my lungs filled with air, my mind cleared and a sort of void surrounded me. I can only describe it as a feeling of clarity: I was not going to quit or stop. It wasn't fitness or strength (that leaves you within three or four days on course), I had simply reached a point where my self-knowledge fused with my intentions. I felt as though they couldn't get me. I wasn't scared of failing because I'd reached a mental state of indifference, kind of like in that movie *The Matrix*, when one of the characters says, 'Do not try and bend the spoon – that's impossible. Instead, only try to realise the truth . . . There is no spoon.' There was nothing the instructors could ask of me that I wouldn't undertake in order to achieve the end result. And I guess ultimately that's the goal of CDAT, to find those individuals willing to sacrifice their own interests and preservation for the greater good of the mission, the team and, to a certain extent, those in society who cannot or will not offer the same.

Cresting the dunes at Palm Beach on Sydney's Northern Beaches, I was imbued with a sense of pride that I had made it this far. But the fat bitch had not sung yet and there were still 'miles to go before we slept'. Up and down, up and down; what fresh hell was this? How much longer were we expected to undertake this Sisyphean task? Then the whistle was blown and a wave of relief swept over me; there was respite, at least for now.

Looking down the bedraggled line to my left, I saw that the Chief Diver, Johnny Vroom, was checking each candidate to see if they could continue. Vroom was a legend in the Branch, a man to be feared and respected in equal measure. As he approached me I felt okay and wasn't too worried, but I noticed that the candidate next to me, Number 10, had his eyes closed and was wobbling at the knees. 'This bloke's about to spear in,' I thought. 'He'll be finished in the next two breaths and when he awakes in hospital "off course" (a fate considerably worse than death), he'll be majorly pissed.' So I grabbed him by the scruff of his shorts with my right hand and supported his left shoulder with my left.

'The Vroom', as we affectionately called the Chief Diver, approached and looked Number 10 up and down. 'You all right, Number 10?'

No reply.

'What day is it, Number 10?'

'Tuesday,' came the muffled reply.

'It's Monday, Number 10 . . .' Then the Vroom looked at me. 'Is this bloke okay to continue?'

Without hesitation I replied, '*Yes!* I mean, yes, Staff, he is; he's fine.'

The Vroom's gaze moved to my puppet-like grasp on this obviously spent individual, then he said, 'All right, but you look after him', and walked off.

'Shit,' I thought, 'I'm struggling to get through this ordeal, let alone carry this bloke.' But I checked myself and thought, 'No, fuck ya, that's what this is all about. Get your mates through, help the lads, and in time they'll be there to pick you up when you stumble.'

As it turned out, the bloke recovered relatively quickly with a bit of water and a rest on the bus travelling to the next location, and went on to receive an A pass. Not that the bugger ever thanked me for holding him up that day, thereby enabling him to continue.

'If you can keep your head when all about you are losing theirs . . .' Those immortal words by Rudyard Kipling are repeated ad nauseum to every growing man in his formative years. I've come to see them through different eyes – tainted eyes, maybe – for appreciating this poem requires a certain amount of idealism. How I say that line to myself now, especially in light of my selection experiences, is, 'If you can keep your head when all about you are keeping theirs too!' You see, to succeed and rise to the top when those who surround you are 'losing their heads' is quite easy; the real challenge is to be considered worthy among those individuals, be they student or teacher, when none of them are 'losing it' but are excelling and achieving. Or, as divers say, 'killing it'. Therein lies the challenge.

Asphalt as far as the eye could see. We had reached the top of the mountain and, surprise, there was no helicopter to meet us; we'd reached the end of the second Groundhog Day, or Day Eight of CDAT overall. Personally, I laughed my ass off, as did Canada, at some of the other blokes' reactions when informed we'd be carrying the stretchers for the next twenty clicks, an addition to Day Seven. Guys actually thought we'd get a helicopter . . . Brilliant!

We all pushed on through the bush onto the tarmac road used by the Rural Fire Service to access these backwoods destinations. The four-man teams surged ahead; every couple of kilometres they would lower their stretchers to give their shoulders a much-needed rest.

The task became steadily more difficult for my team. With only three members, putting down and picking up the stretcher was harder than the actual carriage. As we painstakingly hoisted it up yet again, something in my mind must have boiled over and, surprising even myself, I said to the boys, quietly, 'Lads, let's not put it down.'

The suggestion seemed crazy as we had no idea how far we still had to travel, but it kind of made sense as we were a long way behind the others. Somehow, and I'll never know why or how, but that suggestion galvanised us. It became an all-encompassing mantra: 'Don't put it down!' Our world shrank and our minds gained a singleness of purpose. With eyes fixed on the road ahead, we picked up our pace, and passed one group, then another, then the third, until we were well ahead of everyone else. Blood trickled down my arm where the wooden handle bit into my already worn shoulders but the goal was absolute; no questions were raised.

'Don't put it down.' It sustained us, gave us strength and purpose; the days that lay ahead mattered not; the ones completed were forgotten in an instant. We shared a total unwillingness to look facts in the face. 'Don't put it down . . .'

Nearing our destination, at the Basin near Akuna Bay, we simply ran out of road. An old wharf lay in front of us and, with a collective sigh, we lowered the stretcher. The early morning sun glistened off the water and birdsong heralded a new day. We were alone, far beyond the chaos of CDAT, and there was a stillness in the air. Not a word was spoken, just a weary glance exchanged between mates.

I can say now without a shadow of doubt that in that moment I was content, calm and happier than I'd ever been – or probably will be again – in my life. I can only describe it as ease of heart and I'll never let the memory leave my tangled insides.

Then came a voice, soft and rumbling but commanding: 'There's some water over there, boys, if you're thirsty.'

Our heads flicked around; we must have looked like startled meerkats. It was the WO; he'd been behind us the whole way and witnessed the entire wretched ordeal. He moved around us like a lion stalking its prey.

'What is he doing now?' I thought. Then I realised he was checking our numbers, writing them down.

He strolled down to the wharf, removed his boots and dipped his feet into the cool water without giving us a second glance. Smiles crept across our dirt-covered faces, but we remained silent.

I'm positive that 'Don't put it down' – that single thing, that random decision, totally unplanned, not false, not trying to be tough, just trying to get the task done – is what selection is all about. Inadvertently learning to do something for no other reason than it exists. I don't believe any other course cultivates that approach.

If you can take away one point from this story it is simply that: you don't need a reason, you do the job for the job's sake.

Six

END OF CDAT

'An inability to accept the situation can hamper
efforts to resolve it.'

– HR

I was plummeting to the ground at a rate of knots. What I felt right then wasn't fear but confusion: the techniques I had been shown to slow my descent weren't working, and I couldn't figure out why. And the last resort – the brakeman at the bottom of the cliff – could not slow my momentum either.

When I hit the ground, three things saved me: the first was the sloping gradient, the second was thick vegetation and the third was Salty's body, which absorbed half the impact.

'Fuck, you okay, bro?' was the first thing I heard as I rolled over.

'Mate, what the fuck happened?' My concern for Salty, uppermost in my mind, quickly evaporated when he laughed, and told me to get my dumb ass off him.

Then it hit me, a sickening pain in my hands. Looking down, I could see that my gloves – special rappelling gloves reinforced with hardened leather – were half-melted away. Gripping the index finger of my left glove with my teeth, I eased it off, then did the same with the right glove.

It was immediately apparent what had happened. Trying to slow my descent by gripping the rope and moving it from the right side of my body to the centre, in order to lock on the roller device, had failed. During that crazily fast drop I had sustained third-degree burns across both hands.

The debacle could have been prevented. The physical training instructor (PTI) in charge of the roping exercise had used rope that was simply too thick to roll efficiently through the descent device. Consequently, the first few participants to struggle off the edge of the cliff had crept down slowly in small surges. Instead of admitting the fault, the PTI said pompously, so that the CD instructors could hear, 'Ha ha. Looks like these blokes are scared to go off the cliff. Ha ha ha!'

'What a wanker,' I'd thought. Any idiot could see it was a matter of friction on the roller system. So, me being me and not wanting the label of 'scared' to be bestowed, I asked the PTI to use fewer rollers on my turn, allowing the rope to slide more easily and therefore speed my descent.

As it turned out, it made it impossible to slow myself down, and trying to do so had caused all the damage to my molten mitts.

The possible impact this would have on my progression through CDAT was going to hurt worse than the physical pain. Walking around the corner, away from any instructor's eyes, I surveyed the damage and considered the repercussions.

To put it mildly, my hands were fucked! There was still a week to go; I needed to perform chin-ups three times a day just to eat. Before every meal, twenty overhand dead-hang chins were required. Add into the mix many hundreds of push-ups, and . . . The wounds would have no time to heal; I would have needed 'Wolverine'-type healing ability to get them back to normal. And the risk of infection was high.

'Well, lesson learnt,' I thought and proceeded to tape up my hands each night, trying to hide the full extent of the injury.

Although I managed okay, the chin-ups were agony. Each time I drew my chest to the bar, the freshly dried skin ripped off like the top layer of soup as it cools in the bowl.

The remaining days of CDAT were punctuated by runs, long fins and a particularly annoying climb to the top of Barrenjoey Lighthouse, heaving with us the bloody canoes, I might add.

To a man, our bodies had wasted away considerably; after two solid weeks of no sleep, little food and daily testing of physical and mental limits, we'd reached the end. But our minds, vulcanised by the challenges faced and overcome, were now ready for the round-table judgement that would shortly decide our fate. Each of us would either have a chance at receiving that black beret or would fail in our quest for inclusion among the diving fraternity and pack our bags for home.

'How do you think you went?'

'Bloody hell,' I thought. 'They always ask that; what do they want me to say?'

I knew what I wanted to tell them. I wanted to say that the fact I could walk up the fricken stairs into this office to attend this round table was a bloody miracle! 'I'm half-starved, half-drowned and I can hardly string two words together. My hands look like Welsh rarebit. I've got feet like a leper and a brain like Swiss cheese. Just fucking end it already and tell me if I passed!' But I said none of that.

Somewhere, somehow, I'd absorbed some excellent advice for situations like this one – interacting with superiors in the military. I knew to keep my eyes and ears open and my mouth shut. I rarely expressed what I truly thought – for a few reasons. The first is purely a respect thing: you're there voluntarily, you can leave at any time, so don't blame the instructors for your own inadequacies. Secondly, it's their club: if you want in, do as you're told, don't ask questions and endure; these tests exist for a reason and don't rock up if you don't like it.

With that in mind, I simply raised my weary head and said quietly, 'Okay, sir, I think.'

'Well, son, you did better than okay. We're giving you an A pass and recommend you go on the next available course.'

My heart exploded inside my chest; a wave of relief swept over me. I couldn't believe it. I gingerly stood up, thanked the assembled brass and stepped out of the room. I had just passed arguably one of the hardest selection courses in the Australian military; the trials of a nine-month course lay ahead, but I was over the first hurdle.

I was floating on air as I went out into the early morning sun and onto the wharf, where the others were packing up their gear. Canada walked over and shook my hand, and walked away down to the water's edge.

'You don't even know if I passed!' I yelled.

He smiled – a rare event – solemnly looked back and said, 'Mate you passed when we got on the bus to attend dis madness, ay!'

I laughed and jogged down to give him a hand with the heavy Zodiac that now seemed light as a feather.

Perhaps now I'd be able to sleep, at least for a bit, before the nocturnal demons returned to haunt my repose and holler from the blackness, 'You'll never pass course, you'll never pass course . . .'

Seven

BASIC CLEARANCE DIVER COURSE

'Softly tread the brave.'

— *Ivan Southall*

Standing on my head in eight metres of water for the better part of an hour wasn't the best start to clearance diver course. Though it was educational. For one thing, it was forcing me to rethink my adherence to the adage, 'There are no stupid questions.' Following it had landed me in this situation – that and my limited knowledge of dive physics, which had prompted me to ask how the water stays out of your dive helmet. In typical CD fashion, the PO instructor in charge boomed at me, 'Well, Diver O'Brien, as you're not willing to wait for the classroom lesson, I'll show you!'

As it turns out, it's the simple principle of 'positive pressure' that ensures water stays out of your dive helmet, and it is but one of the many principles and laws we were about to learn in the nine-month long 'basic' clearance diver course.

With the gruelling but rewarding selection phase behind us, we prepared for our education as clearance divers: Basic Clearance Diver Course (BCD). The process was divided into the four broader elements of the Branch: underwater battle damage repair, mine countermeasures, maritime tactical operations and explosive ordnance disposal. Each stage was carefully paced and merged into the next. Many other skill-sets and subjects were also covered.

Each section of the course involved an incredible amount of theory. Diving is not an exact science – men are simply not meant to venture beneath the waves – however, with education and training comes understanding.

One of the first principles I grappled with was Boyles Law – really one of the most important principles in diving, and learnt verbatim by every CD hopeful. It states that if the temperature remains constant, then the volume of any given mass of gas is inversely proportional to the absolute pressure. Don't worry, I won't go into diving theory and physics – plenty of people have filled encyclopaedias on the subject, and it can get a bit boring. Suffice to say that the basic principle of breathing compressed air and having nitrogen diffuse into your soft tissue is one of the main problems with the aquaman lifestyle. Rise too quickly and you will not allow those bubbles to diffuse out again. Those bubbles will place you squarely in the hurt locker and this is the essence of what makes diving so inherently dangerous.

Well, that and jellyfish; fucking jellyfish!

Despite my hour spent at eight metres, courtesy of my dive helmet question, I continued to ask plenty of questions, often to the annoyance of my instructors. Firstly, I did it in order to avoid the embarrassment of a fuck-up, and secondly to give myself every chance of passing. Some blokes merely wanted to be told that a particular event occurs, whereas I wanted to know *how* and *why* the event occurs, in order to better undertake the task.

Perhaps this approach was unnecessary in some cases – at times, on the job, you just get the brief and run with it – but where possible I generally like to know why! I found that knowing the task and understanding the theory behind it could vastly contribute to the end result.

The way I looked at it – and still do – passing dive course, or any selection for that matter, takes a combination of philosophy, strategy and training. Any one of these by themselves will get you part of the way, but it takes an understanding of all three to truly face the mirror and be ready.

The fear of returning to my pre-diver, uninspired lifestyle was a visceral spur in my daily need to learn all I could and strive for success. I couldn't go back now. I was committed and I needed to stay one step ahead. Dixie Ford had asked me, over eight months earlier, when I had dared to sign up, 'So you want to be a frogman?' You're goddamn right I do.

Looking at the CD rate badge high on the right arm of the instructor's overalls was also a daily reminder why I was here. They didn't hand those things over without a fight.

Learning how to use all the tools, helmets and associated breathing equipment, along with the recompression chamber, was a steep learning curve, as steep as bloody Awaba Street, the heartbreaking hill they made us run up barefoot every morning carrying an enormous rope. But I was really starting to enjoy course; it was everything I'd dreamed of: challenging, educational and generally nuts!

At night we would still have diving physics homework, and I found this particularly hard as after a day at Dive School you were so spent you could barely climb into bed, let alone study.

Getting to sleep was often a challenge for me. Inscribed on a banner at Dive School was the saying, 'Some men fear the ocean; the ocean fears some men.' Frequently I lay awake at night contemplating its vast implications, and what it meant for my immediate future.

I never ran out of things to think about on those nights when sleep eluded me. Even having passed CDAT, Dive School was still an intimidating place.

During my time in the military I noted the very real but quite indescribable 'flux' that surrounds everything. There were always these distinct metaphysical barriers around you and those you served with. Depending on what you've done, haven't done, passed, failed, partaken in, you'll be put inside or outside certain circles. These circles – let's call them constructs of endeavour – exist everywhere in the military world; they cross all borders, envelop everything and, depending on your general level of awareness, you could pass in or out on a daily basis without ever having realised they exist. It's about acceptance and earning a level of respect. You couldn't just rock up everyday and 'phone it in', you had to excel every day if you wanted to stand out in the Branch.

Every course is given a course number. Ours was 53 – BCD 53, to be exact – and upon receipt of said number, it was each course's duty to develop a T-shirt, get it printed up and make sure everyone in the entire course wore it every morning to PT. It was supposed to display some sort of symbol and a saying that you and your mates could share.

Salty and I took on this duty as we had strong feelings about it. Ivan Southall had written a book about the wartime bomb disposal teams that gave rise to the Clearance Diving Branch. *Softly Tread the Brave* was the title, and we thought that reviving that as a saying would be an honourable nod to the old and bold.

Coming up with the symbol was left to me, and I cast around for something that'd look good on a T-shirt, as well as embodying what our course was about. After much deliberation, I nominated the flying hellfish symbol, from Grandpa Simpson's commando unit in *The Simpsons*. I think the creators of the show had based it on some old US Navy SEAL symbols. To me, it perfectly represented the general mischievous nature of the boys and, besides, it looked cool!

Wearing our brand new hellfish T-shirts for the first time at morning PT felt amazing. I'd never been part of such an exclusive group in my life, and I knew that the T-shirt with the letters BCD 53 printed over the heart came with enormous responsibility as well as pride. We were the latest in a long line of men who had volunteered to undertake hazardous duty for the navy, stretching all the way back to the Second World War P Parties in 1945 and the brave men of Z Special Unit.

All the lads on our course were good blokes and we were shaping up to be a great working unit. By this stage, the members of BCD 53 were Houston, Pepper, White, Borthwick, Peaper, Smith, Archibald, Baron, Clancy, Maihi, Henwood,

Barr, Damian, Healy and O'Brien. Huck and Strongy had both sustained small injuries so went onto the course immediately after ours.

We launched into Dive School with a week and a half coxswain's course. Essentially, this entailed getting your boat licence and becoming familiar with the dive boat and Zodiacs. After that it was straight into the underwater tools phase, learning the use and maintenance of a wide array of equipment, including hydraulic and pneumatic tools, as well as underwater welding and cutting. Becoming proficient with all this stuff on the surface was hard enough; taking it underwater and passing a test within four or five weeks seemed next to impossible.

Practice, practice, practice – that's the only way to get good at anything; we put in countless hours underwater in our newly learnt surface-supplied breathing apparatus (SSBA). Utilising the MK 17, MK 18 Kirby Morgan dive helmets was an amazing experience and a steep learning curve.

The deep diving phase, with its complicated decompression tables and recompression chamber emergency procedures represented another large amount of information to take on board but I was learning fast.

On my first descent to fifty-four metres beneath the white caps, I was paired up with Salty; you always dove with a buddy, plus as a back-up there'd be a man dressed in on the surface. Salty and I made bottom and settled in to the surrounding pressure of 6.4 ATA (atmosphere absolute pressure, aka atmospheres), a combination of the 5.4 atmospheres of sea water depth and the one atmosphere of air pressure we experience on the surface. Reporting back topside via the in-helmet comms system that we were okay was the first procedure. The next was to turn the valve attached to the side block of our helmets, allowing a blast of fresh air to cool our face and clear any condensation that may have built up on the inside of the viewing window.

Gazing towards the surface, I could see my dive hose, or umbilical, spiralling upwards into the light blue void. It contained my air hose, comms cable and kluge, a simple air hose used for remotely measuring depth. Around me was a landscape as barren as the lunar surface I'd seen in those Discovery Channel documentaries. There wasn't much to get excited about; that is, until I saw Salty trying to bury himself in the silty seabed, laughing hysterically as he went.

When enough nitrogen has built up in a diver's bloodstream – from the surrounding pressure plus breathing compressed air – nitrogen narcosis can set in, causing a state much like drunkenness. The condition can be overcome with concentration and training, but we were fairly new to all this and Salty's antics, although at first they seemed weird, started to become funny to me as well. Without understanding why, I too began to laugh.

Our hilarity was shortlived: we received an instruction to prepare to leave bottom. You didn't have long at that depth if you wanted to avoid a long decompression schedule. As soon as I felt the predesignated four pulls on our lifeline umbilical, I gave Salty the chop (the signal to ascend) and we headed home, gently returning to the surface at a rate of eighteen metres a minute so as to avoid the bends and allow the nitrogen to diffuse out of our system. Our heads started to clear and the reason we were previously cracking up now seemed a mystery.

The deep is a strange place and it would take some time for us to learn its secrets and adjust to a world of more than one atmosphere.

During one of our final tests on cutting, welding and general underwater tool use, I became embroiled in a particularly embarrassing incident and learnt a real lesson in how different things can seem underwater. The incident perfectly demonstrated how the simplest task could become a shit fight if you didn't think about every step – because of the rule of three, whereby any task, no matter how basic, becomes three times as hard when conducted underwater.

The task in question was to cut a hole in a piece of steel with the Broco cutter, a type of thermal lance that works not unlike the light sabre from 'Star Wars'. You then had to grind down the edges with a hydraulic disk grinder, apply a cover patch and, using a mad tool called a Ramset gun – which uses a 9mm cartridge – fire a nail through both bits of steel, thereby fusing them together; this was to be done in each corner. Then we would weld the edges, completing a simulated ship's 'hull patch'. The key to doing all this successfully was to set yourself up comfortably, lay out your kit, be methodical and carry out the task in the allotted time, after which your job would be taken up to the surface for inspection.

This task seemed to embody all that I'd come to associate with a quintessential navy diver and I was keen to do well. Initially, everything went smoothly; however, when it came time to shoot the nails, or fasteners as they were called, into my patch a little problem arose. This is what had happened: following through on some sage advice, I'd located a reasonably flat surface on which to work. I'd placed on it my two bits of steel plate and set myself for the nailing. Bang! Bang, bang, bang, no dramas.

'That thing looks sweet,' I thought, with astonishing hubris.

When I went to pick it up and take it over to the underwater welding bench that was set up only three metres away, I noticed a small but significant problem: I couldn't lift the bloody thing up!

'What the fuck!' I thought, totally confused. I'd been down there for over two hours by that stage, and as you get colder and more tired, it becomes hard to concentrate.

Then it dawned on me: the nails had gone straight through both bits of steel plate and into the seabed, fused for all eternity.

'Fuckkkkkkk!' What the bloody hell was I going to do now?

Time was a factor and I was already behind schedule. I skirted around the area and, despite the limited visibility, determined that my nails hadn't fused to the seabed but to a freaken enormous bit of old steel plate that must have been lying down there for aeons and was now screwing me over. This thing was huge! About five metres by eight metres and ten millimetres thick. I simply did not have a way to remove my job from it.

Thinking quickly, I requested cutting equipment in order to remove the section with my work on it and carry on with the welding. No joy, request denied. The cutting equipment was being used by another diver on his project some ten metres away.

'Think! Think! . . . Screw it,' I said to myself and, with all my strength, lifted the edge of the large plate and dragged it over to the welding bench, quickly welded the edges of my job in the middle, then dragged it back to the wharf. What now? How was I to explain the situation to the instructor on the other end of the coms?

'Ah, topside, this is Diver One.'

'Go ahead, Diver One.'

'Ah yer, ah, request a rope to be sent down to retrieve my job?'

'Diver One, this is topside. Just bloody carry it up with you. What's the hold-up?'

'Um, well . . . just send down the rope and you'll see.' What else could I say? They were expecting a 60cm × 60cm piece of steel, not the bloody *Titanic*!

Half an hour later, and with the help of no less than eight of my course mates, I hauled this monstrosity to the surface for inspection.

Many seconds passed; the instructor stood there in silence, shaking his head. 'Well, Diver O'Brien, I can honestly say I've never seen that before.'

To make things worse, some CDs from Team One were on the wharf collecting gear to take back to base. This was the team I hoped to be posted to if I graduated; they were eyeing off my handiwork and laughing their arses off! You couldn't blame them, it was pretty funny.

To my amazement the instructor then said, 'The welds actually look good. Get a crowbar, pry that thing off there and we'll see if it holds water.'

'Jesus,' I thought, 'that's good of him!'

As it turned out the job passed and I got a tick in the box for that test, but received 500 push-ups for my trouble – a lenient punishment really.

Eight

MINE COUNTERMEASURES

'Between the devil and the deep blue sea.'

– Anon.

Your mind fills with possibilities and, however unlikely they may be, they can cloud your judgement, compromise your clarity – and make the last breath you take one of frustration at the realisation your death could have been prevented, had you only concentrated harder. This is the reality of training to be a clearance diver. You may not be getting shot at, but every day and most nights you are forty-five metres under the water wearing a man-made, student-assembled life-support system sold to the military by the lowest bidder. You might as well be on the moon, for you can practise all you want – and don't get me wrong, there are safety procedures in place – but you're alone in the ocean deep. A million things can go wrong and they all flash through your head as you concentrate on the task of locating that subaquatic instrument of death, the sea mine.

The word 'clearance' in 'clearance diver' reflects the deep historical roots of mine countermeasures (MCM); mine clearance is still the primary job of a CD. Complicated, bloody complicated, is how I would describe my initial impressions of MCM. It is a vast subject and there are many procedures to be learnt in order to avoid 'transformation into pink mist', a euphemism for a mine blast's obvious consequences.

One of the first thing we learnt in MCM was the acronym MAPS: magnetic, acoustic, pressure and seismic. These are the main ways a mine will actuate – a nice way of saying 'end any aspirations of seeing your next birthday'.

Basically there are two ways of disposal, once you have gone through the painstaking procedure of locating a mine. You can carefully blow it in place, or BIP it, which is simple, and with an infinitely desirable outcome in that it takes care of the problem without exposing any further personnel to danger. Alternatively, if the mine is needed for further inspection or the area cannot withstand a large explosion, then a smaller charge is situated at a predetermined distance and the air spaces within the mine are over-pressurised faster than the components can function, thereby rendering it safe for transportation. There's a heap more to it than that but a good deal of the details are 'secret squirrel'; let's just say MCM requires patience, bucketloads of patience.

As technology has developed, so has the art of mine-sweeping. Straight off we'd had to master a new dive set incorporating a piece of equipment known as the A5800 – a nitrox rebreather built entirely of non-ferrous (non-magnetic) materials, designed for the perilous minefield environment. The A5800's catchphrase is: no bubbles, no sound, no worries.

*

You can hear your breathing now – in, out, in, out, in, out . . . The dive set on your back is heavy with complexity as much as componentry. In your right hand, a 2 Alfa sonar is connected to a headset that bleeps incoherently, mocking your vain attempts to decipher what is a coke can and what is a ship-destroying juggernaut. Your left hand is struggling to contain a plethora of string and floats for the laborious location of said device. The only thing more distracting than the fact your complicated breathing equipment was assembled hastily with tired brains and cold hands is the large weight belt digging into your aching side for the sole purpose of dragging your encumbered form forty metres below into the blackness, in search of something no one wants to find . . .

My breathing had settled and so had the muddy haze surrounding me as my spatial awareness returned, so I started to go through my mental checks. The small red and green blinking light attached to my mask indicated that the partial pressure of oxygen in my rebreather was maintaining safe levels.

It was cold but I'd been smart this time; knowing I had a mindblowing list of things to accomplish while I was down there, I'd attempted to rule out the cold factor and worn a relatively thick wetsuit. As a result I'd copped some glib remarks from the lads. When I pointed out that I was the only one still to have never worn a one-millimetre-thick rash suit under my overalls for our long morning fins, this put an end to the discussion.

The task was to locate the practice, or simulation, sea mine somewhere on the seabed, which we had marked out the previous day. The vis was poor and I started my search half-hoping I wouldn't find the fucking thing. Once it was found, I would have to perform a detailed procedure to establish the mine's position, depth and condition, followed by another set of finicky procedures for clearance, followed by an even more convoluted raising procedure. The whole ordeal could take four to five hours and by the time I'd finished, if indeed I hadn't fucked up – unlikely – I would be well broken . . .

Something incredible had been happening to me during my CD training. In sharp contrast to my inability to achieve anything of merit on the surface of the earth, increasingly I was getting things right underwater. It was becoming my world down there: I felt at home, comfortable, in control; I always knew what to do; I had no doubts, no worries and no demons; the water's cold comfort was mine.

Truth was always a virtue when it came to underwater operations. The contents of a cylinder and the volume of gas you would be breathing were not something subjective. If you were asked whether you had completed a task with those cylinders and, God forbid, you contorted the truth, then your mate could well be breathing your lie. In the Branch, regardless of what the fuck-up was, you got a hell of a lot more respect if you admitted your mistake, took your punishment and moved on – a mindset sorely lacking in the military nowadays. Receiving an official punishment that has nothing to do with your job or your training can make you angry and alienated – I've seen it many a time. But dealing with things 'in house' and receiving a punishment that may be swift and brutal but which contributes to your training: a) makes you not want to fuck up, and b) achieves something by its completion. Back in my day, this was how everything was dealt with. Fifty push-ups here, one hundred push-ups there – they were the currency the Dive School traded in, and it was not uncommon to have smashed out a thousand by day's end.

One incident occurred about halfway through our course. Some of us got into a fight on the piss. I forget who was at fault but you can guarantee Canada and I were involved. When the Chief asked who it was, we owned up immediately and the whole course got run jumped for the next two hours straight, holding a Zodiac above our heads most of the time. This was something that teams often had to do. By this stage we were used to the pain and it didn't affect us much. Canada and I thought we'd won, but after the run jump, the Chief made the pair of us stand still while the whole course did 500 push-ups. To this day, I've never felt worse in my life. It was the single most effective punishment I ever received in the military. Without any of us realising it, we had come to care not for personal pain or injury but deeply about our course mates. This was no accident; there's a reason those instructors had got to where they were.

Compared to other branches, the cost of training a clearance diver is one of the highest in the military. Consequently, nothing during training is an accident; you get away with nothing, even when you think you have – the instructors are always a step ahead of you because they did the same things when they were in your position.

That was the first and last time Canada and I needed to be singled out for punishment. Forcing us to watch our mates suffer was the only effective thing they could do to us, and they knew it. After it was over though, not one of the boys said anything derogatory about us. They did the punishment without complaint or ill temper; they knew how much it killed us.

As a diver, your life literally rests in the hands of everybody on the site, regardless of skill, rank or position. Even if we never went to war, blokes could and did die during training through mistakes made under pressure. We were taught a valuable lesson that had practical implications: fuck up and others will suffer.

The task lay before me now and though I knew its difficulty, confusing panic was replaced by calm. It felt like everything was happening in slow motion as a deliberate, measured system of steps kicked in – easily controllable, calculable and cold. I'd attached the lift bag and secured the towing line to the massive hunk of steel that I'd located an hour earlier, and was now returning to the surface, retrieving a mountain of string and floats used in the marking and location procedure.

Suddenly I paused mid-water feeling a restriction around my leg. To my horror I was tangled in the miles of thin marker line. I couldn't believe it; I'd been so careful and methodical; it was a mystery how the entanglement had occurred.

Then I remembered the timer . . .

Beneath me, the actuation mechanism attached to the two-tonne mine and lift bag would shortly initiate on its own, filling the lift bag with compressed air. And although there were no live explosives involved, what amounted to a hot air balloon attached to a VW was about to inflate and shoot forty metres to the surface, taking me with it. Ascending to the surface from forty metres in less than a second is, to say the least, undesirable.

Feeling the pounding in my chest and the strain in my head, I realised the situation was life-threatening. Resisting the urge to panic, I threw my head forward, kicked with my free leg and completely inverted. As I was turning and producing what can only be described as an 'aquatic yoga downward dog roll', I whipped out my knife (one of the three I had strapped to me – one can never have too many knives!) and swung at the obstructing rope. Severing the line in a swift ninja roll and quickly righting myself, I headed safely for the surface. I made it in just enough time to see the yellow balloon hit the surface, indicating that the task was complete.

As a diver, you can't wipe your forehead of sweat and say 'Phewwwwww', especially with a mask and rebreather on, but I did permit myself a reaction. I'm sure you get the drift.

Nine

EXPLOSIVE ORDNANCE DISPOSAL

'The best way out is through.'

— Robert Frost

Sun Tzu's *The Art of War* tells us, 'Know thyself, know thy enemy.' Well, I've read that cryptic fucking book four times and I reckon Sun, a revered military strategist who died over 2500 years ago, was onto something. The book is really hard to understand but there's a lot of brilliance in it. Two things in that quote strike me as absolutely true. *You* are the enemy. Also, I think old Sun might be suggesting that your weaknesses are the enemy's strengths and vice versa, but your own inner turmoil or lack of confidence can be far more damaging than anything.

Little by little, the course was whittling away these tendencies of mine. I may never be fully rid of self-doubt but clearance diver course sure drills it out of you. By the end of my Shoalwater Bay experience, I would certainly 'know myself' and then some.

There's a turning point on CD course, designed specifically for the purposes of finishing off the weak, and I was acutely aware that the three-week EOD (explosive ordnance disposal) phase was it. It was to be held on the imaginatively named Triangular Island, a small dot in the otherwise vast military training area of Shoalwater Bay, off the coast of Rockhampton, Queensland. It is used specifically by clearance divers for underwater demolitions and large-scale EOD. At only about 3.5 kilometres across at its longest point, it is tiny, but it is an excellent training environment. Although every bloody thing about basic course was a giant test, if blokes were going to crack and decide the life aquatic was not for them, then this would be the time and place they would do so.

For BCD 53, the signs were good. All the lads were fusing together into a solid contingent of divers. Our course had been doing well; we had a good rep with the instructors and we were feeling capable and confident heading into EOD phase. I was glad. As so many of us were from different backgrounds and areas of the navy, it was imperative we gel prior to this phase. If there's one place you don't want to come unstuck and have a domestic with your classmates, it's during underwater demolitions.

Before we even set foot on the island, aspects of our upcoming training endeavour were becoming evident. For instance, we knew that two fully laden semi-trailer loads of ordnance and explosives were awaiting our arrival. It looked like every day would be filled with scenario-based mission profiles emulating those in which a CD might find himself. I overheard a particularly obtuse instructor saying that if there were any mistakes with this stuff, then 'Goodnight, the fox'. Thanks very much; that said it all really.

In this area of the world there are massive tides, and each time Poseidon pulled back the waves, a giant plateau of mud would be revealed. It extended out two kilometres and surrounded the island in a halo of hardship.

The area was perfect for conducting underwater demolition and quite often we trainees would spend the morning hauling and manhandling a symphony of ordnance out into the mudfields. Then when the waters rose, we'd dive the 'problem' as if we had just found it.

One of the hairiest experiences of my career happened in this place. For the exercise in question, Salty and I spent a good part of the day shifting and stacking depth-charges – eleven to be exact – into a pyramid shape. They were heavy bastards, about forty kilograms each, and had no fusing system. Essentially, they were just each a lump of bang; remember that a single one of these suckers can take out a submarine!

We carefully primed each one with two sticks of plastic explosive (PE), drew the whole thing together by securing the tails of the det cord sticking out of the PE and were ready to see the fruits of our labour – the whole thing being blown to smithereens – later in the afternoon.

As we had set it up, Salty and I were afforded the luxury of going out in the boat with the assistant instructors to 'put fire on', in other words to light the fuse. We would then head two kilometres away to witness the explosion while the rest of the course and remaining instructors waited patiently in the bunker for our confirmation of detonation and the all clear.

I swam over and initiated the fusing system, got back in the boat and awaited the roar of the outboard motor, expecting to be whisked away to safety.

Putt, putt, putt, sputterrrrrrr! The bloody thing cut out about one hundred metres or so from our pyramid of death! 'Shit,' I thought.

Salty started the heavy donk and we surged on.

Putt, putt, putt, splurttttt! Shit, shit and double shit! The motor stopped again, and we were a mere 400 metres from where I'd lit the fuse.

Taking in the cool demeanour of the assistant instructors, I thought, 'They'll know what to do; they always do.'

After pumping the gas a little and giving her full throttle, we finally began to gain some distance on the angering beast.

'Um, bro,' I said, 'how far away do we need to be from this thing?' A perfectly reasonable question, no?

The instructor gave me a sidelong glance, continued playing with the motor as it spluttered and struggled to maintain momentum, then mumbled, ''Bout two K.'

'Right then. I guess we had better get going then, eh.'

The meandering pace we were setting with our painfully sick donk definitely wasn't going to cut it. We needed to get a wriggle on.

At 1.5 kilometres out, and with forty-five seconds to go before our pyramid did its thing, Salty looked across at me and I could see he was a little worried. My blind faith in the CD on the boat remained unwavering, until he turned around and I detected a hint of concern creeping across his face.

'Right, boys, jump in; wait for the blast to rip through the water. When you feel it on your legs, hold your breath and get under the boat. Not before, as your lungs might implode! Oh, yeah, and don't come up until you hear all the shrapnel finish.'

'You can't be serious!' I thought. 'Was that part of the bloody drill? What the fuck!'

But before we had a chance to discuss it further or even jump out of the boat, BANG! A plume of water rose over thirty metres, a shockwave rippled through the water around us and we watched as giant black shards of shrapnel whistled through the air.

Bloody hell, what a show; it was exhilarating! When I looked down I could see flickers disturbing the water as shapes appeared to tumble toward us. These, I'm told, were pieces of fist-sized steel slicing horizontally through the water with the ease of a skimming stone on a pond. Imagine what they could do to your face! They were a terrifying spectacle. A couple of chunks landed around us but nothing hit the boat.

We looked at each other in silence as slowly calm returned to our surroundings and the water settled.

'Mmm, that was a bit close,' muttered the instructor.

You don't say . . .

Our three weeks or so on the island drew to a close, and we started to pack up for the long trip back to Sydney. A comprehensive evaluation had been done on all the individuals on our course; it turned out we had all passed and done well.

You wouldn't have thought it to look at us. We were a motley crew. Having washed in salt water the whole time and worn only one set of camouflage uniform, we could even smell ourselves. But sitting there on the beach waiting for the naval landing craft to retrieve us, we felt as one for the first time on course. It may only have been T-shirts that made us a course before, but now we truly were one.

*

How does a person remain standing when with every fibre of their being they wish to lie down? Most people would argue that the answer is somewhere among our hopes and aspirations. I would put it to you, however, that the solution is darker, less shiny, sinister even.

I could feel it welling up inside me, a sick stifling nausea, a stubborn angst not to let 'them' win, not to be afraid. It was akin perhaps to the obstinacy of an embattled petulant child, raising his fist and declaring an undiluted willfulness *not* to go to bed. It's not a 'yes' for me, it's a 'no' . . . 'No! I won't quit, you fucks!'

Go on, hit me again. It matters not, for strength lies not in the attack but the ability to withstand. Inflict what you will; I might not win but neither will you . . .

Ten

MARITIME TACTICAL OPERATIONS

'There's no such thing as friends. Just degrees of liability.'

– Chief Diver

You plunge into the dark swirling nothingness, concentration temporarily immobilised as the frigid waters numb your brain. You feel stunned, but as the warm oxygen fills your lungs your focus returns and the task ahead takes precedence. A glance to your left reveals the phosphorescent outline of the encumbered form next to you, then you remember: someone here is awaiting your choice of direction, depth and pace. You're on a tactical swim surviving on a pure oxygen rebreather. The burning in your legs soon matches the fire in your chest and your goal of swimming two thousand yards (1.8 kilometres) in sixty minutes seems impossible. Welcome to maritime tactical operations (MTO).

Ask any navy diver what he remembers about clearance diver course and the answer will invariably come back,

'MTO, mate; fucken MTO.' The reasons are as varied as they are painful, for MTO represents 'the sharp end' – a level of training and endurance so challenging that it is left, understandably, to the end of course. It is a rite of passage not easily forgotten by those who undergo it.

There are two parts to MTO; well, possibly three if you count learning the LAR V dive set, a pure oxygen rebreather manufactured by Draeger: a fine bit of kit, user-friendly and durable as fuck; diverproof, as they say. The first part is clandestine beach reconnaissance and beach clearance. The idea is that when a mission calls for a large seaward approach, numbers of divers covertly check out the area beforehand. Following a grid system of sorts, groups of divers carry out a detailed assessment of the possible landing area. To be honest, I found it incredibly laborious and complicated, and it took a great deal of practice to get right. There are so many moving parts that it requires timing, coordination and a bit of luck. The second component of MTO, and the noticeably more gung ho of the two, is the attack swim, or silent approach, towards a ship or coastal installation to plant explosives or gather information. The training for this basically involves swimming your arse off for hours, day and night, until you achieve the required goals of speed, accuracy and task completion.

A certain smoky haze always surrounded everything to do with MTO, as it was a seldom-used but curiously much-respected element of the clearance diver training experience. Among the Teams, it somehow held a top-shelf reputation. Whether that is justified or not, I cannot say; neither do I know why it has that mystique. Whether it's as a result of historic reckoning or self-imposed internal elitism, some activities seem to separate themselves from the rest, even within a structured environment. MTO was one of those topics that organically grew its own mystique.

As MTO was held in such high regard, achieving a high level of success in this final trial became a personal goal.

Also, rumours had begun circulating about a secret new unit being formed within the military that would involve some of these skills. Information was tight, but that didn't stop a couple of us from wondering what this shadowy company was up to and, more importantly, how we would get a piece of the action.

I was in a little bit of bother . . . The shaking was becoming increasingly violent and I could not have been far off that point we all were taught to dread, when your body enters its final phase and simply stops shaking. The cold had taken all my thoughts, feelings and sense of self; I was finding it hard to concentrate and even had trouble remembering where I was and why I was there. It was a beach clearance training operation and hypothermia was setting in.

My dive buddy, Maihi, was laughing at me, I could hear him. That's the strange thing about rebreathers: if you've been diving for long enough and have had enough practice, you can actually hear sounds in the small air space in the breathing loop. It was unmistakable: he was laughing at my shivering carcass. He had taken the wise step of adding a few extra layers of wetsuit, knowing full well we would smash our part of the operation and be waiting, idle, back at the pick-up point. And yes, we had flown through our task and were now sitting at eight metres freezing our arses off.

Minutes ticked by and still the other teams did not arrive. My condition worsened, but there wasn't much I could do. Calling off the dive wasn't an option: exercise or not, we treated it as if it were real, and the consequences both practically and socially for calling off a dive on account of being cold were far worse than being shot! So I sat there singing the hits of the 1980s in my head, willing myself not to spear in and float to the surface like a dead mullet.

At last the other teams arrived at our position. We had probably been down there on the long side; even the instructors were concerned. The lead diver gave the chop, a signal to ascend, and we headed to the surface in unison.

What a relief to finally be moving again; I could feel the blood returning to my chicken-like legs. When I hit the surface I noticed one of the other pairs of divers having trouble: there was a bit of commotion that finished with a black form being dragged from the water into the waiting Zodiac. It turned out that another of the guys had become next-to-hypothermic. His temp had dropped so far that he experienced an oxygen hit, where oxygen toxicity causes the body to go into convulsions; we call this the 'Funky Chicken'. The bloke was promptly removed from the water and the medical staff treated him on the spot. All I could think was that this meant the end of our mission, the dive and our night in the freezing black liquid – but there was no such luck!

The instructor lent over the edge of the Zodiac and said, 'We're taking this bloke in. You fuckers get back down there, finish the job, then swim home,' and off they went.

The boys and I looked at each other, reinserted our breathing pieces, lowered our masks and headed down again.

Yee-har! How good was Dive School!

'There's always another hill', so the saying goes. You're goddamn right there is. Not one week away from graduation, from finally receiving our badge, and there were further unsettling 'grass is greener' rumours around. We'd heard whispers of a secretive selection for the new anti-terrorism unit. Details were sketchy and we realised that no one was going to talk to a couple of new guys, let alone lads still on course. There was no choice but to put it out of our minds and focus on the job at hand: surviving MTO. And that was a pretty big job.

During one of the infamous two-thousand-yard swims, my lifelong battle with jellyfish continued. We were about halfway through, and I was on track for a passing time nicely under the sixty-minute mark – a feat I had not yet accomplished – when I swam directly up the arse of a lion's mane jellyfish. Instant pain gripped every inch of my exposed skin, and there was more of it than usual as I was wearing a short-sleeved three-millimetre-thick wetsuit in order to gain more speed. I could feel my neck and glands swelling and my already laboured breath shortening.

Shit, shit – I was spearing in.

But aborting the dive wasn't an option; completing it in the allotted timeframe was a prerequisite for passing out, and I'd be dammed if an invertebrate was going to stop me. Taking a few deep breaths and ploughing on, I reached the beach – barely.

Gasping for air, I crawled onto the sand, and the first thing my swim buddy, Maihi, innocently said was, 'Hey, bro, did you see the size of that nasty jelly?' Catching sight of the swollen pulp where my face used to be, he realised the situation. 'Fuck, mate, do you want me to get the medic?'

I can't remember my answer but I was later told that my response was something like: 'Time, time, did we get the time?'

Yes, I had made the time, which gave me some solace. I spent the next three nights without the luxury of sleep, thanks to the incessant itching of my swollen arms, neck and face. Fuck, I hate jellyfish!

We were nearing the end of MTO and logging up full-mission profiles on a nightly basis – drop-off by Zodiac, surface fin, subsurface dive to target and task. The six of us whose turn it was to dive next gathered in for the brief, with our other course mates prepping our kit in the background of the dive vessel. The instructor's face was serious – he looked as though he was about to issue orders to the *Enola Gay*.

'Right, lads,' he began, 'the target is the beach at the afore-mentioned coordinates. Once in the shallows, you are to exit the water and head up the beach ten or so metres, then line up and sing a song of your choice as loud as you can.'

The boys and I looked at each other, not sure whether to laugh or simply nod our acceptance and mirror his stern delivery. There was no time to think it over.

'Right, in the water. *Go!*' came the order, and we complied.

Swimming as a pack, we were tight, fast and on target. We had this shit down by now. The group of six consisted of the better guys on course, headed naturally by the irrepressible Salty Pepper. Salty didn't make mistakes; he was perfect. It had shown through again and again. By way of confirmation, the bloke received the highest marks in each of the testable components in every phase.

Hitting the surface, we prepped our equipment for the walk up the beach, fins in hand, anticipation at a fever pitch and our song choice undecided.

Once we'd lined up and were staring into the blackness and what we presumed was empty bushland, Salty took charge. Standing at full attention, at the top of his lungs he belted out, 'SIX O'CLOCK I'M GOING DOWN, THE COFFEE'S HOT AND THE TOAST IS BROWN!' an easily recognisable Cold Chisel line from a classic of Australian rock. The lads were onto it faster than a fat boy on a Smartie and sang in unison, 'HEY, STREET-SWEEPER, CLEAR MY WAY, SWEETHEARTS' BREAKFAST, THE BEST IN TOWN! WHOOOOOO OHH OHH, OH, BREAKFAST AT SWEETHEARTS!'

At the completion of our task, we sniggered a bit but remained standing in the magnificence of our isolation, staring at the dark back of beach and its silent bushland. Suddenly we heard, 'Waaahoooooooo', CLAP, CLAP, CLAP, CLAP, CLAP. This burst of spontaneous applause was followed by more shouts of approval: 'Whooooo!' CLAP, CLAP, CLAP, CLAP. Then it dawned on us: we had been sent to serenade a group of Team One clearance divers out bush on a training mission. Obviously our instructors had been informed of their presence in the area and wanted to send their mates in the teams a little light evening's entertainment.

The lads and I turned around, momentarily stunned, though a little amused, before heading back into the lapping waves – masks on, fins on, mouthpiece in. Then away we went, disappearing into the swirling black pool, leaving behind no trace of our having been there. Other than the faint echo of laughter, that is.

The clock kept winding down on our time on course. Unbelievably late in the piece, we discovered that the head diver had a trick up his sleeve for us. We cruised into the wharf after a long hard day of diving; in mere hours, we were supposed to wrap things up and head back to HMAS *Penguin* for graduation the next day. We had been conducting the last few weeks of training at Pittwater Annexe, as is the custom. Out of the blue he rose and addressed all fifteen of us. 'See that wet stuff under the boat?' he boomed. 'Get in it!'

Without hesitation we took to the water like otters spotting a cray, such was our level of indoctrination. We were expecting a final beating and were braced for it, but instead he casually crouched at the tailboard of the boat and said, 'Well done, lads, well done, but I've a final test for you.'

He instructed us to drag the boat back to the wharf 'to save fuel' – yer, right! That was a mammoth task in and of itself without the addition of an outgoing tide. But we persevered. With a large rope and on weary legs, we towed its almighty mass. Observing that the remaining instructors on the boat were grinning from ear to ear, I had an inkling that something out-of-the-box was afoot.

Back at base, we were ordered to dress in full tactical MTO dive gear ready for a ship assault. Hurriedly we complied, then jogged out to receive our orders with our rebreathers hanging around our necks. Next, to our amazement, we were ushered onto our 22-seater bus and, without a word of explanation, driven to the local movie theatre.

'What the bloody hell is happening here?' I wondered.

These were the instructions issued as we disembarked: 'Due to the fact you have two hours left to go to achieve the required oxygen breathing time, and as we can no longer stand the sight of you, you will go on gas and breathe from your dive sets while watching the latest Hollywood blockbuster. We will go to the freaken pub and lament your inevitable graduation tomorrow.'

At that, and amid a great deal of laughter, our instructors departed.

The boys and I cracked up, slapped each other on the back, and there were handshakes all round. For the life of me I can't remember what movie we watched as I think we all fell asleep, such was our exhaustion. Most of us were injured or broken in some way, shape or form but, latterly, with the passing of each remaining day of course – and therefore the opportunity of punishment – a corresponding buoyancy had crept into all our spirits.

Graduation was approaching and we could taste it. Soon, with a simple handshake, the clearance diver badge would be handed to us and that which we prized above all else, the black beret, would sit atop our weary heads. Maybe I would be able to relax on a bed of fluffy laurels, unwilling or unable to want anything else . . .

Yer, right. There was always another hill, another question asked, another door unopened and only the faintest whisper to indicate that something else lay at the end of the ever-lengthening rainbow . . .

*

'United and undaunted' is the clearance diver motto and the day had arrived when it was to become ours. Graduation was a ceremonial occasion so we were required to wear our white dress uniform. Being divers we hardly ever wore the thing; they had a hard enough time getting us to wear shoes, but for this we did our best. We met up in Salty and Canada's room to check our rigs; Stealth and Houston joined us there as well. None of us could take our eyes off the blank space on the right arm of the ceremonial uniform where in mere hours there would be a clearance diver's rate badge. Spic-and-span in our ceremonials, as we strolled down to the Senior Sailors' Mess on that bright Friday morning, our jubilation was evident. This was it; the day had arrived, a day at times I thought might never come but come it did. Standing there next to my mates, with whom I had shared so much, it was hard not to feel invincible, capable and proud.

Throughout my teens and adulthood, on so many nights I've woken up sweating, charged with adrenaline, but with the faint memory of a nightmare that I can't quite remember, nor do I want to. I know the gist of it: the fear of mediocrity, the fear of an unfulfilled life, of failing my friends and family, of letting down my mates – it haunts me. There's a scene in Arthur Miller's famous play, *Death of a Salesman*, where Biff Loman tries to convince his father, Willy, that he is a failure and not worth the faith Willy has had in him since birth. It's an awful scenario, and my whole life, I have dreaded the possibility that I might one day stand in Biff's shoes. I never want to feel weak and ineffectual, letting down my father like Biff does.

Though that dread cuts me down in my dreams like a silent shot from the dark, I soon forget that fictional sorrow when I sit down with my mates at the pub and we recall what we have been through on course and what we did to get that badge.

Funny thing: it doesn't matter who you talk to, someone will always say they did it harder or tougher or they did this or that; whatever. They're probably right; I've never been shot at.

All I can say is that clearance diver course was hard. I had to fight every bloody second I was there. Some guys killed it; some blokes are born operators; I am not. I have to wake up every day and steel myself not to fuck up, not to fail. I have to concentrate and focus my limited ability in order to maintain the standard, answer the question and fight through, because if I relaxed for a second, it might cost me more than I'd be willing to part with . . .

Eleven

TEAM ONE, HMAS *WATERHEN*

'Keep your eyes and ears open, and your mouth shut.'
— *Chief Diver*

With a few days R and R before we were posted to the Team, the boys and I decided to take it easy, maybe go on a picnic in the park and play a quiet game of croquet. Ha! Not bloody likely! We got on the piss hard (sorry, Mum). I awoke Saturday morning to a staggering Canadian, who burst into my room and handed me a Corona, our chosen beverage at the time.

'Here ya go, ay bro. Drink dis, ay.'

Fucking Canada. 'Right then, to the Branch,' I said, downed the amber liquid and promptly got dressed. Part of being a clearance diver is that when you have down time the bonding continues, and it's usually down the pub.

That night we headed into King Street Wharf, opposite Darling Harbour. After course, we were allowed to move off base into our own accommodation and most of us stayed north of the bridge, so there were more than a few of these boozy cab rides into the city. We were being reasonably well behaved until Canada and I got into a light-hearted discussion about who was the weakest: 'Every bloody time, Canada,' I thought.

Keen to prove his point, he exited the bar and climbed the stairs leading to Pyrmont Bridge, the fifteen-metre-high walkway that spans the harbour inlet. Yelling at us from halfway up, he launched himself into the water, to the cheers of all the boys and the patrons of half the waterside bars that lined the area. As he exited, he continued with the assertion that I was weak as piss.

In the spirit of the night, I shook his hand and, with a wry smile, agreed, then added, 'Just wait here a sec.'

Bemused, the boys – and half of Sydney I was later informed by my mates, who never exaggerate – watched as I ascended the stairs then climbed the extra eight metres to the top of the bridge, took up position on the guard rail, a further metre up, then executed a one-and-a-half turn somersault into the water below, surfacing to the almighty roar from the now surrounding crowd.

Hauling me out, Canada let out a rich, husky laugh and shook my hand. 'Dat was okay, bro, ay.'

Divers, bloody clearance divers!

Australian Clearance Diving Team One HMAS *Waterhen*, 'the chosen'. Any confidence we had gained during the previous months would have to be kept in check, as we were about to enter a world where angels feared to tread. Joining Team One wasn't what you would think: there was no official welcome, no one showed you around and I'll be damned if

I can remember any handshakes. You were simply expected to start work and know your job. If you were lucky and had managed to form any friendship with anyone in the course before yours, you might get a few hints on what to do. But basically it was sink or swim. My take on it was that you had to be quick on your feet, volunteer for every task, be the first into work and the last to leave.

'The lions in their dens tremble at his approach' is the inscription on the Moroccan bravery medal of the Order of Ouissam Alouite; I saw it in the movie *Patton*. I try to repeat that to myself when I feel trepidation: it reminds me of what I would like to be, of my wish to be brave even at times when I am not. My apprehension at becoming part of the Team was overcome by my excitement; this was what it was all about, getting into the Teams and plying your trade as a CD. Salty had been sent to Team Four, along with Houston; Canada, Stealth and I went to Team One, as we'd requested.

But we were still baby divers; we were only to speak when spoken to, and we had to complete a few extra skillsets before our unofficial probationary period ended.

Fast roping, a useful insertion tool for waterborne operators, was the first of these skillsets. To acquire it, I spent over a week training at the navy base in Jervis Bay, near Nowra, and it could be a bit hairy if you hadn't done it before. A large green hawser rope made of relatively soft fibres would be lowered from a helicopter and you would swing out and slide down it like a fireman's pole. Although sliding down a rope seemed like a simple task, unlike many other activities, there were no added safety lines or back-up procedures. It was only your grip on the rope that prevented you freefalling forty metres to the deck below. On one occasion my feet came off the rope and my legs flew out at a right angle, leaving only my hands attached. It was an anxious millisecond before I could sort that one out!

Another thing I quickly got under my belt was a significant weapons training period: the Teams had recently converted from the Aussteyr to the M4 assault rifle. This added the M4, the chosen weapon of most Special Forces (SF) units, to a constantly growing list of tools at our disposal.

That would have pissed off the regular navy no end, I'm sure. These factors, and many others besides, combined with the fact that we CDs all wore Australian DPCU – aka camouflage – like the army, set us well apart from the grey navy, and they hated it. Good; bloody great, if you ask me. I make no apologies for my view that CDs should be a separate unit. It's a different world and the larger navy should simply recognise that, thank us for our services and continue on their merry way.

Life in Team One, I discovered, was never boring. A typical day would start with hard and fast morning PT, then operational-readiness training, and weights in the arvo. During any given week, we could be called upon to perform any number of tasks. The fact that we were 'jacks of all trades, masters of none' meant our day-to-day activities varied enormously. One day you could be fixing the giant propellers on a warship, and the next you'd be blowing up ordnance in the Solomon Islands.

On one particular day we received a job near Shark Island, where the navy had a degaussing range. This is a series of underwater sensors that alter a ship's magnetic signature to make it less vulnerable to attack. Essentially, the task was to add some new sensors to the steel base structures on the seabed. The sensors consisted of big cason-type cylindrical tubes that sat on the deck like a 44-gallon fuel drum, with a flange on top for attaching the bolts.

It had been a while since the old sensors had been removed, so the site required thorough preparation before the new sensors were to be brought in. As it was a reasonably sizeable task, we decided to use the surface-supplied breathing apparatus, which included the MK17 Kirby Morgan dive helmet, among other things. Needing a large platform to work from, the Team decided to take *Seal*, our large dive vessel. It was a beauty of a ship: sleek, grey and about twenty metres long; it looked totally badass.

My dive buddy – a Chief Diver – and I were to suit up and would be deployed below to clean up the flanges and undo the old bolts with a shifter, so they would be ready for the next set of divers to fit the sensors. Our two helmets were equipped with internal communications so I could talk to the Chief, who would take up a position ahead of me. The plan was that I would tell him when I had completed undoing the bolts on each platform and we would then move on as a pair to the next set. He was metres ahead of me, cleaning with a wire brush so I had access to the nuts and bolts. We had been going for an hour or so when I encountered what you might call a little trouble . . .

As I reached across to undo my hundredth bolt for the day, a large slimy octopus arm shot out of the dark void and wrapped itself tightly around my forearm! It was fricken huge!

'Jesus!' I yelped, as the thing tightened its grip on my limb and tried to drag me into its pit of death! When I pulled against it, I was shocked at how strong it was. Our tug of war commenced and I was huffing and puffing so much, the guys on the surface must have thought I was dying. Pausing, I leant over to look down the hole as the creature struggled with its obviously oversized catch. The bastard's eyes were too big for its stomach, I told myself as I peered inside to try and get a good look at this would-be Kraken. There it was: a large eye, as big as an apple, staring directly at me!

'You cheeky bastard,' I thought, as I drew my knife and prepared to deliver the coup de grâce! Then I had second thoughts: he was only defending his home; who was I to judge? Besides, he had fought valiantly. So I put away the ten-inch blade and retrieved my shifter. After a couple of loud bangs on the side of the steel casing, he retreated as fast as he had attacked. Living inside a steel drum is fine for protection, until some bugger rings your bell with a five-kilo spanner!

Upon returning to the surface, thoroughly fatigued, I might add, having grappled with this monster for the last hour or so, I tried to tell the boys what had taken place. Knowing my propensity for exaggeration, they doubted my story and gave me no end of shit – and calamari jokes all the way back to base. My dive buddy, the Chief, was no help at all, denying the story in its entirety.

By the time we stepped onto the wharf, I had all but started to believe I'd imagined the whole thing in a nitrogen narcosis-induced haze when the Chief leant over my shoulder and whispered, 'How fucking big was that octopus, ay.'

Bastard! So he had seen it too! I knew it! But what could I do? I just laughed, as did he, and we strolled back to the confines of Team One HQ in the cool afternoon sun, totally spent, laughing hysterically.

After a few months in the Team, a couple of us started to feel more comfortable and began probing for info about the rumoured selection for this new unit. It was all a bit cloak and dagger and my curiosity was well sparked. Over beers on the weekend my mates and I would hypothesise as to what was going on, but without any real intel, it was difficult to understand. I guess that's how the powers that be wanted it. It worked, 'cause nobody knew a bloody thing!

Stepping back and looking at the wider context, the Teams, and quite literally the world, were still adapting to the coexistence of two frontiers of war: a highly public, long-running and recently enacted war in Iraq and the silent and ever-present internal terrorist threat. Most of the Western world was gearing up heavily against these two threats post 9/11. I won't go into the politics of it all; neither will I pretend to know the reasons why Australians go to wars like Iraq, though I believe it's so we can all continue to have the right to question if Australians should go. The one bloody thing I will say is that domestic counterterrorism basically consists of defending those who haven't chosen to be involved against those who *have*; it defends non-combatant civilians. That, my friends, is a fight worth engaging in, and bloody well justified, whatever your politics; imagine if you were taken hostage.

As one of the many consequences of all this, the Clearance Diving Branch was splitting. Well, that's the way it seemed to me: I'd barely joined the Team when it was announced that a bunch of guys were being sent to Iraq to clear the stretch of water around Umm Qasr, the port on the main maritime supply route for the Coalition, rumoured to be heavily mined. The mostly senior guys in this deployment were being drawn from Team One (based in Sydney) and Team Four (based in Western Australia) to create a brand new entity, Team Three, a collective operational team tasked with mine clearance and general explosive ordnance disposal. The mission was every CD's dream and everybody wanted in, me included. This was to be the first rotation and, hopefully, there would be a second, but something else was in the air.

My observation, and others might see it differently, was that blokes who more than likely would have gone to Iraq were not part of the deployment. Among these were some legends of the Branch, as well as the latest young guns, guys I'd caught glimpses of and heard about but not really met. Why weren't all these switched-on dudes collecting their desert cam issue alongside the others about to deploy?

Gradually information came to light about something separate and new: Tactical Assault Group (East). Realising who was involved, it became clear, especially to Canada and me, that it was the path for us. Army black roles, domestic counterterrorism, Special Forces – these were all buzz words being bantered about. It was evident the time was coming when we would have to choose which stream we wanted to pursue. Yes, I would love to consolidate my skills, stay with the Branch and play with sea mines *but* . . . Another selection, Special Forces, and a chance to work at an even more elite level . . .

'What do ya reckon, Canada?'

'Ya fucken know what I think, bro.'

And I did. I needn't have asked.

We both approached the Warrant Officer of the Team and made our intentions clear: we wanted in, what did we have to do? Little did we know the chain of events that would be set in motion; be careful what you wish for, ay . . .

'Team One for fun, Team Four for war.' Yer, right-o. The light-hearted competition between the east and west served as our inspiration to train even harder.

It had long been a good-natured joke that WA-based Team Four was somehow more geared toward operational readiness and we inferior eastern cousins were unmotivated – that we were out in Sydney, on the cans, chasing chicks and living in nightclubs. Nothing could be further from the truth. Well, maybe we gave things a nudge in some areas from time to time; the opportunities were few and far between though. In actuality, we were the online, or ready to deploy, team that year and had all the overseas trips.

My first trip was to Singapore for a dive symposium. Representatives from all the Coalition Forces clearance diving teams around the world were getting together to discuss equipment, tactics and generally get on the piss. Above all, what it offered me was a chance to impress the other members of the Team – not so much the brass or the chiefs – I wanted to make my mark with the lads. Like any tightly knit unit, the Team was a microcosm of society at large: you had your cool kids, your geeks and your arseholes. I figured that where you fell in this bell curve, especially during your first trip away, could very well cement your position for life.

The trip was great; we saw how other international units conducted their operations. I can't say that we learnt much else, however, unless you count the ability to scull beer through a rebreather hose connected to a dive mask and funnel! What did hit home to me was the high standard of our own Australian forces compared to those of the rest of the global community. At this stage, we may not have matched some of the others in operational experience, but our training was second to none. Another interesting revelation was the level of status we seemed to enjoy with other clearance divers. I'm not trying to sound wanky, but they loved us over there. It was almost like being a celebrity. At one point I thought some of the Asian participants were going to ask for our autograph!

In all seriousness, the unit that most impressed me was the Kiwis, the Royal New Zealand Clearance Divers. These blokes were as hard as nails. It seemed that despite our sporting rivalry, the Anzac spirit was alive and well in Singapore that year; we got on like a house on fire and spent many nights drinking and singing with these warriors of the deep. They had a very tight team, and most of the blokes had their Branch tattoo inked on their chest – it was an image of a traditional Maori warrior spirit holding a mine overhead. Needless to say, I thought it was very cool. Witnessing them do the haka was a privilege. It gave me chills. You wouldn't want to come up against any of those guys in battle, I can assure you.

The Singaporean Navy had a pretty sweet set-up that included a massive pool, fifteen metres deep at one end, with an impressive fake warship built on the side. It was used for mock ship attacks and stood eighteen or so metres high. After a few beers, the Kiwis and I started to wonder aloud whether anyone would have the balls to jump off it.

Well, you can see where this was going. The next day – which I dragged myself through with a mind-numbing hangover – one of the Kiwi CDs reminded me of my earlier nocturnal boasts, and the game was afoot. The pair of us snuck over to the pool enclosure at sparrow's fart the following morning and checked for any onlookers. Registering the height of the thing, I started to have my doubts, but any misgivings were cast asunder as soon as I saw the bloody New Zealander start climbing.

'What do you think you're doing?' I asked.

'Goin' up, ay, bro,' came the reply.

'Not without me,' I thought as I scurried up behind him.

We reached the top, and as with all these things, they seem like a good idea at the time – but in reality the shine is quickly removed.

'Fuck bro, she's high, ay,' said the Kiwi.

As I nodded my agreement, we noticed all the Aussie divers and their New Zealand counterparts cresting the hill and walking towards the pool. This had just got a lot more interesting!

The boys spotted us, and hoots of approval started drifting our way. My Kiwi mate said, 'I'm not letting you take the glory,' and promptly flung himself off the top, smashing into the water feet first.

Cheers went up from the crowd and a smile crept across my face as I braced myself for the dive. With an almighty leap I jumped, spun into a somersault and entered the water in a dive, surfacing to the sight of the Aussies applauding me enthusiastically. On exiting the pool, the Kiwi and I shook hands and laughed as everyone else came over and joined in on the joke. That's how the Anzac spirit is, in my experience: blokes doing their job but having fun in the process, with a bit of rivalry thrown in for good measure.

The culmination of the Singapore exercise was a round robin demonstration of the different CD skillsets. The most interesting of these, I thought, was the Frenchies' use of a water canon to smash into oblivion a car containing an improvised explosive device (IED).

On completion of all the serious stuff, the final event was to be a biathlon comprising a two-kilometre ocean swim followed by a ten-kilometre road run. Each country was to select three members to compete. Even though I had developed something of a reputation for fitness, I was apprehensive when I was selected as for the past couple of weeks, all I had done was drink!

When all the divers – from over twenty countries – assembled at the start of the biathlon course, there was a fantastic atmosphere. By about halfway through the swim, I wasn't feeling remotely fantastic; I was hitting the wall, and my chances of a favourable outcome were diminishing with the falling tide. However, I kept swimming – there was no choice; I was halfway out to sea! When I exited the water, according to what information my water-logged brain was able to process, I was halfway back in the pack with a ten-click run to come. All those Tiger beers and tequila shots now seemed like a bad idea. The South Korean Navy SEALs were leading the race. I'm told their American counterparts trained them; it certainly seemed plausible as they and the New Zealanders were killing it.

Suddenly I got my second wind and started progressing through the pack, though I held no genuine aspirations until about the third lap. The Aussies on the sidelines shouted that I was catching the leaders. Then I heard a comment from the Warrant Officer of the Team: 'You better fucking win, Obi!' and I put my foot down and surged ahead for the final lap.

Now I could see the leaders, two South Korean SEALs. I felt like my head was going to explode, but all this effort wouldn't be worth it if I didn't win, otherwise I might as well have been sitting in the grandstand with a tinny in my hand! The struggle continued and I passed one of the Koreans, but when the guy in first place saw me coming, he legged it for the finish line. He was amazingly quick. I just couldn't catch him, and he crossed first as I came in a respectable but disappointing second.

The race was done. I approached the winner and extended my hand. He promptly removed his issued T-shirt – a prized possession of divers – and handed it to me, saying in heavily accented English, 'You run good, almost like me!'

I laughed and, after shaking his hand, handed him my own blue-and-gold crested T-shirt. 'You run good too,' I said.

I may not have won but I felt happy, really happy. Here I was, a helluva long way from home, racing Korean Navy SEALs, diving, drinking and hanging with Maori warriors. How fucken good was it to be a diver!

*

It was the last thing I expected early on a Sunday morning at dive headquarters on HMAS *Waterhen*, better known to us as Australian Clearance Diving Team One: a call from George W. Bush. Well, not from him personally. The Team had been called out to assist with the visit by the President of the United States to our nation's capital, Canberra, in the ACT. On the Texan's program was an appearance at Parliament House; so he would be crossing Lake Burley Griffin on Commonwealth Avenue Bridge and returning on Kings Avenue Bridge. This plan necessitated a team of clearance divers to systematically and methodically search every pylon, the length of the two bridges, before he passed over them. A few lucky members of the Team would even have to clear out the culverts and static ponds surrounding the area, just in case.

It was a massive operation and as the water was only ten metres deep and the dive time prolonged, the decision had been made to use the Draeger LAR V Pure O_2 dive set.

Lake Burley Griffin is a man-made freshwater lake, and this presented a few special challenges. Firstly, fresh water is significantly colder than salt water and it was the middle of winter. Secondly, being man-made, the lake-bed had previously been bushland and was covered in old trees and many other entanglements.

Despite these difficulties, it felt awesome to be on a real job. Things had been quiet lately and going on a road trip with the boys was a welcome change. We arrived in Canberra and set up base at the HQ of the Water Police, upriver from the bridges.

This was to be an 'on call' task, conducted in quick time, and each team of divers could be called on at the drop of a hat. When the notification came through from the Federal Police that the big cheese was shortly to cross the aforementioned expanses, we would be required to leap into action and clear the area of any potential IEDs. However unlikely the possibility of terrorism may have been, it was useful training for us, and a chance to participate at an international level, coordinating with other agencies.

When the time came to stand to, it was a cold wintry morning and the boys and I loaded the Zodiac with all the necessary gear to complete the search. This task was made considerably more enjoyable by the proximity of the Australian Women's Rowing Team, preparing their boat only metres away. You've never seen divers at their best until you've seen them trying to impress a bunch of Olympics-bound athletic lassies!

As luck would have it, I was charged with searching the bottom of the pylons. This meant I was to go the deepest of the string of five divers – the deepest meant the coldest. It was fricken freezing down there yet in order to gain the speed and agility of movement I needed for such a search, I chose not to go with the standard thick wetsuit, but instead I would just run with a three-millimetre version.

It was a blind search – as most are – and the diver's saying of having to search with your ten eyes was never more apt. Rounding each pylon I had to battle through the remnants of ancient trees and shrubs. It was a bloody fight to keep up with the lads above, not to mention the deal with the creepy sensation of rotting foliage and branches, which felt like sea goblins' arms and legs grabbing at me. It was all I could do to control my temper as I clawed my way forward. Every time I moved a centimetre or two through the debris, I had to actively stop myself from imagining it was scattered with dead bodies and cattle carcasses.

It took a total of three hours to search an entire bridge, then we'd head back to the Water Police base and await the next call-out. Old George must have forgotten his keys at Parliament House on more than one occasion because we searched both bridges day and night for four days. By the end of things, I was absolutely smashed. The constant up-and-down and breathing of oxygen played havoc with your ears and sinuses.

Our team finished the job and met up with the other divers who had been on the 'stagnant pond and road culvert patrol'. Canada was one of them and when I asked how his week had gone he responded with his usual abruptness, 'Fucking Yanks! That's the last time I dive in a sewer!'

On our return to Sydney from Canberra, I was involved in a small incident that did nothing for my promotion prospects. One of my good mates and I were mucking around, as we were wont to do after a long day. Initially we were mock-fighting and generally being stupid, then we thought it was an excellent idea to start playing with knives . . .

In the Divers and other areas of the military, you would occasionally do some fighting drills or learn Close-Quarter Fighting (CQF) but these opportunities were few and far between. Consequently, neither of us had the skills to be practising any type of real disarming techniques. That didn't stop us. We were going through a few joking knife drills when, as I turned quickly to my left, the bloke's hand slipped and his six-inch knife blade drove straight through my forearm!

Blood shot across the room, and I could see a giant slash through my arm; two white walls of flesh lay open like an unzipped pencil case. Planting my free hand on top of it and pulling the wound together, I thought momentarily that it may be not that bad. That hope was rapidly extinguished when the lads came over to check on me. Gasps issued from the onlookers when I momentarily removed the hand.

'Fuck me! This isn't going to look good!' I thought.

There was a mass exodus from the room; nobody wanted to be involved in this cluster fuck. I couldn't blame them.

The knife-welding maniac and I came up with a solid alibi that I had cut my arm on some glass and I then proceeded to drive myself directly to hospital. When I asked Canada to drive me, he had roared with laughter!

At the hospital I spun the glass-cutting fiction and the medical staff prepped me for stitches. The wound was going to require ten internal stitches and fifteen external ones – not a bad outcome for a bit of horseplay. Dickheads, both of us!

They told me that when they gave me the appropriate amount of anaesthetic, I would have to stay a while for observation. But I had a party to get to that night, so I asked the doctor if I could forgo the anaesthetic, have him sew me up as is, and I'd be on my way.

The doc gave me a funny look and said, 'You can't do that. There is no way you could handle the pain, and besides, you couldn't keep your arm still.'

'Challenge issued and accepted!' I quipped.

I managed to hold still but it hurt like a motherfucker! On the plus side, it gave me a sense of confidence to know that if I ever had to sew myself up, I would be able to manage it.

After the procedure was finished, the doctor suggested I do some psych counselling, as it simply wasn't normal for someone to endure that much pain. I thanked him and left for the party. Time was a-wastin'.

Twelve

PRE-WORKUP TRAINING

'Softly tread the brave.'

– Ivan Southall

Eventually, the powers that be sat down with a few of us keen beans and gave us a brief on what this new unit was all about and what the process for selection was. The secret unit we had heard whispers about – called Tactical Assault Group East, or TAG (East) – was to be made up of CDs plus commandos trained by the SAS (Special Air Service) and assisted by commandos from 4RAR (4th Battalion, Royal Australian Regiment). Its formation was enacted post 9/11, in response to the increasing threat of terrorist attacks and hostage-taking on our own soil.

There already existed a force to deal with this: the SAS (TAG [West]). But because of heavy operational commitments and the fact that these true warriors were increasingly required in theatres of war overseas, the Australian government saw fit to create a new unit and base it in the east.

Combining navy with army to form a crack unit was not unprecedented: CDs had worked with SAS in the past, albeit with varying degrees of success. Initially, the decision-makers had planned to use only commandos, train them in Close-Quarter Battle (CQB) and a few other black arts and essentially keep it in-house, as commandos were already part of Special Operations Command (SOCOM), army and Special Forces. The CDs – lamentably maybe – were not. Although I'm not sure of the finer details, luckily for us the powers that be concluded that if specially selected CDs could pass the 'Barrier Test', or Special Forces Entry Test (SFET), CQB, Advanced CQB, Reinforcement Training (REO) as well as a few key skillsets, then the new TAG unit would benefit from having a diving capability, ready to go: water platoon, much like a packet of dehydrated warriors, really! Just add H_2O.

It was spelt out emphatically that the blokes who wanted to attempt selection for this new unit would have to jump through a few hoops. That was fine by me. There were still eight weeks until the next SFET. Up until now, my CD experience had been tough but I had enjoyed it and was relatively good at what I was doing. I was at home in a water environment and comfortable beneath the waves. But as has been the case my whole life, as soon as I get comfortable, I bloody well throw myself out of my comfort zone in order to see if I can take on the next thing. I was about to enter one of the more challenging sections of my career. My process has always been to go ahead with whatever path seems the hardest, for then, even if you fail you know you tried; 'almost' is a bitch.

Before the Pre-Workup Training (PWT), or test preparation, began, I concentrated on getting my head in the right place. To sustain me through what I knew would be hard times, I chose for my mantra: 'I'd rather be the worst of the best than the best of the worst.'

This brings up an interesting question: is ignorance bliss? Would you rather misguidedly think you're the best, and have no knowledge of those better, or have the perfection of others revealed to you, even though it might mean you subsequently see yourself as a failure? Like in the movie *Vanilla Sky*, do you jump off the building and confront the reality of your situation or remain in a waking dream where things are great but false? Or as stated in *The Matrix*, 'You take the blue pill, the story ends, you wake up in your bed and believe whatever you believe. You take the red pill, you stay in Wonderland, and I show you how deep the rabbit hole goes. Remember: all I'm offering is the truth. Nothing more.' Personally, I'd rather know, really know, even if that means possibly being unhappy with the truth.

My desire to make TAG was paramount and I was aware that I would have to go through a lot to succeed. Nothing worth having is easy to obtain; I'd known that all my life. In fact, it has always been an article of faith with me to earn my achievements 100 per cent, and never to squib. On my original CD course, part of the designated uniform was a hooded jumper featuring the branch emblem. To me, it wasn't right to wear anything with the CD badge on it until I passed, as I believed this privilege should be reserved until after graduation, when you'd earnt the right to wear it. In order to stand by what I believed, I had to freeze my arse off, but that jumper was all the warmer once I'd earnt it.

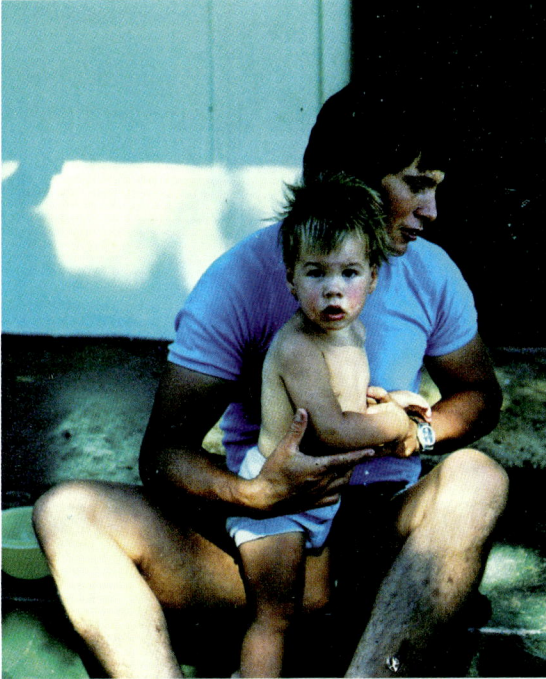

With Dad, circa 1982, on the front steps of our farmhouse, 'Marree'. Dad always encouraged me to be an adventurer.

My brother Phil (*far left*) and me (*far right*) playing for our local rugby club, the Young 'Yabbies' – both wearing our cerise and blue St Joseph's College socks, a point of pride. Just quietly, that bloke in the striped jumper smashed me seconds after the photo was taken.

The old and the bold conducting fast pick-up drills.

MIDDLE: CDAT and the infamous 'canoe carry' up to the Barrenjoey Lighthouse. Note the numbered vest: you keep that shit on for two weeks straight and do not want to give it up, even at the end.
BOTTOM: Pittwater Annexe, the cradle of clearance diving, known only to the few.

TOP: 'Big Bang Beach' on Triangular Island, named for obvious reasons.
MIDDLE: Standing in front of a propellant burn. I'd been wearing those clothes for two weeks straight and hadn't slept in just as long.
BOTTOM: 'The Hellfish' aka BCD 53, smashed but undaunted after completing the mud run.

TOP: Group shot of BCD 53 at the end of our 'tools' (deep air) phase. Learning to cut and weld underwater was cool, old-school diver stuff.

MIDDLE: Getting ready for an SSBA dive on the 'deep air' phase (*left to right*): Smoutch, me, Stealth, Canada.

BOTTOM: Diving the Nitrox Rebreather A5800, conducting diver recovery drills. The object on the mask is a small light indicating your partial pressure of oxygen; it has a large effect on your staying alive.

Tactical diving: prepping for a caving ladder climb onto a wharf . . . real frogman shit!

MIDDLE: The 'sharp end' of Maritime Tactical Operations. BOTTOM: During my MTO training, the weapon of choice was the M4 assault rifle (5.56mm). It's compact and accurate but annoying to clean after a saltwater bath.

'The Hellfish' on our final MTO phase, wearing the trusty LAR V (*left to right*): Houston, Maihi, Canada, me, Salty, Smoutch, Peaper.

Ex-crocodile at the Shoalwater Bay training area. The boys from AUSCDT ONE are about to conduct a beach clearance. That's me standing in the middle, with what I told the lads was my 'Ninja Turtle' face camo.

TOP: Surface-supplied breathing apparatus: entering the water and dealing with nitrogen narcosis. Fun times!

MIDDLE: An MTO diver underwater equipped with a 2Alpha sonar device. It takes a lot of training to get used to all the kit.

BOTTOM: The lads lined up ready for a tactical swim: there's no such thing as sharks, cold or can't!

RIGHT: A typical day's training in TAG at Holsworthy Base, Sydney: 'Bang it in!'

CENTRE LEFT: 'Spy rigging', a fast-extraction technique; not for the faint of heart.

CENTRE RIGHT: Making an entrance, so to speak, on the MOE house.

BOTTOM: Operators lined up for inspection, balaclavas donned to protect our identity.

'The boys in black': you don't want them knocking on *your* door, trust me.

Water Platoon Team One; me on the far left. The rest of the lads are still serving, hence the blacked-out faces; just makes them look cooler really, LOL.

Whiskey One Three (W13): my Assaulter days, on exercise in Perth, Western Australia. I'm holding an HK MP5 A3. I should say 'barely' holding as I was about to collapse when this photo was taken – I was so buggered.

Water (Whiskey) Platoon, Charlie Company, after a long day of 'rope and blow' training and stronghold takedowns. I'm second from the left on the rope, just hangin' out really.

Commercial diving days. This was a big job for Energy Australia in Sydney's Botany Bay. A five-hour dive in freezing water was not uncommon.

Pirate-hunting in the Red Sea. I was bored but I had to remain switched on, just in case.

Maritime security off the coast of Yemen. Posing (literally – yeah, I know) with a PKM 7.62mm.

Out in the oil fields of Nigeria. Listening to the iPod helped take my mind off the appalling conditions.

Brothers in arms. Canada (*right*) and me on my first trip to Afghanistan. I'm holding an AK 'Krinkoff' version – smaller and more compact than the 47.

Kickin' back in the office in Kabul with a tricked out AK. They were long hot days out on the road.

My mate Salty Pepper on operations in Afghanistan with 20 EOD. This is what clearance divers are now engaged in – using their skills to counter IEDs in a land-warfare theatre. Salty stayed with the Branch and completed his advanced course, whereas Canada and I wanted to be gunslingers . . . to each his own.

Rogue trader. In Helmand Province, Afghanistan, running with the USMC (2MEF) in my black-market body armour and carrying a borrowed M4 rifle and without permission from my company to roll out past the wire – as if that would stop me . . .

En route to Tikrit, in the north of Iraq (*left to right*): our local fixer (not someone to be messed with), the recon TL (one helluva tough guy) and me (not so tough really).

It was a privilege to visit such archaeological sites as the ziggurat in Nasiriyah, southern Iraq.

Putting some rounds down range near Muthana, Baghdad, with the Sig 552, wearing my 'I'm a contractor' get-up. It's a bit clichéd, I know, but what can ya do?

Double-O-nobody. One of the rare – hated – occasions I have to wear a suit. Not sure my tie matches the rifle.

Similarly, after I'd left school, I was playing rugby for my hometown of Young one time and I discovered that in the rush to pack my kit bag, I'd inadvertently thrown in a pair of my brother's prestigious First XV socks. It was an innocent mistake, as when rolled in a ball, the tops are the same colour. Rather than sneak onto the field dressed in socks that I didn't have the right to wear, I played barefoot on that cold Condobolin day. My teammate looked at me as if I was from another planet. 'They're just socks, mate,' he said. But he didn't get it; to me it was more than that. Honouring tradition makes these things all the more valuable if you ever do obtain them.

What I'm getting at is that I was expecting PWT to be tough, and I was up for it. As it turned out, PWT was just for starters. Elsewhere in the military, you can simply put in your paperwork and opt for a chance to do the Barrier Test, but the divers – being divers – decided they didn't want anybody to disgrace them by failing. So they set up their own preselection before allowing army selection!

Mad, right?

Well, that's the Branch, and to carry out this harrowing tactic, they enlisted the services of some of the hardest men I have ever met. They were blokes who had been both CDs and SAS: imagine that. Back in the 1980s when there was a sort of crossover, and some CDs went online with the regiment, these blokes had done the cadre and patrol courses to be part of it. This was a slightly different process to the current arrangement, where we would 'only' complete Barrier and CQB.

The preselection course was three weeks long. We were separated from the rest of the Team and trained in the army way of doing things. Basically, we went through a combination of long pack marches, webbing runs, navigation, weapons drills and generally getting physically and mentally smashed, so that when we got to selection, the Branch would be confident we'd pass.

Canada and I were the two most junior divers present. As you can imagine, we got a bit of stick from the others and even from some blokes not on the course. But the rules were the same for all comers: 'You want in? Then throw your hat in the ring and prepare to be judged like the rest.' We got through.

There's a quote I can't quite remember about there being no glory in pointing out the failings of others, but that true value is in the attempt, and the honour belongs to those who lie battered and broken on the field, having tried. Well, that poem was read out to us before we started PWT and it was the instructor's way of telling us not to listen to the naysayers, but to keep going.

DH Lawrence wrote, 'I never saw a wild thing sorry for itself. A small bird will drop frozen dead from a bough, without ever having felt sorry for itself.' In my civilian life I used to occasionally fall into the trap of self-pity but there was no time for it in the defence force. To feel sorry for yourself was a death sentence; if I was to succeed with these 'wild things', I would have to become one.

As things at PWT started heating up, so too did my apprehension. That's when I started singing to myself in my head, 'I wish I had a river I could skate away on . . .' I heard the actor Robert Downey Jr sing these wistful Joni Mitchell lyrics once, and during my more solemn moments, I sort of press play in my mind; sometimes it's the hits of the '80s or a Ben Harper playlist: the idea is to calm yourself. That might not be the most macho thing to admit, especially in a military book. But in the interests of full disclosure and honesty, I often do this, whether it be twenty metres down in the black water or sitting in some pigeon-shit-infested warehouse trying to remember the right amount of explosive to use for a door charge.

I think I may have already mentioned the crystallising properties of pain: how it can both distort and focus your mind in the time needed to take a breath, how it occupies that space between friend and foe. Well, PWT was no different. It was pain incarnate and gave me a newfound respect for those camouflaged pongos known collectively as the army. Night navigation was just one of the many tasks I found challenging. Well, to be perfectly honest, navigation in general fast became the bane of my existence and I was 'geographically challenged' more than a few times before I learnt this most necessary of skills.

Fear gripped me as if the grim reaper himself had placed his bony hand around my sweaty throat. I'd never known anything like it. My stomach turned and I felt like I was going to spew. My eyes were the size of saucers; I'd been jolted wide-awake even though I hadn't slept in days.

I was partway through a night nav ex (navigation exercise). Half an hour earlier, after hitting the third of my eight marks for the night, I had taken a deep breath, knelt down and placed my rifle next to my weary right knee. I'd checked my bearings then headed off into the dark jungle to find the next checkpoint.

Now I was trapped in this moment of horror as the stark realisation hit me: my rifle? Where the fuck was my rifle? I wiped the sweat from my brow with the back of my right hand

What a fucken switched-on operator I was. I'd just left my rifle somewhere in the undergrowth.

There I was, trying to be selected for Special Forces, and I'd managed to lose my weapon. I could hear the voice – a deep voice – in my head there and then:

Able Seaman O'Brien, you've passed every test, killed every challenge, eaten up all adversity and walked trium- phantly across the finish line first in your class, but just one teeny tiny small point . . . Where's your fucking weapon! What are you going to kill the enemy with? Your razor- sharp wit! Or maybe a burst of searing sarcasm!

It was pitch black. All I had to go on was the hope that if I worked out the reciprocal bearing and walked that exact same path back where I'd come from, I might, just might, have a chance of finding my weapon. Either that or say hello to 'Miguel Sanchez' resident of Mexico! I hope that's a non-extradition country.

Like a hungry lion stalking the only living antelope left on the planet, I crept back. I have never panicked in my life, but I can tell you I was bloody close; any military aspirations I had would swiftly disappear if this puppy got out.

After twenty minutes of painstaking backtracking, I felt my boot touch something. I quickly placed my hand down and felt the cold steel and recognisable features of a gun barrel. 'You fucken beauty! Holy shit!' Relief washed over me and I picked up my weapon and kissed it like a long-lost lover. I had never before, nor would again, felt such overwhelming love for an inanimate object.

It might sound weird but, as divers, we never really carried guns that much; you can rest assured that if they were my fins, I wouldn't have left them behind! So rule number one to all prospective military wannabes, maybe get it tattooed on the inside of your eyelids so you don't forget: 'Don't lose your weapon!'

The next day consisted of gruelling pack marches and hour upon hour of PT. Then we partnered up for another nav ex, one considerably longer and harder than the previous night's. I was with Canada, which I considered fortunate, as he was good at everything, whereas I could get lost in my own backyard.

The distance was hard but we were doing okay. About four hours in, Canada kept dropping back and had become even less chatty than usual.

'What's up back there, big fella? Things getting too rough for ya?' I enquired.

Not a word, not even a 'Fuck you, Obi' came back in reply. That was strange I thought. Then I heard what could only be described as an atomic bomb and Mount Vesuvius erupting at the same time. I trekked back and poor old Canada had his kit off and was simultaneously spewing and shitting all over the shop, enough to scare any surrounding wildlife away, I can tell you.

'Fuck, bro. You okay?' I asked. He was in a bad way, courtesy of the local army cuisine no doubt.

'Mate,' he murmured, 'I've been shitting and spewing for the last couple of kilometres. I think I've got food poisoning.'

I felt so bad for the guy, but as we were CDs, I offered the usual words of brotherly encouragement: 'You weak cunt, do you want a saucer of milk?'

Even in his weakened state he managed a small laugh; however, I was acutely aware that when he got better he'd kill me for that comment.

I'd never seen the bloke falter – and never have since – he's one tough monkey. After much protesting I managed to convince him to let me carry his pack and rifle, a fact I remind him of to this day. But it was futile, and after a brief discussion I decided we should knock it on the head and trek back to Base Camp.

Canada wanted to go on. 'Mate, we have to get a few more checkpoints,' he argued, between ungodly spasms of shitting and vomiting.

Once again I explained the situation; I suspected he was becoming delirious. 'Bro, we're five kilometres from camp; you're a fucking mess. If we make it to this ridgeline and follow that fence, we can get you back. And besides, this is just practice for the test, not the actual one, so don't go damaging yourself now as next week's the real deal and you need to be on your game.'

Begrudgingly, he agreed and we headed back, me with my dodgy navigation skills, using a bloody flashlight, making more noise than a fricken brass band, and leaving a trail of shit-stained destruction behind us. Two divers out bush – real secret squirrel!

I can only imagine what my brother, who was in 3RAR,

or any members of the army at large would have thought had they witnessed this sorry sight.

As most athletes will tell you, there is a point at which your training can either positively or negatively influence your results on game day. As PWT drew to a close, we were completing the entire list of the Barrier Test events in under two days, then repeating them, just to see if we could. I had a sneaking suspicion we were overtraining . . . if so, fatigue wasn't far behind, and fatigue could have disastrous effects.

Thirteen

THE BARRIER TEST

'Don't let the bastards get you down.'
– Second World War saying

'Three point two' sounds like quite an innocuous number. However, it was the distance in kilometres of what is known as a webbing run. To this day I have scars on my thighs from where my heavy equipment chafed against the skin during those exercises, causing the phrase 'pain barrier' to be branded on my heart. Whatever hardship you've endured since, no matter how many times you've done a three point two, you can't tell me that it isn't ball-tearingly hard, running as fast as you can with eight kilos of unwieldy kit around your waist, carrying your rifle and wearing GP (general-purpose) boots of lead – it levels all men. Even if you killed it and got a good time, your whole world would be crashing in every bit as much as the guy who came last. It was simply that kind of test; by the end, your arse was hanging out regardless of your fitness level, because it required all your effort.

The SFET, or Barrier Test, was nothing if not compre-hensive. It consisted of a fitness test encompassing the usual push-ups, sit-ups, chin-ups, the 2.4-kilometre run, a few navigation theory tests, a fully clothed swim, more psycholog-ical testing, the aforementioned 3.2-kilometre webbing run, enclosed space and height tests, something called mechanical aptitude testing – whereby you'd be shown several weapons drills and then tested to check your assimilation of infor-mation – and a four-hour practical navigation exercise. Last but not least was the fifteen-kilometre pack march carrying around thirty-seven kilograms. This was all to take place in around three days at the end of October.

The test was held at Singleton Army Barracks in Central New South Wales and was run by the Special Forces Training Centre, which was staffed by commandos and headed up by members of the SAS. To say I was intimidated is an under-statement. That said, I wasn't one of those wide-eyed suck-ups who had pictures of the SAS all over their rooms; though you've got to respect the achievements of others!

As much of this book is about selection, I should contrast the naval selection process with that of the army, as they are very different beasts. Like anything else, each has their own strengths and weakness. Navy specialised testing boils down to: how much can we put you through? Who is the last man standing? How depleted can you become and not fall over, then in that state how do you conduct yourself? The object-ive is to select a suitable piece of clay that can be moulded and built into the sort of operator who can pass the required testing. The army's way of testing was much more black and white, almost mathematical: here's the time, weight and distance, now go. It seemed to me, at the beginning at least, that it was a highly objective process, nowhere near as subjective as my naval selection experiences. The army drew a line in the sand and you either crossed it in the right time or you didn't; no existential crisis there, ay!

When I turned up at the Singleton Barracks with ten other divers, something was wrong. Well, maybe not wrong exactly, but not what we were expecting. At the first brief, a burly sergeant as wide as he was tall gathered us together. He reminded me of a warrior dwarf from 'The Lord of the Rings' movies and I made a mental note to stay well away from any potential swing of his axe! When he ran through, in basic terms, how the test was to be conducted and what the times were, it was different from what we'd expected: the goal posts had changed. There were some worried faces among us, none more so than mine. Even the army guys were looking around at each other with questioning gazes, wondering – like all of us – whether games were afoot.

What it all boiled down to is that before the selection in question, the test was supposed to be 'relatively hard'. The one we did was 'crazy' and the subsequent ones were 'bloody hard'.

The facts as I see them about the Barrier Test, with the benefit of hindsight:

1) The three-hour navigation exercise with no kit was replaced by a ten-hour jungle ordeal, with twenty checkpoints, carrying a pack of around forty kilograms
2) The fifteen-kilometre pack march was changed to a twenty-two-kilometre march

3) The 3.2-kilometre webbing run was conducted in boots – not runners, as it was before and after this test – and with a shortened cut-off

4) Qualifying times for the swim and 2.4-kilometre run were reduced

5) Last but not least, the selectors failed blokes left, right and centre for all kinds of unexpected stuff, including not registering your first twenty or thirty push-ups; some blokes didn't have these included in their total and were sent packing.

Of course, we didn't realise all this when we first arrived, but it became evident to even the most clueless observer that there was a storm a-comin' and it was bringing hell with it.

In relation to the above, before any readers get their camouflaged panties in a bunch, for the record I don't consider any of it unfair. It's their club and they can do to candidates what they want; if you want to be selected, you deal with the changes. I'm simply stating that a significant change in the standard of qualification was introduced at this moment. The fact that *it did change* also reflects that testing was – and still is – an evolving process; not all tests are conducted the same way; that also applies to the navy's CDAT.

On reflection, I believed, like the others, that I'd trained hard and could adapt. My biggest worry was the scaled-up navigational exercise as I had the sense of direction of a dead lemming and could picture myself stumbling if I wasn't careful. Also this test was normally run by the commandos, with a couple of regiment guys overseeing everything, but you would have had to be blind not to notice the increased number of sandy berets (SAS) that surrounded us and the lack of green ones (commando). Let the games begin . . .

My arms felt like they were going to fall off. The burning was terrible but the anger inside me was worse. The bastard counting out my push-ups was only counting every third one and by the time he got to fifty, I reckon I'd actually done well over a hundred. But you don't 'argue with the ref' on selection, so I kept a lid on it and somehow got through.

When I eased myself back up from the prone position once the test was over, it was the middle of the first day. Already we'd completed the 2.4-kilometre run and the dreaded 3.2-kilometre webbing run in the desert heat. Next cab off the rank was the swim and I needed to prepare myself.

As I recovered I tried to bring myself to a mental zero. In my previous selections I'd developed this process myself: I'd remove all thoughts of what I'd just done and try not to over-analyse what was coming up. It was like placing myself in a kind of bubble or void, so any challenges could be faced without surrounding static or interference. Without being too 'hippy' about it, my view is that overconfidence in what you've achieved or doubt about what remains unachieved can affect you negatively and hamper your efforts.

Casually glancing across the line, I noticed Canada having his turn for push-ups; a massive army PTI was standing over him counting one of about every five. 'They're out for him,' I thought. God knows why. It happens all the time in selection. Some bloke doesn't like your face and you're gone, no matter what you do. By my count Canada must have done at least 150 before he went down. Rage swept through me. Momentarily, I fantasised about running over there, grabbing that tight-shorts-wearing motherfucker, dragging him to the pool and seeing how long he could hold his breath!

But that's not the way it worked, and I watched as Canada was ushered over to where the other failed candidates were assembled. He wasn't alone; at least five or six of our diving brethren had already been knocked out via similar nebulous decisions, along with a good portion of the army guys. Out of an original 150, only about fifty remained. It almost seemed as if some directive had been passed and they wanted to thin the ranks of people getting through as soon as they could; I'd never know.

When it was time for the next phase, we were herded like cattle to the pool. Walking past Canada on the way, I mouthed the words, 'Sorry, bro', and he nodded and gave me a fake salute. I could not believe he wasn't about to get in the water too; Canada was the best soldier I knew. I would have been angrier but I was still in the fight; there was no time for sentimentality.

As they arrived at the pool, for the first time I saw those army blokes squirm but there were smiles on the faces of the remaining divers. If there was one area where we had the upper hand, it was in the water. The first group of army guys jumped in for their swim. You shouldn't laugh on selection but I damn near wet myself observing some of them; it was like watching the Pharaoh's army crossing the Red Sea in full armour. But before my brother – the one in the army – starts getting uppity, hold off: we were soon to enter the bush for our ten-hour nav ex. You can bet your bottom dollar those guys would have their revenge on this little black duck. Divers don't play well in the weeds . . .

Any satisfaction I might have gained from my showing in the pool was short-lived as for some reason, whether by accident or design I know not, the pool was over-chlorinated yet no one was allowed to wear goggles. By the end of the swim I was blind: it makes my eyes water even thinking about it. Ordinarily, this might not have been any great problem but we were about to enter the lecture hall to receive a brief and do our nav theory test.

Suddenly I was dealing with two issues that could drastically impair my progress. Firstly, as an SAS sergeant was giving the briefing in the hall, there were other SAS blokes walking around, generally observing, so I needed to concentrate. Secondly, my eyes were burning badly and had all but closed up. Prior to entering the room, on the advice of some brilliant army bloke, I'd even tried pouring milk over them. The guy's probably still laughing now, several years later, having watched this clearance diver pour a two-litre bottle of milk on his face. Good one, mate!

As the talk continued, so did the burning and I periodically rubbed my searing sockets for comfort. When some SAS bloke patrolling the aisle screamed at me, 'Can't you even keep your eyes open when the sergeant is talking, you weak fuck!' I was stunned. I would never have fallen asleep and shown such unmitigated disrespect to the sergeant during his briefing. It was no use trying to explain that to the gentleman, so I just sat upright and took those words of encouragement on the chin. 'I'm sure that will really help my chances,' I thought, but tried not to worry about it as I squinted and focused on the theory test.

Partway through the test I very nearly came a cropper again. The patrols continued up and down the aisle. My head was down and I was working hard to finish the test when I noticed something that almost stopped my heart. We were allowed to use calculators for the sums, and carved into the cover of mine for all to see was a rather accurate drawing of the SAS's emblem: a flaming Excalibur, or winged dagger as some call it. What the fuck! Who had done that?

Then it came to me: I had taken the calculator from home. It must have belonged to one of my younger brothers, who'd probably drawn it on there, as kids do, like their favourite footy team logo. I was horrified. If one of these operators spotted it, I would be laughed out of the course and probably receive a punch in the head for my trouble. Quick as I could, I grabbed the edge of my steel ruler and scraped it out.

'For fuck's sake,' I thought, 'that could have been nasty.' A military emblem is a sacred thing and should always be treated as such.

Onto the nav ex. When entering the jungle, I was initially taken aback by how thick the vegetation was. You could have fallen into it and never touched the ground. It was nothing like the relative cow paddocks where I had learnt nav only weeks before.

Anyone with even a basic understanding of navigation knows that it's all about paces and bearings. Paces and bearings, that's the mantra. Work out the direction you have to travel and the distance, and off you go, skipping along the yellow brick road.

Some blokes are happy out in the weeds with the heat, the bugs and nice lush greenery while carrying your house on your back, whistling 'Dixie' all the way. I, unfortunately, am not one of those lucky individuals. Consequently, I took a pragmatic approach. Each checkpoint of the twenty or so was supposed to take anywhere from half an hour to one hour to reach, depending on your accuracy, endurance and skill. The way I saw it, if I could achieve ten checkpoints, I might still have a chance because of my relative success in the previous events.

Sadly, things went south within minutes, and I don't mean due south, as I had no idea what fucking direction I was heading! Struggling from the get-go, I found it hard to maintain a straight line through this quagmire and became increasingly frustrated. This is how mistakes are made: you get vexed and you start to lose concentration and suddenly you're in a world of hurt, with no one to blame but yourself.

We'd been issued with a GPS for emergencies and in case the staff couldn't find us. It was taped up and sealed so that if you did use it they would know. But I can tell you now that even though I'd lost my bearings and got hopelessly lost, not once did I consider using it. They would have to find my corpse years from now, with that thing still wrapped tightly. To use it meant instant failure and a good deal of embarrassment.

To put it mildly, I had a rough trot. At one stage, I fell through the thick foliage into a dry riverbed. My pack pitched gracefully over my shoulders as I went down and drove my head into the sand upon impact. Several minutes passed when I lay there, all fucked up, looking at the small gap of light in the canopy, thinking how shit I was and wondering what

I had got myself into. I was momentarily defeated. Assessing the damage, I realised my kit was all smashed, I'd scratched my eye pretty badly and I'd also thrown my shoulder out a bit.

But it dawned on me that I had to get up and find my way to at least one checkpoint! It was too easy to picture the headlines: 'Body of Idiot Diver Found Out Bush – Cause of Death: Stupidity'.

Through a bit of luck and some painstaking calculation I limped into my first checkpoint. It had taken over four hours and I looked a mess, a dirt-encrusted, vegetation-covered mess.

There was a rather wiry, diminutive SAS corporal sitting at the checkpoint. The picture of composure, he had one of those 1980s moustaches, and his thousand-yard stare made me brace for what was sure to be a scathing appraisal of my presentation. To my surprise, he said with a smile, 'Geez mate, you're doing well, you must be almost finished!'

I raised my head, swallowed some of the blood that was collecting from my fat lip and answered, 'It's my first one, Staff.'

He looked at me in bewilderment but, with a tinge of empathy, said, 'Shit, mate, you better get a wriggle on. Do you know where you're going next?'

It didn't take an Einstein to see what this crack soldier was thinking: 'What is this navy idiot doing out here?' But to his credit and my everlasting gratitude, he gave me some words of encouragement and helped me with my next bearing. 'Good luck, kid,' he called as I slunk off towards the next checkpoint.

Concentrating hard for the next six hours, I managed another four checkpoints, giving me a grand total of five.

Well, five and a half if you count the walk back to our start point, and I do.

Back in the truck, I listened as many of the army guys commented how hard they found the ex, and it did give me a little solace. But above all I was spent, absolutely buggered, and there was two hours' rest before the start of the twenty-two klicker.

Back at base we all headed off to prep our gear before the march. When I looked in my tent, there sitting on my bag lay a folded fresh pair of GP socks, with a note attached. Clean socks! I'd only brought the one pair, and they could have walked home all by themselves by this stage. I picked up the note, which read, 'Bro, here's a fresh pair for the march, sorry I couldn't be there. Canada' . . .

Four hours give or take was the time allotted for this little tiptoe through the tulips, and I would need every second of it if I was going to pass. The twenty-two-kilometre pack march was the last event of the Barrier Test, and even in my depleted state I still thought I had a chance. Pack marching is a highly specific skill and requires a kind of Olympic walker-style shuffle. The army guys have got it down to a fine art. It may look funny but that waddle of theirs hurtles them down the dusty road with enough momentum to rival Robert de Castella himself.

Early on, I settled into a sort of ambling gait, but it was evident that I was too slow. How did I know this, I hear you ask? Well, quite simply, every man and his camouflaged dog were passing my arse! The pack dug into my shoulders and all I could do was shift the pain to different areas, but at no stage was I comfortable. Each step I took felt like I had broken every bone in my foot and my dream was slipping away in what seemed like slow motion.

As I topped the final hill, a mere 700 metres from the finish line, a truck pulled up next to me and a voice boomed out rather unceremoniously, 'Time's up, mate.'

I was crestfallen. It wouldn't have taken more than ten minutes to finish the entire ordeal yet they told me to throw my shit in the truck. I'd failed.

I won't lie – there's no point – I was close to tears. Since joining up over two years previously, I hadn't failed a single test the military had thrown at me. The prospect of returning to the Team and trying to explain to those people – who'd put so much effort into my preparation – that I had let them down was almost too much to bear. It was no consolation that only one diver had managed to pass. I took the loss very personally.

Canada and I could have sat down over a peppermint tea and talked about it, but we didn't; neither of us is that type of person. We always knew what the other one was thinking and it needed no discussion. We knew what had happened – we hadn't prepared enough – and both of us needed to accept that and move on.

The bus ride home was like being present at my own funeral. I wallowed in self-pity. I blamed no one but myself, and it was tearing me up. I had the weekend off so was able to drown my sorrows, then dragged myself into work on Monday.

Blokes slapped me on the back and generally gave me support. It didn't ease the pain for me though. I guess it's like a boxer: they all think they're going to win when they step into that ring, and when they step out beaten, the suffering and self-doubt must be massive.

An unlikely saviour snapped me out of my anguish. He was the Warrant Officer of the Team and had served with the regiment 'back in the day'. After our daily afternoon meeting, called O Group, this unlikely champion of the fallen, whom we hardly knew, approached Canada and me. In that quirky tone that all old divers have, he gave us the following speech:

'Boys, come 'ere, ay, ay. What's up? Heard you just came off Barrier. Well, here's the forms to do it again. Fill the fuckers out and have 'em on me desk by the end of the day.'

Canada and I were stunned; we thought the powers that be would make us wait a good long time, if the bosses even allowed us to do it at all. My ego was still in traction and I wasn't even sure I *could* step up to the plate again so soon, but this WO had different ideas. There was no cooling-off period as far as he was concerned: we hadn't quit, we just hadn't performed well enough. He was basically saying, 'Do the fucking thing again, ya bastards.'

I think in unison, Canada and I said, 'Yes, sir', and took the papers from his mallet-sized hands. He had already signed at the bottom, authorising our return.

Fourteen

SECOND BITE OF THE CHERRY

'Never compromise, not even in the face of
Armageddon.'

— Watchmen

In the movie *Pulp Fiction*, Marsellus Wallace says to Butch,
'The night of the fight, you may feel a slight sting. That's pride
fucking with you. Fuck pride. Pride only hurts, it never helps.'
Maybe it was foolish pride or maybe I'm just a glutton for
punishment, but the Barrier Test had become my Waterloo.
I'd be damned if I'd fail my second attempt.

Also the Branch – being the Branch – insisted on another
PWT, though with some changes. The last one had been run
like a selection and, while it was awesome, by the end of it
I think we were all a bit fucked, to be honest. This time, not
unlike in a marathon runner's training, the intensity would
taper off a little prior to the event. Exhaustion combined with
the slightly 'modified' selection criteria had caused something of
a shortfall in our pass rate. This time round, although still hard,

155

PWT would be geared more towards passing the upcoming test and not smashing the boys to see who could take it.

Many of those who came off that first Barrier chose not to return. I don't blame them. There can be a myriad of reasons for not making it over any hurdle, let alone something as gruelling as that test had been. And I'm not talking here about finding excuses, I just mean that you can hold your head high in the knowledge you did your utmost, take the results as proof that it wasn't for you and move on.

Failing your second attempt was a completely different matter, for then those around you could – and in my experience invariably would – throw all sorts of labels at you. It's a weird phenomenon, 'cause you'd think that people would give you props for standing up and running back into the proverbial fire. But things don't always work out like we want them to, do they? The world is not fair and I had the very real fear that if I failed again, my reputation would be finished.

This PWT was hard but more measured and specific. Specificity is a training principle that I believe in strongly. Cross-training is all right, but there's nothing like *doing* the thing that you are going to be *doing* in order to prepare for it. This may not always be possible, especially if the task ahead is full of unknowns, but where you can do so, repeating the task parrot fashion will give you the best result.

The one thing I did a little differently, and this fits in with the above, was that I practised a shitload more pack marching. I was going to make damn sure, no matter how stuffed I was, that I would be able to run twenty-two kilometres with a forty-kilogram load. Canada and I even spent our Saturdays marching up and down the Pacific Highway on Sydney's

North Shore in an attempt to strengthen this area of our game. Because the second Iraq War was running hot by then, as we marched past 'Joe Public' with packs and wearing camo pants, we would often hear people yell out, 'Say no to war!' and 'Iraq's that way, man!' Given that we were training to be part of a unit that would defend *them* against domestic terrorism, it was quite amusing.

For this next Barrier Test – the second bite of the cherry, or 'retread', like the tyre – I wasn't anywhere near as intimidated as I had been that previous attempt. Going in, I felt confident – not arrogant. I knew what to expect and I had my mind right, which is the most important thing.

I passed the initial fitness test with pretty reasonable scores; hit the pool and the theory tests out of the park. Now I had to face my demons: the dreaded nav ex was next.

Recognising my relative weakness in this area, I had devised a cunning plan: essentially, I held the compass in front of my nose, walking to each checkpoint one foot in front of the other like a tightrope walker. It was slow going but I hit them all dead on and ended up with eleven out of the twelve: not bad for me; most days I was lucky to find the fridge in my own kitchen with my nav skills.

Finally it was down to the twenty-two klicker, that monster of a walk that screwed me last time. On the truck ride there, at about two in the morning, I felt nervous. Then I got chatting with this enormous army reserve guy who was going for SAS selection. He kindly gave me half of his protein bar. Thanking him, I smashed it down, though without much faith in the promises made on the wrapper: 'All the energy of thirty nuclear bananas!' Yer, right.

When the whistle blew, most guys started into that familiar duck-like army waddle, but the guy I'd been talking to in the truck just fucking took off like a bat out of hell.

'Fuck this,' I thought. 'This bloke's got the right idea: give it everything, smash the shit out of yourself and do whatever you can to limp over the finish line, leaving nothing behind.'

It was everything I'd been told *not* to do by my training staff: 'Don't run, you'll only tire yourself out.' But their advice hadn't worked for the first Barrier Test; I'd walked too bloody slow! I couldn't walk like those army guys but I could run. So I thought, 'Fuck it, I'll stay behind big fella and see what happens.' Besides, that protein bar was really kicking in by now!

So I totally went for it. Of course I couldn't run the whole way. I did taper off occasionally and walk, but not for long; every second I felt I could, I took off sprinting.

I remember the army blokes laughing, probably thinking, 'Look at that mad bastard, he won't even finish if he keeps that up.'

But I was bloody terrified of failing again, and that drove me on. I stayed close behind the big reserve guy until right at the end, when he lost me. Until then he could probably feel me staring at his back; I never took my eyes off him. I was like, 'This guy is going to pass; I'll let him be my pacer.'

Suddenly the finish line was in sight. I crossed it at a jog, unable to quite comprehend that it was over. Surely I had finished up front in the top fifteen, at least. I collapsed on the ground, drenched in salty perspiration. An SAS guy came up, threw me a cold Tetra Pak of fruit juice, said, 'Well done', and then walked away.

That drink scarcely made a dent in my thirst but I couldn't have been happier: the monkey was off my back and so was that fucking pack.

Having now passed the Special Forces Entry Test, we would be placed in a holding pattern until the next CQB (Close-Quarter Battle) course, which was the gateway to TAG. Successful completion of CQB would result in an invitation to TAG's water platoon, where clearance divers were posted once qualified.

Despite the hurdles and adversity that still lay ahead, delirious would be how I'd describe the mood on the trip home. All the guys who had failed – which was a bloody lot – had already been RTU (returned to unit) so on our trip home, the only ones on the bus were those of us who had passed. Throughout the bus the sense of achievement was palpable. Every bloke on it would have had his own reasons for putting himself through all of that, but I'm damn sure there was some commonality among the group; there definitely was for Canada and me. Yet again, the two of us had had to see if we could, just to see if we could . . .

The CQB wasn't panelled for another month, so while I had a bit of down time I was put forward for COMSURV (combat survival), another specialised course. Clearance divers hadn't done it for a while – something to do with bureaucratic issues that I have no idea about – but it was a course that CDs had traditionally taken part in, and one highly regarded within the military establishment. I for one was keen to get it under my belt, not because it progressed your career or anything, but I'd heard stories, and it sounded cool: no food, no shelter, running from dogs, more training, more tests, more selection – what more could you want, right?

Spaced over three weeks, the course combined theory with plenty of practical content, and was conducted out of an air force base near Townsville, Queensland. Over several phases, a range of techniques, tactics and principles of survival were covered in different settings, including arid or desert, coastal, group jungle and solo jungle. As it was the first one run for a while, we had quite a few divers on this course and the remainder of the participants were pilots; it was only offered to people who could conceivably find themselves behind enemy lines.

The basic principle of survival is to give yourself every chance of being rescued. This can be achieved by setting up a large visible signature, like a fire or a colourful display – by that I don't mean a production of *The Pirates of Penzance*, just any visual indicator. The next thing is to establish communication through whatever electronic means you have. Then there are the basics of shelter, food and water. All these and many more nuggets of information were drilled into us, but the tactics will vary significantly depending whether you are in enemy territory or in your own. As you can imagine, there's no use setting up a bonfire to invite the enemy to roast marshmallows and sing 'Kumbaya'!

Everyone participating really enjoyed this course, especially us CDs, as the level of training we already had allowed us to shine. At some stages the instructors got the shits with our joviality and their inability to smash us in the early PT sessions up Townsville's enormous hill. But we learnt a lot, and I believe we gave the instructors the deference they deserved, all except one, that is . . .

This bloke was an ADG, or airfield defence guard, kind of like the air force's army. Now, I have absolutely nothing against them. My younger brother Matt was an ADG and I respect him and his achievements greatly. But this guy was a total spanner, his demeanour was that of an arrogant school bully, and some of the stories he told sounded totally implausible. Like I've said, it's not on to claim anything you haven't done, yet this guy's confidence was unshakeable even when straight-out lying to the class about his feats, such as telling us that he'd done selection with the US Delta Force. So the boys and I were just waiting to take him down a peg or two.

That opportunity arrived sooner than we'd hoped when during a classroom session he began one of his ramblings, making outrageous claims about the ADG's exploits. One enthusiastic young flight cadet asked, with complete sincerity, 'Gee whiz, how many ADGs are there?'

In response this bloke placed his hands firmly on his hips, poked out his chest and while looking into the distance stated, 'Well, there's not many of us left!'

Straight away I yelled out, 'What, like the Jedi!'

The room erupted in hysterics; people were rolling on the floor laughing and the poor bloke could not get the class back under control. He went and complained to his boss and I was reprimanded by my XO (executive officer), who was in the class as well. Fortunately he saw the funny side of the incident and it was all swept under the table.

The whole course was a huge adventure and the escape and evade (E&E) section was one of my favourites. Working in a group of five, we had to avoid detection by the soldiers combing the terrain with dogs, which we managed to do by climbing high into the mountains and taking the long way to our checkpoint.

Probably the most challenging part of the course was the last solo phase as by this stage we were weak, having not eaten much, and had a list of tasks to complete in order to satisfy the criteria for passing. We had to build a shelter, a signal fire plus enclosure complete with wood-drying rack, a bed of sorts and latrine facilities. Not knowing how long we were going to be out there, I was determined to make my camp the Taj Mahal of survival areas. The only sustenance I had remaining was a small packet of green cordial crystals; I was relying on them to give me the energy required to undertake construction of my dream hut.

First things first, I made a fire. No, not by rubbing two sticks together; I'm not MacGyver, the TV action-adventure hero. I had a flint and steel, a survival tool that makes sparks. The skill lies in having the appropriate fuel to get it going, and then keep it going. When the fire lit I was able to boil some water, which was very satisfying, as up until now I'd had to add iodine tablets to any water I'd found, which made it taste like there was a hospital in your mouth. I added the green cordial that I had hidden in my pants and downed it. Whoa, baby! You wouldn't believe what a little sugar can do for you when you've had nothing to eat for three days. After seven hours, I stood back and looked at what I had done, and it was good (couldn't resist a little biblical allusion there).

Unexpectedly, the weather turned icy and Townsville experienced its lowest temperatures on record. Even with a fire I was still mighty cold, but I got through the night by cooking up little lizards I'd caught and some baby yabbies I snaffled up in the adjacent creek. It was all quite fun, even though I found being alone with my thoughts slightly freaky. It would be easy to get a bit weird, sitting for hours staring into the fire, watching it flicker and dance, entranced by its controlled chaos.

The next day an instructor came by to grade my efforts. He was really impressed and said I'd done a fine job, even if I was a bit of a smart ass in class. I thanked him, then he added that he'd never seen anybody sweep the forest floor and rock out pathways to the toilet and make furniture like I had. 'Cheers,' I said.

Before heading off, he commented that he'd come by later with a camera and take some photos as examples to show future classes. This gave me a bit of a buzz but also misled me into thinking that it was all over and they'd be picking us up that arvo for extraction. So like the lazy grasshopper in the fable I lazed around all day instead of gathering wood for the upcoming freezing night.

When the sun fell, it was plain that we were, in fact, spending yet another night out in the 'J'. I realised I could no longer venture into the woods to collect firewood as I might get lost and then I'd be up shit creek.

The night grew cold and the fire started to die down, so I looked in my emergency survival pack, which I had painstakingly assembled back at the Team base. I'd made sure to include a space blanket, one of those folded-up silver-covered 'joeys' that are supposed to keep in your body heat. There was a kind off 'poooft' sound when I shook it open, and all the silver warmy stuff disintegrated in front of my eyes, floating away like flecks of silver snow into the night air. The thing must have been fifty years old. I was left standing there holding a large and absolutely useless piece of clear cellophane.

There was no option now: I was freaken freezing, and surrounding me were the wood furnishings and shelter I'd made with such care the previous day. Without hesitation, I systematically threw it all on the fire, effectively burning my whole camp to keep warm; Bear Grylls, eat your heart out.

Early the next day, when the instructor returned for our extraction and to take snaps of my 'ideal spot', he was shocked. 'What happened to your camp?' he asked.

From my patch on the ground, where I lay curled up, smeared in dirt and soot, I said, 'I burnt it! I burnt it all!'

After we'd shared a laugh about that, he told me he'd already graded me, so that was no dramas, but there would be no photographic glory for me. Oh, well.

It just goes to show you that, in selection, you should never assume anything!

Fifteen

CLOSE-QUARTER BATTLE (CQB)

'There's a reason they call it Special Forces.'

– HR

I won't lie; I was shitting myself. Once again I was facing something I desired with all my heart yet, somehow, I felt woefully out of my depth. It wasn't the case that I was under-prepared – I'd done everything humanly possible to be ready – but there was no denying that CQB has one of the steepest learning curves in the military world.

By reputation, it's cut-throat; there's hardly any time to assimilate what you're experiencing: you either pick it up immediately or you're gone. And I could see the reasons why. The skills and training involved high levels of danger and although safety measures were put in place, this was as real as it got other than actually going to war. We're talking fast, complicated moves, with live bullets and no margin for error. Plenty of commandos, clearance divers and – even in their own REO cycle (reinforcement training period) – SAS members had trouble completing the CQB component of training. Many candidates had to attempt it two or three times or, worse yet, were told not to come back at all. I did not want to be one of those candidates.

People constantly ask me why I put myself through so many fear-inducing situations like that, and the answer's hard to convey, but partly it's about 'asking the question'. Where others might baulk at stepping out of their comfort zone, risking everything for no apparent reason, leaving their loved ones, their couch, I want to answer the question. People lie, all the time, especially to themselves; I try not to.

If ever I were to run away from a fight, I would hate myself for it. Facing the fear and losing would always be better than not facing it at all. All you can do is stay in the fight and, like Tom Petty sang, 'You can stand me up at the gates of hell but I won't back down.'

The TAG unit was part of 4RAR Commando, presided over by the SAS and referred to as Charlie Company. The secrecy surrounding its creation, daily events and training is still in place, so you'll have to forgive any gaps in my account or lack of detail (secret squirrel, sorry).

Initial training consisted of four weeks: two weeks of Basic CQB, which dealt mainly with weapons drills and shooting skills and concluded with a test – or, to be more accurate, a culling of the candidates – then two weeks of Advanced CQB, which covered room-floor combat, elements of method of entry (MOE) and specific drills.

I returned from COMSURV a fortnight before CQB started and having been on the brink of starvation, I was looking forward to a bit of a break from pressure. Maybe kick around the Team with no specific duties? Negative! It turned out that the Branch had other ideas. Thanks to some upper-echelon concern about the shooting prowess of us divers, they'd decided to create *another* selection course – called CDSEC, or Clearance Diver Skills Enhancement Course. That's right: yet another selection prior to selection. It was to take place at an army base on the outskirts of Sydney. As most of the divers lived on the North Shore ('Near the waves, bro') we were allocated a 22-seater bus to drive us from Dive School every day.

Initially, my response was, 'Come on, let's just start', but I was about to discover that I was wrong. Compared with the commandos we'd be joining at the upcoming course, we CDs were way behind with our shooting; this CDSEC proved to be the best idea the Branch had come up with, equipping us with valuable shooting skills prior to the real selection. There was one down side though. It *was* a 'selection' and if you were deemed unsuitable, then you could say goodbye to your chance at TAG. More pressure.

Another pressure – although more subtle – surfaced in the form of rumours that getting out to TAG and into Water Platoon wasn't solely about your ability. You had to be good, that wasn't in question, but allegedly it was also about being 'one of the boys'; it was important, though not officially, to be seen in general terms as a good bloke, part of the in-crowd – a team player, in other words. In real terms, this was just one more thing to think about.

Shooting fast and straight takes masses of practice, repetition and patience, as well as adhering to basic principles of marksmanship, grip, stance, trigger manipulation and sight picture. It may seem rather simple, but when you're up on the line a mere five metres from the target and you miss the fucking thing . . . words cannot express the frustration. I quickly realised that shooting is also an art and nothing but serious training would enable me to make that shot at over twenty-five metres when it counted.

'Couldn't hit the side of a barn door with a shotgun' would be an apt description. Thoughts that the fucking barrel must be bent or something went through my head as the Chief Diver in charge of our training – one CPO Welsh – inspected my target. 'Does your husband shoot too?' quipped the Chief.

A few of the boys were doing okay but I couldn't shoot for shit! This posed an interesting dilemma, like in *The Simpsons* episode when Bart, spying on some kids with binoculars, is put on the spot by Millhouse: 'I thought you said you could read lips.' Bart replies, 'I assumed I could.' Well, I had assumed I could shoot and that all the 'other skills' would be the problem. Once again I was up against the wall.

Chief Welsh was a terrific guy and, to my surprise, had some level of respect for me; I'm not sure why. He generously offered to coach me on the finer points of shooting and by the end of the course I was at a respectable level, though by no means Wyatt Earp.

A validation (or VAL) shoot was the immediate goal of all this range practice. The VAL was a shooting test designed to examine speed and accuracy over varying distances and with various weapons systems; it incorporated movement, accuracy and speed. If you dropped more than one shot at each range, you failed. There was no 'That's okay, mate; have another go, darling.' It was fucking 'Fail!' You might be granted another attempt if you were ridiculously talented in other disciplines, but the benchmark was high and you had to pass this test a couple of times a week all the way to the end.

Initially, all prospective candidates had to pass the test with just the iron sights on their long gun, and wearing a gasmask that gave you the vision of a cataract-suffering bat. Somehow, I got through.

Twelve guys started CDSEC and on the last day, a Friday, they selected eight of us to go on to CQB, Canada and I among them, to my surprise. Despite my early lacklustre shooting, I had passed the last two VALs, and the Chief seemed to think I had the ability to pick it up.

It was tough for those who hadn't made selection. Upon returning to the School that afternoon, still clad in our tan-coloured mechanics overalls and numbered brassards – the training uniform of prospective TAG members – we alighted from the bus and headed to the HMAS *Penguin* Junior Sailors Bar for a beer to console those not coming forward with us. Naturally, there are dress regulations for the base bar and I'm pretty sure none of us came close to meeting them: we were all covered in sweat and gun oil and were barely able to walk. As we filed through the door, some ranking sailor stood up and made a beeline for us, presumably to inform us of our 'mistake'. Halfway to where we stood, staring at the ground, our bodies slumped, a perceptive baby diver who happened to be in the bar placed his hand on the guy's arm and whispered in his ear. Immediately the sailor sat down, allowing us clear passage to the bar. I don't know what the guy said, but I'm sure it was words to the effect of 'I wouldn't, mate.'

'Slow is smooth and smooth is fast' – repeat these words in your sleep, oh weary traveller, for they will serve you well. Although this mantra and plenty of others were running through my head, I don't think I spoke more than two or three sentences all weekend. I didn't answer the phone and I found it hard to eat. CQB was starting Monday morning, and the gravity of its impending arrival weighed heavily on my already loaded shoulders.

Canada came over on Sunday night, and we cracked a couple of Coronas and chilled on my balcony.

'How ya feelin', bro?' I enquired, knowing that I probably wouldn't receive a response – well, nothing that would allay my fears anyway.

However, without an ounce of self-doubt and without so much as a twitch changing his façade, Canada sipped his beer, gazed at an already fading sun, and replied, 'She be right bro, ay.'

We're not in Kansas anymore, ay, Toto! The army was a very different place to what I was used to, and there was no denying we were firmly in its grasp. Army guys are a breed apart, and by that I don't mean bad. The army takes things that are serious and treats them as such; the navy has more of a laissez-faire style, which is no less effective, just differ-ent. In the Dive Branch, when it came to learning incredibly

CLOSE-QUARTER BATTLE (CQB)

dangerous equipment and/or procedures – where you needed to understand it all plus learn to handle the pressure – the instructional technique was more of a 'Hey, bro, this is how you do this if you don't want to die', whereas the army was more, 'Right, it's like this . . . do that' implying the 'if you don't want to die' part with the sternness of delivery.

My plan was simple: do as I'm told, learn fast, and make no mistakes. Looking back, I realise I was wound tighter than a drum. They said to Maverick in *Top Gun*, 'You're holding on too tight, man.' Well, that was true of me when I turned up for CQB. Although I didn't want to admit it, I felt nervous because I was terrified of failure – CQB has one of the highest failure rates of any military course. To be counted among those that couldn't make it would be a major concern for me. That fear was my constant dark shadow – it followed me everywhere.

The ideal state for serving with TAG is to be calm and somewhat relaxed, yet ready to unleash energy effectively in an instant, should a situation demand it. You've got to step and move like a prize-fighter, because if you plant your feet and let the fog envelop you, you gonna hit the canvas, daddy'o. But that knowledge, and the confidence to apply it, was some way off in the future for me.

TAG was divided into three groups: the Land Platoon, made up of commandos; the Water Platoon, made up of clearance divers and a few SAS lads; and the Sniper Platoon, which had elements of both. Instructors and assistant instructors for the CQB course came from all three of these sections; at the top of the command structure were SAS members, followed by commandos and CD officers.

Operators 'on team' with TAG were used as DS (directing staff), and the ratio of commandos to bubbleheads (divers) didn't exactly stack up in our favour. Not that it would have made a difference, as on occasion Water Platoon staff could be harder on us, purely to show there was no favouritism. There was no hiding on CQB.

The course was run in a kind of vacuum; CQB had its own criteria – a set of standards and infringements. To become an operator, you had to measure up to those criteria. Each instructor had a notebook and by the end of every day it would be full of notes on all the candidates. On the surface it was black and white but paradoxically, the criteria were also open to interpretation.

Criteria One: Safeties – a safety could be called on you for anything from lasering (pointing your barrel in an unsafe direction) to not having your safety catch engaged at the appropriate time, and everything in between.

Criteria Two: Dangerous occurrence – this was highly subjective and encompassed any shortcomings in responding appropriately when an event occurred.

Criteria Three: Awareness – this was the most subjective area and gave the instructors an all-powerful wand that could be waved at anything they noticed; generally, it added up to a bloke not being good enough.

Criteria Four: 'Validation shoots' – as explained earlier, these are tests of your shooting skill.

On top of these four main areas of judgement, there were countless other hoops to jump through, not least of which were the morning drills, or DPs (dry practice).

DPs . . . the very thought of them still chills me to the bone: lining up in full kit, body armour and gasmasks, armed with both your primary weapon (HK 9mm MP5) and your holstered secondary (HK 9mm USP). You would stand poised, ready to respond instantaneously to the commands of the staff carrying out the stoppage drills and alert to any movement that could occur in an indoor combat environment . . . and that was merely the tip of a very nasty iceberg. The experience of DPs is quite unlike any other I have gone through in my life! There are a thousand eyes on you and the smallest mistake is picked up in a nanosecond by the numerous staff.

In between high-paced DP drills, which lasted anything from one to two hours, we would be ordered to run 100 metres in full kit around the toilet block – or shitters as they were usually called – and back. You took off trying desperately to gasp some air through your gasmask and praying that when you got back to the line you didn't pass out from lack of oxygen. My vision narrowed on more than a few occasions.

After this horrendous activity, there would be a small break during which we would grab a quick brekky. Every morning without fail, a huge box of bacon and egg burgers would materialise; they had melted cheese on them and were the absolute pits. We called them CT (counterterrorism) burgers. Believe me, if we managed to get a bunch of these things into any terrorist stronghold, they would give up pretty fast.

Barely would I have scoffed my brekky and placed the last round in the fourth of my magazines, when we'd be called back up on the line, and would be firing and away again. No shit, the slide on my pistol actually cracked. That shows the level of intensity of the training; it was a non-stop head-fuck.

Everything I had done up until then in the armed forces, no matter how edgy, had always allowed for some mistakes, some wiggle room. Not out here though; definitely not on this course. But we were about to find out why as we headed into the next phase: room-floor combat.

The RFCR (room-floor combat range), or 'kill house' if you want to get all American, was the reason for the unwavering standards held on course. It was like a wooden maze with a roof on top. Its interchangeable internal moving walls could be configured to any desired layout, providing an ever-changing architectural hellscape to confuse and befuddle the brain.

Running around the RFCR in the dark, firing real bullets alongside five blokes you may not even have met, takes a high level of skill. Every time we stacked up at the door ready to enter the room, or dominate as they called it, I would feel sick, physically ill – not because I was scared but, quite honestly, because I didn't want to be the one to fuck up and *kill* one of my mates. It sucked up all your concentration. It was both physically and mentally demanding on a scale I've yet to see paralleled.

Tap tap. Tap. Tap . . . I would tap the stock of my weapon on the chest plate of my body armour. Tap tap, tap, tap . . . It was my way of switching my mind into the right gear to enter the house. I don't know why I did it; it must have been a nervous twitch or something. Every time I have to do something hard, I still think of that idiosyncratic action: tap tap, tap, tap . . . 'Harden the fuck up,' I would tell myself.

I wish I could say I was killin' it, kicking arse and taking names, but it wasn't the case. Although my shooting wasn't too bad, I wasn't picking it up fast enough, and speed is the real trick to CQB. I was struggling and we were only doing basic stuff – beginning to learn how to open doors, go around corners and climb through windows and the like. With the appraisal of our skill level at the end of the second week there was to be a massive cut in numbers. The second two weeks of CQB – Advanced CQB – were held in Perth, right under the eyes of the SAS, and they didn't want to take anybody who wasn't going to cut the mustard. Advanced CQB ramped it up considerably.

After cleaning our weapons on the Friday, there was nothing else to do but wait patiently for the verdict as to who would be going to Perth. This little pause in the space–time continuum exists on all selections: a moment between unrepentant happiness and unmitigated failure. Everything stops; you think of nothing else in life – not your house repayments, not your wife, your dog, your car, your cat; the Earth stops spinning and you hover in purgatory awaiting the call for judgement.

'Green Twenty!' My number was literally up. Green was the colour of my armband, twenty the number on it; the purpose of the brassards was to enable the staff to grade our performance anonymously.

I ascended the stairs to the instructors' office; it felt like being led to the gallows.

'Right, mate, you've just scraped through. You're going to Perth.'

They said a bunch of other stuff but that was all I heard. I was going to the next phase, but only by the narrowest of margins.

Sixteen

TASTING FAILURE

'Blood and brass.'

– Directing Staff

The procedure was to leave a coloured-light device called a cyalume stick behind after you'd cleared a room full of paper terrorists, or tangos as we called them. According to the navy staff on course, it was so subsequent teams would know that particular room had been done. When I heard the same question asked of the army staff, the response was slightly more, shall we say, 'poetic'.

Question: 'How do you know a room has been cleared?'
Answer: 'There'll be blood and brass all over the floor!'

Rightttttt. Ooookayyy.

It's not that I didn't appreciate how the army did things; on the contrary, they could be a damn sight more professional than the grey navy, that's for sure. It's just that they had this gung-ho attitude to everything they did. Although it served them well from an operational standpoint, I don't believe it enhanced the training components that much. Sometimes the bloody-mindedness could get under your skin.

This story – from CQB – highlights the difference in mentality between army and navy. It was about food: each day our lunches would arrive via bus, packaged in those small foil tubs with the cardboard lids, like you see in a chicken shop. There was hardly ever any choice, and from day to day the kitchen staff cooked much the same dishes, hence our dilemma. The navy blokes didn't wish to eat the same thing every day, but there was no way of telling what was in those foil tubs. So, in the spirit of 'improvise, adapt and overcome', as you approached the collection area, the simplest way of determining the contents of this culinary Pandora's Box was to lift the lid slightly and peek inside. That unleashed an uproar from the army ranks: 'LID-LIFTING CUNTS!'

'What the fuck?' I thought. 'What are these clowns on about?'

Well, in the *army*, you line up and take the top box and get what you are given – even if it means consuming the same lunch every day for the rest of your life!

The topic polarised the camp. It was Landies vs Wateries: 'You can't lid-lift, blah, blah, blah . . .'

'Why the hell fucking not!'

Into the fray entered the head commando, a softly spoken, polite bloke (um, yer right): 'Well! What do you do in the navy? How would you pricks solve this problem?'

I took the question, as I believed I knew the answer. 'We write the contents on the lid, sir.'

As we began the third week of CQB it was clear to me (and the instructors) that I was falling behind. My general awareness just wasn't good enough and frequently, as soon as we passed through the door, I found myself confused, disoriented and generally not up to the level required.

Realising your own limitations is a hard pill to swallow, and I didn't want to give up; I thought I could get through if I concentrated and ground it out. But things didn't even plateau, and the required learning curve had the gradient of Everest. My plight worsened at one DP session on the Friday of Week Three, when we were doing stoppage drills – where you go through the process of running out of ammo, reverting to your pistol, then running out of ammo again. As I reached for my new mag and went to slam it home, as per the drill, I totally missed! The mag went sailing across the room in front of everybody! Everything was silent until I heard an instructor walk up behind me, lean in and say, 'You can't kill anybody without bullets!' My heart sank and I knew I was on the chopping block.

We had one day off before the start of the final week. Canada was as sick as a dog with the flu and had to keep removing his gasmask in between run-throughs to spew in the toilets. All colour had drained out of his already pale face.

'Mate, you doing okay?' I asked.

'She be right, ay,' was the only reply.

Ironically, what he said was true. Whereas I was fully fit yet struggling to keep up, Canada was doing really well and was set to pass the course no dramas, even though he was dying. The bloke was a freak!

At the beginning of the fourth week the urgency of my situation became glaringly obvious. Up until now we had maintained our groups and respective coloured brassards i.e. Green Team, Red Team, Blue Team, but when we formed up on the Monday we were put in different groups. As I surveyed the room the *Sesame Street* song rang in my ears: 'One of these things is not like the others, one of these things just doesn't belong.' While all the other teams had the same colours and relative members, my team, goddamn it, was a motley crew made up of six individuals with five different colour brassards between us! The term used was Rainbow Six, an ironic play on the title of a Tom Clancy novel about Special Forces (really funny). The humour was not lost on me: we were the 'loser' team. I had heard about this process beforehand and I knew its terrible implications. This team would be watched like a hawk by twice as many instructors as the other teams and have extra pressure applied until each of us cracked and were failed.

My days were numbered and, although I didn't want to admit it then, I realise now that the instructors' assessment was right; I didn't have it what it took, and they knew it.

Surviving the next two days was a bloody miracle; through sheer determination I held on; two members of Rainbow Six weren't so lucky. Then came aeroplane drill, the last test, held in the most perilous environment of the CQB training arena. No mistakes; no ifs, buts or maybes; one wrong step here and I was going to be on a real plane heading for home.

I sat through the brief for aeroplane drill feeling like a worm on a big fucking hook. It was highly complicated; the intricacy left no room for ad lib, you might say. For us remaining members of Rainbow Six, this one go at the plane was a final chance. Looking back, even that was generous.

On entering the mock aeroplane I immediately fucked up the drill. I'd been in a confused state even before I started. One of the instructors called me aside and told me to take off my gear and meet him in the office. My shoulders slumped and I couldn't take my eyes off the ground as I complied with his commands. It was as though I was outside of myself watching this dejected figure crumble. I'd never felt worse; it was over.

Entering the office, I tried to hide my crushing disappointment and prepared for a dressing down with respect to my performance. 'Don't cry in front of the SAS!' I told myself. Luckily I held it together.

Three people were seated around a table: the head of TAG, an SAS officer and an SAS Warrant Officer, and to my amazement they were kind and comforting, asking me to sit down and praising me for having no safety breaches or dangerous occurrences. But, they said, my awareness was not up to standard, and they felt I was not learning fast enough. I agreed and, to my surprise, they told me I was welcome to retake the course in six months and gave me a few more areas to work on.

Rising to my feet, I thanked them for the opportunity and we shook hands. In reality, I couldn't imagine taking the course again . . . not for a while anyway.

My only consolation was that my good friend Canada made it through, although in some sense this seemed to magnify my failure. I was genuinely happy for him, even if it was hard to show it right then.

The plane ride home was a depressing experience. I felt tired, deflated. When I asked the hostess for a beer and retrieved my wallet, she informed me that this was an international flight, due to the plane's previous destination, and consequently alcohol was free.

Right! I must have downed twenty beers. When I got off in Sydney, I could hardly make it home. Not the best way to deal with disappointment, I know, but that's what happened.

Seventeen

A CHANGE OF DIRECTION

'There's no problem that can't be solved with the proper application of high-power explosives.'

– EOD saying

Back with the Team, my mates were great. Everybody knew what a bastard of a course CQB could be, and the fact I'd got to within a couple of days of the end shielded me from any really harsh criticism. Over the next week or so I took a few days' leave and did some light duties. I still felt the sting of failure; it rested far too heavily on my shoulders.

Technically I had been posted to Team One the whole time I had been pursuing a spot in TAG, so I was up for a new posting. It had been nearly two years since I'd made the Team and new postings were supposed to be allocated at around the eighteen-month mark. Still marinating in the disappointment of my ill-fated attempt to join the boys in black, I thought I was resigned to whatever fate the geniuses at the posting cell could come up with. There were really only two options:

I could be sent to a mine hunter (small-arse boat) to work for the mine warfare section – an exercise in futility, without much dive time: a fate worse than death for a CD – or I could be sequestered to Dive School as an assistant instructor, a position I felt would suit me well.

To be honest I was shitting myself – no matter how they try to sell it to you, going to a mine hunter was no place for a serious diver. For me it would be like being put on the shelf; it offered no chance to practise the plethora of skills I'd been trained to employ. I wasn't intending to dodge it; if it came I would accept my fate and do my time in 'diver prison' if need be, but I wouldn't welcome it.

As luck would have it I was posted to Dive School. I was ecstatic; it was a brilliant place to train, teach baby divers what you had learnt and generally hang out. And six months, baby; that's how long I had to wait until I could opt in again for TAG selection. Yes, any hesitation I had briefly harboured was gone; that Tom Petty song was roaring through my head at full volume. Wait I would, but it would not be idle time. I had a responsibility to take my position of instructor seriously, as any product that gets turned out from the School reflects on the teacher.

For an instructor there were two aspects to Dive School. On the wharf, near the water, you could roll your overalls to your waist, wear sunnies, soak up the rays and rain down hell on those brave enough to enter your domain: pretty cool really. What a life: teaching blokes how to dive, do weights and drink lattés on the deck overlooking the bay ('Everybody wants to be a diver!'). No wonder that's where I wanted to go. Then there was that other part: 'up top' at the Explosives Ordnance Disposal (EOD) School, where the hours were long, the graft hard and the entanglements plentiful. Par for the course with EOD were long trips away to Marangaroo, an army base near Lithgow, and Shoalwater Bay in Queensland, the Branch's explosive ordnance learning areas. Up top basically amounted to a hell of a lot of work in less than ideal surroundings: preparing lessons, taking care of a gargantuan inventory of equipment and having your arse hang out completing tasks so that the basic and senior courses ran smoothly.

And the card I was dealt? – EOD.

There was one bonus to this posting, and it was an interesting one: not only was the new Chief of the EOD section a former TAG member from the old days, he was earmarked to return there shortly as the Whiskey Bravo (or big man on campus). Fate had handed me the chance to serve directly under the bloke who would soon be running water operations at TAG.

As soon as I launched into my role as an assistant instructor, the full scope of what it took to train a clearance diver became apparent to me. It is a mammoth task that requires a lot of hard work on behalf of the instructors, a fact I'd probably taken little notice of when I had my face in the sand.

Among my new responsibilities was the course's early morning PT, a job I relished, as fitness was still my forte and an element I saw as essential in a CD's training. I must admit I did push the guys hard, but not from the sidelines: I always participated in every activity myself. The first month or so we spent up near Lithgow, over the Blue Mountains to the west of Sydney. It was a terribly cold winter and I would take the guys on frostbitten early morning runs up the fire trails and into the hills, sometimes carrying water jerries or sandbags on their shoulders. There was no rest for the wicked when it came to PT.

Instructor was the term, and instruct was what I did (well, assistant-instruct to be precise). I made sure the lads knew everything they were supposed to, forwards and backwards. No way was I going to have some clown rock up to the Team not knowing his shit and saying, 'Obi taught me.' No, sir.

One aspect of my job was to sort the wheat from the chaff, so to speak, and in the first few weeks I could already see a few blokes cracking, even though I was giving them every opportunity to prove themselves and then some. Each generation says it, and I know it's a damned cliché, but these blokes had it easy compared to when I went through. (Ha! I know some guys would be disappointed if I didn't mention that.)

To test my theories about who was weak and therefore might let the Team down when it came to the crunch, I developed a few plans. I wanted each of those guys to know exactly how far they could push themselves – and how much that CD badge was worth. It wasn't a bloody attendance course.

Standing chest deep in a frozen dam holding my rifle overhead wasn't how I wanted to start my morning, but the boys had been making a few too many mistakes, and the PO had told me to take the lads out and 'encourage' them to get their act together. All this may seem a little harsh but I needn't remind you there are no second chances when it comes to explosives.

'This is a voluntary course!' I shouted to them, as my body became numb and my eyes glazed over. I knew I could keep going and they would have to follow if they wanted their own black beret. 'You can get out any time you wish!'

Nobody moved and I felt proud of them, even if I didn't show it (as an instructor, you never did – more is the pity). 'Do you really want to be here? Is it worth it? Ask yourself!'

The boys stood frozen but silent, like terracotta warriors stuck in time. I could feel them galvanising as a team, even if it was a team *against me*. I would pay the price if it meant their cohesion, their focus; if the determination not to be beaten would sink into their souls, never to be forgotten, never regretted, maybe even appreciated . . .

The last rotation I did at the School before reattempting selection for TAG was at the infamous Triangular Island in the Shoalwater Bay training area for underwater demolition. If I thought I'd done hard yakka while a student, I was wrong, because being an assistant instructor, the work was as endless and taxing as any selection. Not only were there baby divers to oversee but we also had an advanced course of CDs learning to be Petty Officers. They were put though a gamut of testing, all of which – at the behest of the senior trainers – me and one lucky offsider had to help set up every day, as well as run the camp and give lessons to the Basic course.

It was for one of these exercise set-ups for the POs' course that the other Second Dickies and I headed out into the bay one particular morning. Cruising along in a large aluminium tinny called a bomb boat, we had to drop ten missile payloads called warheads into the search area for the students to find and the POs to assess. The POs would then render them safe or BIP them. The warheads were cylindrical lumps of explosive with a hole in the middle about the size of a small garbage bin. Normally they would be attached to a missile behind the nose cone and guidance system – in front of the propellant chamber and rocket propulsion system.

The Chief in charge of training had told us in no uncertain terms to mark the warheads with styrofoam floats, as the water was mud brown and the tides in that part of the planet are nuts. Diligently, the boys and I attached the floats to the mini-fridge-sized barrels of explosive with string and, in a sporadic fashion, rolled them off the side, each about ten metres apart. We prepared to return to the beach for lunch, job done – well, that was what we thought until we noticed one of the floats drifting away, far away. When we zoomed over and grabbed it, after winding its string to the surface, we realised to our terror that it wasn't attached to anything! There were blank faces all round. What the fuck?

We had no dive gear on board and no way of knowing where the missing warhead was without a fricken mine hunter. Someone suggested that we zip back to base and grab some dive gear, but that would mean informing the very scary Chief Diver that we had lost his precious warhead! Not advisable, I can assure you!

I looked at the boys and stated without a skerrick of humility that I would free dive and find the fricken thing. The other guys looked at me with the most doubtful look since Orville Wright said to his brother, 'Let's go, Wilbur!', then all nodded. Stooging back to where we thought the warhead might be, they held the boat steady and I got my kit together. I slid into the turbulent brown liquid with the weight of the boys' expectations enough to drag me to the bottom of the surging ocean. Taking a couple of deep breaths, I focused and calmed my heart rate. Then emulating an otter, I turned inwards, bending my torso forwards and kicking my legs hard, and dove for the bottom some twenty metres below.

A few fruitless attempts later, with a pounding heart I went down for one last try, pushing my hands out in front of me, holding the string of the float and finning with everything I had. 'Nothing . . . nothing . . . fuck, can't see shit down here.' *Left kick, right kick.* There was nothing but mud stretching out to an invisible watery horizon. With lungs burning and head pounding, my control over my instinct to breathe waned. The moment had come to head quickly to the surface; I was out of breath, time and patience.

Then, out of the corner of my eye, I spotted the warhead, a mere five metres away. Hell, it might as well have been on the moon: it was pure chance I'd found it and I didn't have a snowflake's chance in hell of locating the thing again, but it was a moot point. I was out of air, simple as that. Five metres or not, tough shit, I was returning to the surface, baby.

I don't know what happened; it was all a blur but I stopped my ascent and dove hard for the warhead. Something in me snapped, and my sense of self-preservation was overridden by the desire not to be beaten by my circumstance. Attaching the line as fast as I could and with little consciousness left, I pushed off the bottom and raced for the surface as fast as my oxygen-deprived body would carry me. The lads said I shot out of the water like a Polaris missile. Fortunately, I surfaced next to the boat and the boys grabbed me as I was about to pass out. They dragged me into the boat and could see I no longer held the float line.

'What happened? Where is it; where's the float line?'

'Where do you think? Attached to a fucking warhead!'

'Yeeeeee! Harrrrrrr!' The cheer went up and never before or since that have I ever received such heartfelt hugs and high fives.

With the job complete, we drove happily back to the beach and the awaiting Chief.

'What took you so long?' he asked.

'Nothing, Chief. All good.'

And it was . . . all fucking good!

The PO in charge of training decided to set up an elaborate training exercise whereby the course could swim in, place real explosives on a wharf and then blow it up; sounds cool, right? Just one problem – there was no wharf!

'Right, you blokes, I want you to construct a wharf in the mudflats next to the boat channel. Oh yeah, and I want it done by morning.'

It was five in the afternoon. I looked around for the fictitious army of engineers he must have been addressing his orders to and saw he was looking at me and two other divers. We were the lucky ones entrusted with this mad task.

'Is he fucking serious?' I said to the two assistant instructors with me. 'Fuck me!'

But there was no use delaying the inevitable, so we grabbed some machetes and rope, a bunch of sandbags and began building what felt like something second only to the bridge over Sydney Harbour.

Five hours later, covered in mozzie bites, mud and sweat, we retrieved the PO from his campfire and coffee and asked him if he would graciously come down to the water's edge and inspect our work. Although I noted a puzzled expression on his face, I was so tired I couldn't hazard a guess at what he might be thinking. All old divers are as mad as cut snakes anyway, so it doesn't pay to worry about their motives – you just carry out their orders. He walked up the beach with us then, with a straight face, said, 'It's on the wrong side of the island.'

What!

'Right, boys, just take it apart and rebuild it on the other side. Good night.' And with that he strolled off.

I dropped to my knees and let the warm mud envelop me as the northerly breeze dried the sweat on my forehead. Dipping my hands into the tiny pool forming rapidly in front of me, I cupped some water and drew it to my face, splashing it over my crusty brow and sweeping my hair back in one movement.

The wind felt cold now and it served to blast awake this weary soul. Slowly I turned around. The two CDs at my back said nothing, but one stuck out his hand and pulled me from my muddy hollow.

Wordlessly, we faced each other – a stoic triumvirate in the dead of night – an order issued, a task at hand and a smile on our faces; the smile of knowing, the smile of purpose, the smile of a clearance diver.

Eighteen

SECOND CRACK AT CQB

'Once more unto the breach, dear friends, once more.'
— Henry V, *William Shakespeare*

Richard Gere plays the mythical Lancelot in a movie about King Arthur and Camelot called *First Knight*. In one scene a villager asks him how to become a warrior. Lancelot looks at the man and says, 'You have to train every day.'

The man nods his agreement, 'I can do that.'

'You have to give up your family, your farm, your friends.'

The man thinks then nods. 'I can do that.'

'You have to dedicate your life to it.'

Still the man remains . . . then finally Lancelot looks away and says, 'You have to not care whether you live or die.'

The man walks away.

Here it was again, that moment of truth: my application to attend another CQB had been approved. The prospect of facing the horrors of selection once more gave me pause for thought. What if I failed again? My mind was consumed

192

with what ifs and unfavourable outcomes. Yet it's a process I've become used to: before any challenge, my thoughts go into a kind of perpetual loop, spinning wildly for a period and then regrouping in a calming well of steely determination. Presumably it is a coping mechanism; I think of every conceivable aspect of the task, feel a swell of pessimism and then attack it as if it were a hostile third party and I need to prove it wrong: *fuck you! Fuck you!*

Harden the fuck up! Just go, just go, relish the pain, welcome the adversity, show no fear, stop your bitching and jump!

I don't know how other soldiers think; I'm not sure what goes through the head of a firefighter about to charge into the flame. I've got no idea how a cop does it – night after night, facing the gloom of the street. Maybe none of that torrent of doubt goes through their heads and they just do what they do. Who could say? The thing is that all that shit goes through my little brain . . . then I do it anyway.

All aspects of my performance on the last course had been raked over; I knew what I needed to work on and was determined not to make the same mistakes twice. Aside from my general confusion, one of the main issues I had was my aggression – or lack of it, to be precise.

By no means am I a pacifist; neither am I a fucking psycho; I know blokes at both ends of the spectrum. Undoubtedly there is a need for a certain amount of aggression when conducting counterterrorism operations. Although that may seem an obvious point to make, there are a great many misconceptions when it comes to this subject – and the subject of violence in general. I'm not talking about the type of aggression you see on a footy field each Saturday; neither do I speak of the aggression you see at the pub on Saturday night. I am speaking of 'controlled aggression', a precise, concise display of force, designed specifically to achieve a task.

Historically, I have never been an aggressive person (except when watching *The Biggest Loser* – 'Run, you fat bastards, run!'). All jokes aside, I needed to learn to use this emotion as a tool, a powerful tool that I could call on when operating at a professional level, in the context of a serious task. I recognised it as a double-edged sword though, something you have to be able to turn off as quickly as you turn it on or fall heavily on that sword. My strategy was to tap into that dark part of myself that wanted to destroy, maim and hurt, that part that we all have but suppress, as is required by social contract theory. It was the switching off that was to be the real challenge.

This time around, the two-week CDSEC was a welcome precursor. I had realised that if I could get the shooting down early, it would free me up to concentrate on the more fluid aspects of the course. Thanks to the unending repetition of it all, I was becoming quite a good shot and by the completion of CDSEC all my VAL shoots were perfect scores. Far from being smug about this outcome, I saw it only as a means to keep the instructors from looking my way, and a head start to what I now understood to be a long, long race.

When I started CQB again, rather than encountering the debilitating nerves I had before, to my surprise it all started to make a lot more sense to me. My brain seemed more capable of assimilating the information and I wasn't nearly as intimidated. Granted, I had the benefit of previous experience, but I don't think it was that alone that placed me in a more favourable position. I think it had a lot to do with my improved mindset – I was more relaxed, more flexible, ready to flow like the proverbial waters through a maze. I looked at each task with softer eyes, able to take in its scope and adapt where need be. The principles of CQB seemed to come into focus. I was getting it, and the bastards wouldn't fault me this time.

According to a saying I once heard, 'You push a sensitive man, and that sensitivity turns into volatility.' The truth of that statement was borne out during the first PT session of the second week, one of the more futile endeavours I've ever partaken in. Even though the diver PT sessions drew their fair share of blood, it was usually for practical application, which cannot be said of this unforgettable army session.

We lined up on the tarmac, dressed in running shorts and the ubiquitous army brown T-shirt. I glanced around and was taken aback to see, not two men down from me, the SAS major in command of the whole unit! What was he doing at student PT, I wondered. The major was a young man – well, young for a major – and he looked as fit as a greyhound. Although I'd not had much to do with the bloke, he seemed nice enough. Later I found him to be an enigmatic leader of men.

The army PT instructor screamed across the parade ground, sending us running. We completed a number of warm-ups and the usual push-ups and so on, then, as we prepared for the next instruction, the PTI stopped mid-sentence, as if he himself had just noticed the major's presence. It was an easy mistake. The major made no big deal of his attendance; he simply wanted to do PT with the lads, and good on him, if you ask me. Perhaps the PTI now felt obligated to make the session harder or make himself look better in front of the major, but next he instructed us to take up a long steel bar each. These were used as weapon substitutes for exercise and I was familiar with their virtues from my diver training, so I didn't think twice about it. That is until he told us to assume the push-up position. Instead of placing our palms on the ground, we were to grasp the bar, holding it below us, shoulder width apart, with our knuckles on the ground bearing our weight.

At this stage I still wasn't alarmed. 'What's a few fist push-ups holding a bar?' I thought. Alas, this was not the PTI's intention.

As we held our positions he jogged out in front of the group at least thirty-five metres and drew a line with his heel into the gravelly earth. 'Right, when I say go, you will walk on your knuckles holding the bar, and race in the push-up position to my location!'

'Fucking hell,' I thought, 'is this bloke for real?' It wasn't that we couldn't do it – of course we bloody well could – but was it absolutely necessary to rip the shit out of our hands prior to undertaking what was already a gruelling physical course, just so this bloke could look tough? He wasn't participating, I might add. The ground was like the side of a highway, made up mostly of gravel and old bitumen, with some sandstone thrown in for good measure. It would have scuffed the bottom of your bloody GP boot, let alone our fleshy mitts.

Grumblings could be heard from army and navy alike as blokes inched their way forwards, slowly at first. But a fire was building and there was nowhere else for it to go. Competition crept into the previously begrudged task and a race ensued.

Incensed as I was at the pointlessness of the task, I raced to the front, blood seeping from my knuckles as I went. Then I felt someone close behind; it was the major. He drove his shoulders forwards, powering past me, slamming his fists into the ground as he etched his way to the line, dragging his feet behind him in the push-up stance.

'Bugger this,' I thought and I increased my speed as well, ignoring the searing pain in my already lacerated fists. Nearing the finish line, I lunged forwards at the last second, narrowly beating the major to it.

We rose at the same time and I stood next to him as the others crept towards us, neither of us commenting. He smiled and nodded in my direction, the only direct communication I would have with the bloke in my entire two years out there. But whenever he walked past me in the halls, I liked to think he remembered the moment . . . Even if he didn't.

Nineteen

ADVANCED CQB

'I feel fear for the last time.'

– Dr Manhattan, Watchmen

The above quote is from a much-heralded graphic novel which later became a movie. I think about that sentence all the time, first of all because I wish I had written it and second and most importantly because I wish it were true.

It's a fiction: you will never feel fear for the last time. Fear is a tool, a tool to be used in pursuit of a goal. If you're not afraid, then you're doing it wrong.

For the first two weeks of CQB I felt like a robot carrying out a set of programmed responses, executing the drills with precision, no errors. I left nothing behind in pursuit of passing the course. I knew what I had to do for this second go; it wasn't a 'black art' beyond my comprehension, it was a course – a course that others had passed, a course that had an end. Much like those computer-generated 3D images with the hidden picture inside, if you stared straight at CQB you missed it, like I had the first time. But if you relaxed, allowed yourself to look through it, then the picture magically appeared and a river of information flowed forth.

It was right at the end of the second week and selections were being made for the Advanced CQB in Perth. While the decision-making happened, a rather poignant moment occurred – well, for me at least. The instructors were about to read the names of the individuals who would be moving forwards; the individual appraisals would follow later. All of us had showered and changed after our last shoot, and as a result we were dressed in civilian clothes. When I moved past one of the sheds to get a better position I noticed that one of the commandos on course was wearing a footy jumper from my high school – and not any jumper, mind you, but the revered black training jumper of the First XV rugby team. Immediately I was awestruck. He was quite a large burly bloke but I hadn't even noticed him before. He must have been younger than me at school and played footy sometime after I had left. I was about to approach him to say g'day but the instructor summoned everybody in. Twenty or so names were called and thankfully mine was one of them. I knew I'd done well this time and was keen to get to Perth, where I could face the ground of my last undoing.

The guy in the footy jumper piped up: 'Ah, sir, sir, you didn't call my name.' My mind was suddenly cast back to school, where that jumper was the ultimate measure of a man.

'Nah, mate, you didn't fucking make it, so fuck off.'

Holy shit, the harshness of what I had witnessed struck a long-forgotten chord in me and I watched in amazement as the bloke slunk away.

It was weird seeing him fail where I had succeeded; that had always been me walking away. My entire world was changing; my entire way of thinking was changing. You can't measure everybody with the same stick. There is no single governing benchmark of success or toughness or worthiness; life's just not like that, a fact both me and this bloke were now largely aware of.

I love movies, I always have; although it's intellectually satisfying to quote Dante or Hemmingway when discussing military experiences, I can't go past a good movie reference. In a movie called *The Way of the Gun*, one of the characters, a criminal drifter, tells a story about what he'd do when asked by God at the gates of heaven why he had lived as he did. Given the chance to confess his sins, a chance for redemption, a chance at salvation, the guy says he would simply look God in the eye and say, 'I was framed.'

For ages I turned that over in my mind, never sure what it meant. I think now I understand: it's about living outside the way of things, about saying no to convention. Taking the road less travelled and making no apologies. Asking no quarter and giving none in return. And there's a place for that; call it arrogance, hubris, even selfishness – you'd probably be right, because it takes that kind of mentality to do certain things others won't. It takes a bastard to do a bastard's job. And maybe TAG was a bastard's job. Or maybe it's just the roguish, irreverent nature of the more specialised areas of the military; it seemed to me at least to be filled with unconventional thinkers and misfits, those who didn't fit in anywhere else. It was as if the tapestry of Special Forces was made up of those who may well, in another life, have been Hollywood-style criminals themselves.

Honestly, the two weeks of Advanced CQB were a blur. My memory usually serves me well, but when musing about that last piece of selection, all I can think of is the pain: the anguish of fighting through the smoke-filled passageways and the ringing of gunshots in my ears. The drills felt like second nature and my aggression was at such a fever pitch that the actions I carried out felt like breathing, like I'd known them all my life. I embraced it, craved it like a drug and I knew that I would pass; I had to. The stringy fibres of nothing that held my self-esteem together were fast becoming interwoven with the fabric of success in this unit, whether I liked it or not.

Stairway drill, partition drill, dynamic moves – speed, accuracy and fluid uninterrupted maintenance of momentum – were the hallmarks of a successful run-through. That's what we called a house clearance. The commandos would always say, 'Right, bang it in,' and we would line up time after time, walking on the edge of a broken razor, honing tested drills in order to achieve the ultimate goal: *Save the Lives of the Hostages.* It was repeated ad nauseam.

CQB and, to a larger extent, counterterrorism differ markedly from all other military operations. There is no cover, no supporting fire; no drawn-out pitched battles give rise to reactionary tactical decisions based on observed weaknesses. There are only the drills. Fight through. As the guy in front of you absorbs the bullets, you move past and shoot the guy who's shooting him. Flow like water through a maze, filling every room with violence, dominating the space and hoping the bad guys shoot you and not the hostages. Don't care about dying, just losing.

It was over. We lined up outside the armoury, handed in our weapons and were directed to where the instructors had set up an office – near the parade ground, just past the accommodation at Campbell Barracks, Swanbourne, Perth, Western Australia. The normally boisterous commandos were as silent as church mice and the thus far excitable divers held their breath, some for a considerable length of time! Army and navy personnel alike sank into the prejudgement void that precedes any selection ending.

Only seconds before I had been brimming with confidence; I'd not chalked up a single safety breach or dangerous occurrence and had passed every validation shoot, but I reflected that for Advanced CQB, there were a hell of a lot more variants and remainders to normalise before you passed.

Several disappointed, bedraggled soldiers walked out of the office as we stood like cattle waiting for the bolt gun. No one said a word, either of encouragement or denouncement. There was a cautious reverence for the fallen; nothing any of the rest of us could say would comfort them.

Having recently been through such an ordeal and walked away with nothing, cruelly or not, I couldn't help thinking that their failure might increase the percentage chance of my success. A nauseous wave of anxiety descended on my previously faux calm exterior as my name, or rather my number, was called: 'Blue Six!'

Fuck, fuck, fuck and double fuck.

As I walked towards the impromptu office of judgement, I made a feeble attempt at humour with one of the nearby divers: 'You got the number of that truck-driving school . . . ? Truck Master, I think it is. I might need that.' My *Top Gun* line may have got a small laugh, I'm not sure; the only thing I was aware of was the thud in my chest. If I failed now, my boat was surely sunk, and no amount of success within the Diving Branch would make me feel better. The crushing weight of this defeat would surely destroy my inconstant self-esteem.

They sat there on their glowing thrones of laurels, having achieved infinitely more than I ever would or, for that matter, could. These warriors, these four horsemen of my Apocalypse, these men who had done so much and now, in comparison, seemed to ask of me so little: 'So, how do you think you went . . . ?'

It was overcast and drafty. I glanced out the window and cast my eye over the barren tarmac, conscious of its stored heat, the growing weariness of the afternoon as it succumbed to the evening's request.

Muffled sentences and the contact of hand with back failed to awaken me. In an eerie trance I made my exit from the office. Past the waiting wounded and towards the gathering. The other divers, apart from two noticeable absentees, had separated themselves; the group of four awaited my announcement as if it were their own fate on the line. Without realising it, I'd been looking at the ground the whole way and hadn't seen the boys walking towards me. Suddenly I snapped awake and confronted their questioning gaze.

'Well?' one of them piped up.

I heard myself answer, 'I made it. I'm through. I'm in.'

It took a couple of hours for it to sink in but the realisation of my goal felt magnificent. The monkey of my previous failures was now firmly off my back and that night's drinking session with the boys felt like that first gasp of air after ascending from a deep free dive.

Things were great, the sky was blue, birds were singing and everything seemed right with the world. But be careful what you wish for.

Twenty

REINFORCEMENT TRAINING

'You have to earn the right to be here . . . every day.'

– HR

'Scooter' (not his real name) was one hell of an operator; the guy was unflappable, strong and best of all 'grey' – a military term for quietly achieving without praise or condemnation. Scooter had passed his first CQB, the one I had so gloriously failed. In fact I never saw Scooter fail anything! He'd even got a bloody chopper licence in his spare time. But despite all this, despite his abilities, despite his absolutely flawless performances to date, he was RTU (returned to unit) during his first month at TAG. I mention this for two reasons: one, to pay tribute to a bloke who – as I see it – never got as much recognition as he deserved and two, to illustrate that even if you passed CQB you had a myriad of other skillsets to learn, master and combine in order to maintain your status as an operator.

Every day was still a test and at any given time you could be sent home for not performing. Unlike many other units, including our own, TAG reserved the right to 'bin' anyone at any moment if they felt they were not maintaining the standard. Even in the Diving Branch, once you made it, once you'd proven yourself, you were cut a little slack and could chill out a bit knowing you were in. Not out at TAG (East) though; not out at Holsworthy, oh no; every bloody day you were under the microscope.

The reasons for this became devastatingly evident as I progressed through the REO cycle, or reinforcement training. It was designed to teach you each skillset and every area of counterterrorism so you would be able to combine the lot at a moment's notice in order to achieve a task.

The new routine of life at TAG was an adjustment; it really was its own world. We REOs were put through a punishing series of work-up trials. Work-ups were a series of exercises conducted over three or four weeks, running through the entire gamut of counterterrorism operations. There were DAs (direct actions), missions where time was allowed for detailed plans on how to attack the stronghold. There were EAs, or emergency actions, where a simulated escalation had occurred and it was imperative that we assault the stronghold right away. I was once dragged behind a Toyota 4×4 as it took off for an EA and I had been using the ablutions!

Our days and nights were filled with all types of training and kit familiarisation; getting used to the NBC (nuclear, biological, chemical) equipment was an ordeal in and of itself. I learnt rather surprisingly that if there was a chemical incident or what have you, we would simply take an EpiPen – the injection devices they use for anaphylactic reactions, such as breathing difficulties after ingestion of food allergens – out of our right leg pocket, stab ourselves, and go the fuck to work! We were issued with all types of cool kit – and, amazingly, price was no object. If we wanted it and it helped us do the job, then we could have it; thank you, Johnny Howard.

Usually we kicked around in beige mechanic's overalls but when we trained we wore a kind of green flight suit that pilots wear. This, I'm told, is because it's fire-retardant, but they did look cool as well. We also had our black flight suits for any real-time ops or serious exercise. Add to this a new lightweight wetsuit issue, full set of personal climbing gear and our own gun case containing our M4, MP5, USP, shotgun, suppressors and Aimpoint sighting systems, and you'd have to say we were well kitted out.

Canada had been out there before me as he had passed his first CQB course and he was a valuable source of information in my initial REO cycle. Being able to hit him up for hints and tips was a great help.

I did notice the still glaring divide between the Land Platoon and the Water one, but the longer I spent there, the more I felt it was a good thing after all: it was good natured and it seemed to foster a sense of competition that drove both platoons to better themselves.

This initial phase of constant training was a window into what my life would now be like. It was all-consuming. Basically, I lived at Holsworthy Barracks, and I ate, slept and drank counterterrorism. The impact of all this on my home life was soon being felt. At first, it was only small comments, but my friends and family, and especially my girlfriend, Alex, were sensing a change in me, a change that wasn't necessarily good.

Joining Water Platoon had its own set of unique challenges. We newbies may have been 'on team' but there was a shitload to learn. The new set of diving drills and procedures were a course unto themselves; MTO has nothing on TAG tactical diving ops. The fast-rib insertion techniques and caving ladder climbs took weeks and weeks of instruction to master, not to mention helo ops with fast roping, which took on a new dimension wearing a gasmask and with all that blasted body armour to carry. Suffice to say that getting to TAG was merely the start; earning your place and staying there was the real trick.

Next up was the Special Forces Ropes Course. I had done some roping with the divers but this was on a whole different level. It required several advanced techniques, not the least of which was the angel jump, a mad way of ensuring a quick descent. You'd let out a couple of metres slack then make a running jump off a platform, freefalling those precious metres and attempting to stop yourself at the required time; that is, before you hit the ground and died!

We learnt techniques like prusiking, climbing with ascenders and how to stop yourself freefalling if your brake failed. This was a nifty trick in an emergency that required you to clamp your hands together above your descent device and pull down, effectively jamming your hands on the rope and then onto the device in order to cease movement. Well, that was the theory anyway.

The final task was learning 'rope and blows', which entailed demolishing a window with explosives while suspended horizontally off the face of the building and then swinging in on ropes to gain access. It was – how shall I put this? – difficult to get right.

Then we had to learn our specialty, the main reason for the REO cycle. There were three specialties on offer, not that you could choose for yourself: the Driving Course, the Sniping Course or the MOE (method of entry) Course.

I was put on the MOE Course, which I looked forward to as I had some experience with explosives and I thought this might give me a head start. As I quickly realised, the way TAG did explosives was a world away from what I'd been taught in the navy. The main difference was that you stood right next to the explosives instead of in a bunker. This put the onus on you to get the charge size exactly right or you could very well die. The tolerances were worked out to the centimetre and gram in proportion to the amount of explosives. As the MOE guy, you copped most of the blast because everyone in the Team stacked up behind you.

There was a hell of a lot of information to assimilate and, unlike the navy, you couldn't write any of it down! Everything had to be learnt off by heart (something I was not good at). I had always relied heavily on notes and studied them when I went home at night, but here they expected you to hear something once and remember it; assimilation of information was the name of the game.

The course lasted two weeks but it was extremely comprehensive and highly technical. You made every charge by hand and you had to do it quickly and accurately. I did enjoy it, except for one day when we were doing internal charges and I made the innocent mistake of positioning myself in the corner, exactly where the blast wave would concentrate because it had nowhere else to go. It absolutely knocked the stuffing out of me. I actually felt my lungs get over-pressurised, and it felled me. The instructor, an old SAS guy, walked over to me and said, 'Get up, you big girl's blouse.'

I complied, but it took me an hour or so to properly recover from it. Apparently, knowing where to stand makes a big difference to your day; nice of them to tell us!

Those other two specialties suddenly looked more attractive: the Driving Course seemed fun but the Sniping Course less so, as it required patience and spending long periods of time in the bush, two skills I wasn't particularly good at.

Canada, who was already a seasoned operator, told me that although the MOE guy was always under more pressure, if you were good at it, you generally got a lot more respect. This was because on an exercise and as the plan evolved, the MOE guy's area of responsibility – the exact charge he had to construct – could change from one second to the next, and the Team's whole mission could come down to their entry . . . or lack of one, for that matter.

Often there would be funny – well, perhaps not at the time – moments when it came to gaining entry to buildings. Once I burnt a hole in my leg while trying to cut through a fence with a Broco cutter! I've seen guys hang upside down on ropes with windows fully intact and pieces blown off the corner of buildings. And footage of a riveting couple of minutes as a bloke tries to cut a door down using a chainsaw with the chain back to front! Just inside the MOE house there is a rather large box-shaped cut in the ground, where some guy let off his charge after the door had already fallen in!

I've had a few other massive fuck-ups myself; that slick, fast Hollywood-style entry, guns a-blazin', is incredibly hard to achieve, especially the old 'swing in through a window' trick. In movies they make that one look real easy, but my entire platoon practised that shit for two weeks straight and I can count on one hand the number of times it actually worked.

I'm not trying to say it's all smoke and mirrors; it's not. Generally, that endless practice and those hair-raising fuck-ups – and even the best operators screw things up in training once in a while – are what precede you 'killing it' on the day it actually counts. That's why you do it, that's why you push it every day, trying to get everything perfect, and in the end that's why it looks cool as fuck. Hopefully all that repetition leads up to that unforeseeable hypothetical date when you get it right, that day when everything clicks, when it all goes off without a hitch and you walk out alive . . . and *they* don't.

It was around this time they issued the new badge with the TAG (East) symbol on it, consisting of a dive helmet over the commando double black diamonds, with a Sykes Fairbairn knife over the helmet, down the centre. Putting that badge on my overalls meant the world to me; it represented the heights to which I had set my sights more than a year earlier. Its attainment had been an obsession, an obsession that had changed my world and my view of said world . . .

I look into the mirror: who the fuck is that looking back at me? I don't know. Sometimes, when I watch those *X Games* competitors I wish I were them. When I see a dad in the street with his newborn baby, I wish I were him. Once I had a key cut at one of those mall key stands, and the guy did his job with such pride and happiness, with such honour that I wished I were him.

But none of that's going to happen; none of that matters.

You're a product of your experiences and that's it; no more no less. It's how you perceive those experiences that matters. Perception is reality, and to date, despite everything, I still have no real idea of what I'm supposed to be.

Twenty-one

GOING ONLINE

'Far better it is to dare mighty things, to win glorious triumphs, even though checkered by failure, than to take rank with those poor spirits who neither enjoy much nor suffer much, because they live in the gray twilight that knows not victory nor defeat.'

— *Theodore Roosevelt*

'Holy fucking shit, I did that,' I mused as I spun around to look at the charred remains of the window that had so unceremoniously imploded, heralding my arrival on roping kit. But my exuberance was short-lived as one of the snipers — fortunately a mate of mine — walked up behind me, put his fingers to my temple and said, 'Bang! You're fucking dead, Obi.'

Lesson One, kids: after having made explosive entry through a third-floor window, swung in and landed on your feet, don't be so bloody surprised and pleased with yourself that you stop mid-assault, forget what you're doing and casually turn to admire the hole in the wall.

Luckily for me, as I said, the sniper playing the enemy was one of my mates, and simply pointed out that next time I should concentrate on the task at hand and follow through with the assault.

Learning how to obtain entry to an establishment was only the start of my new education. There were also the elaborate and sometimes downright dangerous methods we used to travel to places: speed boats, diving, fast roping, repelling, helos or riding atop 4×4s. Fuck, we would have rocked up on a horse-drawn carriage if we thought it would get us to a position quicker. Speed and surprise were the name of the game and we used all types of ninja-like trickery in order to get the task done.

Not long ago, I watched a movie called *47 Ronin* and was amazed to see a tactic whereby the samurai throws a grappling hook on top of the house and has a dude climb the rope with a caving ladder attached to his hip which he then attaches to the house for the others to climb up. It was cool for two reasons: one, the movie is awesome and espouses a lot of the virtues I admire and two, that's exactly how we bloody learnt to do it! No shit; albeit a little more technologically enhanced, it's the same bloody process used to attack a ship at night from the water. I was trained to noiselessly swim in on my LAR V rebreather, tie my diving kit off at the bottom of the wharf or seabed, ascend gradually to the surface breathing out slowly, slip silently beneath the ship, then fire a grappling hook with a compressed-air firing device. Next I would attach myself to the rope and, using a couple of climbing ascenders, literally shimmy up the rope, letting my legs do the work while I trained my silenced weapon on the lip of the looming vessel. Once at the top, I would attach a caving ladder for the others to climb up while I waited precariously in the cover position.

Even after those few weeks of extra training, we REOs were still waiting to be accepted into the unit. But our time of reckoning arrived: the REO phase culminated in a week of day-and-night full-mission profiles incorporating all the skills we had learnt. It was full-tilt bogie, no sleep, Mars Bars, Pizza Shapes and a hell of a lot of bang! We hit the stronghold time and time again from every angle, utilising every skill. Even while I was dead on my feet, the training came through and the skills I'd practically sold my soul to obtain rose to the surface and vindicated the manner of their acquisition.

As an eighteen-year-old, I went on a tour of Europe, in the course of which I engaged in a lot of drinking and trying to tell girls they were 'bella' – in a woeful faux Italian accent. Anyway, I did partake of the occasional cultural sightseeing event. Nothing affected me particularly until I stood before a monument dedicated to the Swiss Guard in Lucerne, Switzerland. Carved out of stone was an amazingly lifelike lion, twisting in agony, riddled with arrows, its face contorted by pain and suffering. The well-known writer Mark Twain, we were told, had once described it as the most moving and mournful piece of stone in the world; it rendered me speechless.

The carving commemorates some Swiss Guards. The story goes that when revolutionaries stormed the Tuileries Palace in Paris, intent on the overthrow of King Louis XVI, the Swiss

Guards stood unwaveringly by their charge; all others who had sworn to protect the king had fled but these brave few took their oath seriously. For them it wasn't about ideology, it was about duty: among the many regiments from different countries guarding the king on a rotational basis, at that moment it was their turn. They fought so fiercely and against such terrible odds that the aggressors offered them a chance to surrender, if they sent out the 'holy bastard'. But the valiant Swiss would have none of it and said instead, 'Come and get us, you fuckers' (or words to that effect). So they were torn to pieces by a million arrows and, to this day, that is why the Swiss Guard are the only ones allowed to guard the guy in the Vatican with the pointy hat.

Like most kids of my age, I was pretty self-absorbed, but I stood there in front of this magnificent statue overcome with admiration for those men. And for the idea of dying for a duty that you believed in – for its own sake – and not for the politics behind the need for such protection.

The idea of selfless courage in the face of overwhelming adversity had long fascinated me but it had nothing to do with my journey towards the Special Forces, which was driven by a selfish desire to be better than others. It wasn't till I finally got there that I truly believed in the cause and the philosophical ideology of placing the lives of others before my own. I can say without an ounce of false pride that I would have thought as the Swiss Guard thought, and that during the course of our training I believe the boys and I embraced this philosophical ideology on a daily basis.

*

Having got through our REO period it was time to get down to the business of preparing for the Commonwealth Games. They were being held in Melbourne, Victoria, and the level of terrorist threat had been deemed fairly high. We were to do solid work in Sydney, after which we would be moving down there to conduct further training prior to the start of the Games and would be stationed there on a more semi-permanent basis for their duration.

My pulse started racing when I was put into one of the teams as an MOE man. We newcomers were all now expected to operate at full pace with the rest of the guys, a task that would have been attainable had my team not contained one of the best operators at TAG.

Matching up with him – let's call him Whisky One 2 – was a hard ask. He was a tall, broad-shouldered lad, slightly older than me, and his name was spoken in hushed tones back at the Diving Branch. The bloke made no mistakes, held court whenever he talked and did not suffer fools. Before we were allocated to teams, I was kind of hoping that I wouldn't be put in his, because of his legendary temper; I had been at the pointy end of some of his abuse when I was on course. Whisky One 2 was full of confidence and unending skill, but he was a harsh guy, with a temper I've never seen matched. To be completely honest, I was a little afraid of the bloke. When we played touch footy in the mornings for PT, I would try and stay at the other end of the field from him so as not incur his wrath. But as it turned out, being a member of Whisky One 2's team was a fortuitous event in many respects. As a baptism of fire, it elevated my skills and forged me into a capable operator. In my time at TAG I was to learn all my skills from this man, and I'll never forget the contribution he made in getting me to the required level of a TAG operator.

One of my first missions at TAG was the recovery of a ferry on Sydney Harbour in a big joint counterterrorism exercise with the police. My platoon came in by fast boat as, simultaneously, the Land Platoon assaulted from Black Hawk helicopters. Jumping onto the boat, the sensory overload amazed me – even after all my training, the craziness of a full exercise blew me away. It was like organised mayhem. Blokes were flying everywhere; there was noise, confusion, but in the midst of all this I saw Whiskey One 2 launch his large frame onto the ship, take up point and lead our team to take the bridge, completely in control and with the speed and grace of a gazelle.

As I stumbled behind, trying to keep up, he wove through the turns of doorways and stairwells, shooting with paint rounds all the would-be fake terrorists with such stunning speed and accuracy that by the time we'd stopped, and before I fully knew what was going on, he'd killed every tango, taken the bridge and reported in. I stood there breathless, a dishevelled mess, having not fired a shot! 'Fuck,' I thought, 'I have got to lift my game if I'm going to keep up with these blokes.'

It was striking to note the difference between guys who had been on Team for a while and we REOs, who were still a few steps off the pace.

Suddenly, I heard, 'Go, go, go; get the fuck out!' as the back of the hulking ship came rushing towards me. Instinctively

I braced for impact and stuck my foot out in a ludicrous attempt to push our helicopter away from the steel uprights, like you do on a boat when you approach a wharf. But we weren't in a boat; by then we were 100 metres up in the air, hovering in a Black Hawk that was swiftly moving the wrong way towards a skyward obstruction.

The Team Leader, having seen the writing on the wall and being the only one to hear the pilots shitting themselves on the comms system, had just ordered me out of the mighty whirlybird and down the fast rope to the relative safety of the ferry deck some fifty metres below. The four blokes behind me were in no mood to hang around either and zipped down the rope at a liberal pace, giving me bugger all time to exit the landing zone and avoid becoming the landing zone for them.

Whiskey One 2 approached me after the ex as he'd been on the comms and heard the pilots' chatter. 'I'm glad you jumped, Obi. I was going to kick your ass out.'

It was my first helo exercise with TAG, and the speed and precision of the pilots stunned me. They were allowed to push things a lot further in Special Forces training missions than in their normal duties. The extent of their ability would be tested when operating with TAG, as they were required to get us on target as swiftly as possible.

Helo ops were only some of the exercises we took part in prior to the Games. We also practised ship underway drills, ship at anchor with a dive option, and roping from skyscrapers. Once we went so far as to stop the elevators of a tower in the city and slid down the greased elevator cables, plummeting into the darkness some thirty floors before attempting to slow down and stop. It was nuts, real James Bond stuff, but when you're doing it you don't think like that. You simply concentrate on not fucking up.

It was a little hard to enjoy some of the cooler elements because of the concentration required; all save for one, 'spy rigging', or the helo hot extraction. This is where a caving ladder is lowered from a helicopter and you hook onto it and go soaring into the sky like Superman. That, I can say, I did enjoy; it was pure fun and I wasn't thinking about the mission much, it was simply a moment of joy and disbelief: 'What the fuck am I doing swinging under a Black Hawk, dressed in black, wearing a balaclava, carrying a machine-gun and looking down on a city where I previously worked in a bloody hardware store!'

Frequently during these mindblowingly spectacular helo exercises I was overcome by my situation; it was almost as though I was outside my body looking in. On the odd occasion we got to fly across the city, my senses would be in overload. We would cruise in from Sydney's west, bank high and right over the Harbour Bridge, my nostrils filling with the sweet salty air, the cold breeze on my face. The bird would then pitch forwards and change position, picking up speed as it dove fully into approach mode, when the sound would change and they'd cut the lights – everything would go black. I would be a ball of nerves until the squeeze on my right shoulder indicating thirty seconds till drop brought me back to reality and I would focus intensely, with the familiar personal mantra of 'Don't fuck up, don't fuck up' echoing in my head. As the helo angled hard forward, I'd feel one of my brothers grip my belt to secure my position at the door, a much appreciated but needless action as the G-forces pinned me firmly to the deck. There'd be another direction change, vertical now, then another hard bank made with lightning reflexes and the near mythical skill of the 171st Black Hawk Squadron.

Onlookers would peer out from their buildings in disbelief as we invaded their civilian lives with our sharp violent ones – unbelievable to them; another regular night for the boys in black.

One particularly long night began with a fast rope insertion onto the top of the defence force building in Pitt Street. Next we had to fight through the office cubicles, snapping off simulated ammunition, or simunition shots at the awaiting regular army 'enemy', securing each floor as we went. Then we had to slide down the inner elevator shaft, racing down the greased cables into the black emptiness below, only to be met by a barrage of opposition at the next floor. The exercise culminated in a return to the roof, where we rappelled down the outside of the building to the empty street below, witnessed only by a few drunk teens returning from a heavy night out. It was your average Tuesday really.

Water ops was our baby; we excelled in the aqua environment, though it still took a lot of practice. One of the hairiest moments for me was when the speedboat I was in for a ship underway drill hit the side of the enemy vessel with such force that the nose of the boat only just popped up and prevented us from diving under the ship entirely. I almost broke my arm in the process. This was a real eye-opener as in the normal military everything would stop after such an event. Everyone would carry on about what happened and halt training . . . but not at TAG. I sort of half-stopped as I assumed that the mission would cease. Especially as the Officer in Charge had gone flying forwards and smashed himself into the bow of the boat and lay crumpled on the floor like a batch of dirty laundry. But the Team Leader cried out, 'Get the fuck on the boat.' This shit wasn't going to stop because of a small case of possible death! That was the first time I realised that this job was for keeps and that we were on a different level.

On paper, we wrapped up work training for the Games, although it was still a month or so before they started and we would relocate to Melbourne. Perfect for a bit of down time and some consolidation I thought. But no such luck. I was told we were about to ramp things up even further and begin an auditing phase. It took the form of one of the hardest trials conducted in the domestic counterterrorism world – called CT Olympics. I had no real idea what it meant or what it entailed but I was about to find out. It was two weeks of hell, non-stop, one exercise after the other, containing every conceivable scenario and involving all levels of law enforcement and government, even up to the Prime Minister himself. No sleeping, no stopping, no dropping, no dramas . . .

I knew these cats had some power but I was blown away by the sheer scope and power of the juggernaut that is Special Operations. The exercise had scarcely begun and we'd already shut down Martin Place train station, flown down George Street in a helo, smashed a ferry in Sydney Harbour, boarded a plane at Sydney Airport and crawled up the side of a warship, all in the space of five days. What next, storm bloody Parliament House? It was access all areas; nothing was off limits in the pursuit of attaining training authenticity. We would hit a target, pack up and go, mobilise and then do it all over again. Every time I thought that was it and we couldn't possibly do any more, there was another briefing, another target, another mission and another hill; there's always another bloody hill.

An interesting part of our SF education was the legal side of things. A lot of guys weren't interested in the briefings and mock trials that we took part in but I found them fascinating. We would cover whole scenarios in excruciating legal detail. We would go through the process of being interviewed by police, and having to account for our actions in the stronghold. It was bloody interesting to see what might play out in real life. What became abundantly clear was that you were accountable, and that any mistake you made wouldn't be swept under the carpet. You had better be damned sure of your actions and confident in the application of your skills if you wanted to avoid prosecution yourself.

The large airlock door of the 747 slid open in what seemed like slow motion, Canada was in front of me and I was smiling inside my gasmask and heavy helmet as I knew he would cop the lion's share of the paintball simunition as I sought to glide past his 'corpse' and take all the glory, smacking the tangos down with a quick four shots from my submachine gun. It was the last mission for the night, and possibly the exercise; we were all running on empty but Canada was still brimming with Energizer Bunny vigour and maple syrup-infused cockiness: 'I'll take the lead position, ay.'

'No dramas,' I said, positive he wouldn't be quick enough to shoot the three army guys playing the bad guys and it would be up to me to save the day.

Canada darted forwards into Position One of the time-tested aeroplane drill and, before I could take up my position to his right, he had taken out the three terrorists with two shots to the face each, blinding them with paint – and no small amount of pain. They had hit the deck before I was halfway into the fucking plane, and I cleared the remaining passage-way at half-pace as I knew it was all over.

Walking back down the aisle I could see the fricken Canuck smiling, even though only his eyes were visible behind the thick balaclava he now wore, having removed his gasmask.

'Think you're shit hot, don't ya?' I growled.

'You know it, bro, ay.'

A giant of an SAS sergeant, the Safety Officer for the exercise, strolled down the plane, having witnessed the scenario, and casually asked who had been in Position Number One and done such devastating damage to his well-placed terrorists.

Canada spoke up before I could get a word in: 'That was Obi, ay.'

'Well done that man,' said the sergeant.

I looked at Canada with a questioning gaze. 'She be right, bro, ay.' That was just Canada, and it was... all right.

We finished the last job for the exercise and were in full assault kit, sitting on a 22-seater bus out on the tarmac of Sydney Airport. I can't remember the last time anyone had slept. There was silence on the bus; the boys were stuffed and ready for a well-deserved rest. As I looked out the window, for no particular reason, I started singing, softly at first, 'Leaving . . . On a jet plane . . . Don't know when I'll be back again.' In unison, all the lads burst into spontaneous song: 'Leaving! On! A! Jet!

Plane! Don't know when I'll be back again!' The bus was alive with song in complete harmony. Exhaustion? Humour? Or just weird? Whatever the reason, the hardest exercise of my life ended in singing and laughter. The hardest and best bunch of blokes I've ever known, singing and laughing.

Things happen fast in this game; blink and you'll miss it.

We'd completed a demonstration of our abilities, and as we lined up in front of the dignitaries, blood slowly filled my glove and the warm sensation that followed disseminated through my entire body. It wasn't so much numbness as hyper-acceleration of all my senses, save one – my sight. My vision twitched and flickered like bad TV reception. My balaclava itched and I had a tiny rock in my shoe that was really annoying.

Fuck, fuck, why am I able to feel everything in my body? Who's talking? Why are we here? Shit, straighten up. Stand still. Shit, I can't clench my fist. Don't fall down, don't even move. Fuck, don't cry . . .

A replay of the demonstration flashed through my frantic mind. I remembered we'd had the right-hand side of the MOE house, I blew the door and we entered. No, hold on; it was the left side; we went to enter and as I raced forwards I was tripped up from behind in the scramble. I hit the ground hard, damned hard, like a rugby tackle. Shit, the embarrassment. *Get in the house, do the job, complete the mission . . .* but then my hand wouldn't hold the foregrip of my weapon. I could barely operate the torch pressure switch. *Shit, target left; engage. Next room. Can't fucking see; bloody smoke from the distraction grenades; target to my right.* Somebody else nails it and I feel grateful as I think I may have dislocated my finger in the fall. 'Clear!' 'Clear!'

Thank fuck that's over. I can't wait to finish this demo so I can put my finger back in place. Then that warm feeling, like someone smashed an egg on your head. *It's just a dislocated finger, no dramas. I've done it before in footy, it's not that bad; shouldn't be hurting this much though.*

We take off our gasmasks, put on our balaclavas to conceal our identity and wait to be called out of the house to the applause of the suit-wearing onlookers. But I'm having real trouble with my mask. Bloody hand won't work; screw it, I'll have to manage with one hand till this charade is over and we get back to the main base.

As we line up and I stand at attention, waiting for the dignitaries to leave, I take a quick look at my hand, at the palm. It looks okay, but the glove seems a little funny. Then the fellow next to me pipes up, 'Shit, Obi, turn your hand around, bro.'

So I do, and the sight of bone and flesh seems to tell my brain that my finger is no longer connected to the aforementioned hand. *Oh, shit . . .*

'Obi, you okay, mate?'

'Um, yeah, shit. I think so. Ah, shit.' I wasn't too worried. 'I could be okay,' I thought. 'Might not be as bad as it looks.'

I figured out that as we had fallen, my MP5 machine-gun had swung down like an axe and the angled magazine had smashed the middle finger of my left hand into the ground. But the adrenaline had been pumping and I'd not really noticed until we cleared the second room.

The situation was starting to spiral out of my control now as the excitement wore off and the pain took hold. 'No dramas, boys. I'll just go see the medic.'

I've got to get away from the lads so they don't see me cave or whimper.

I was positive I could hold my shit together while I walked the thirty or so metres to the medics' ambo that was always on site.

Ten metres to go, I've got this; I can hold on till I get there, then I may lose it. Five metres, yes, just a few more seconds and the tears are bound to flow.

There'd be no one there but the medic, who wasn't a member of the unit, so I might get away with a little emotion. Then, as I rounded the corner, the entire Sniper Platoon was sitting around the ambo having coffee.

Bloody snipers, always slacking off! What the fuck am I going to do now? I'll just have to act tough till I get to the hospital.

The medic called me over. 'What's up, Obi? Hurt your weddle paw, 'ave we?' He started making flagrant baby sounds.

Wordlessly, I held out my hand and he removed my glove and my finger just fell off, held only by a small bit of skin.

Ohhhhhhhhhhhhhh, shittttttttttttttttttt. A collective gasp went up from the snipers. 'Fucking hell, Obi.'

I sat on the tailgate of the ambulance stonefaced, trying not to think about what was happening or the consequences of such an injury on my career. Later I was told that no trace of emotion was visible on my face at all, and after having treated me the medic stated that I wasn't in shock. It's something I have never quite been able to explain but whenever I have hurt myself, which is frequently, I have managed to remain calm. The simple fact is that I fear the reaction to *my* reaction more than the pain itself.

Lying in hospital and later consigned to the couch while my mates battled evil in Melbourne during the Commonwealth Games – not really; in the end they just got pissed a lot – I had plenty of time to think. Not good in my case. I'd been wound to such a fever pitch of adrenaline and risk-taking, combined with a tempo that would make a hummingbird sick. Anyone in that situation would tend to take to a sedentary life fairly badly.

Someone wise once said words to the effect that in times of peace the warlike man makes war upon himself. Inevitably, my thoughts turned to what I was doing in life and what I was actually achieving. My main stream of consciousness settled on the lack of creative stimulus in my life and how I treated people around me, especially my girlfriend, Alex, who I'm sure had suffered terribly through my pursuit of violent fulfilment.

Despite all I'd achieved, I felt hollow and sad, because these days all I did was destroy shit. For a while, the most creative thing I'd done was fashion door charges for explosive entry into buildings, and they had the shelf life of a rice pudding! Also I realised I was becoming increasingly aggressive and self-obsessed; somehow I'd bought into the view that most inhabitants of the world were somehow less than me because of what I did for a living.

These and other realisations hit me like a tonne of bricks. Suddenly I was confronted with the man in the mirror and he was a parody of everything I used to despise in the military – an elitist, arrogant, aggressive wanker!

Sometime later, my friends and family admitted to me that I was different at the time, that they had noticed the unwelcome change in my demeanour, but that they hadn't known what to do about it. I guess I should have realised something was up when the girl I'd loved for over half my life walked out the door and all I could think of was fighting, drinking, shooting and blowing things up. Because of the perceived gravity of what I was doing, I didn't consider anything else important. I almost got shot once in a training exercise (I won't go into that) and had sort of shrugged it off. I used to come home and Alex would want to talk to me about things going on in her life and I didn't care; I was so full of myself and I held my issues to be eminently more 'worthy' than those of others.

That time on the couch was a turning point for me. Little by little, from then on, I began to realise that I had been wrong, and that there is honour to be found in many walks of life, depending on how you look at it.

This is not an excuse and I don't wish to hide behind it, but when you work in that intense military environment and you're not naturally an alpha male, it takes an incredible amount of energy to exist in that world. To go to work every day and night and fight the fight, to amp up and be one of the boys, it wasn't something that came easily to me. It did for some, I'm sure.

The military had done many great things for me but they had taken their pound of flesh, and it was starting to show.

Although the time would come for me to reflect more practically on these issues, I was still in the thick of it, so I stowed that shit and walked on.

Twenty-two

HOLSWORTHY SUNSET

'The fishermen know that the sea is dangerous and the storm terrible, but they have never found these dangers sufficient reason for remaining ashore.'

– Vincent van Gogh

By the time the lads had returned from Melbourne my hand was almost better. I still couldn't make a strong fist but I wasn't going to tell them that. I was keen to get back to work consolidating my skills and learning new ones. We were booked to fly to Perth and conduct an intensive training scheme. It would culminate in a full-mission profile of dive, covert beach crossing and then night assault on the three-level RFCR that the regiment used. It may sound like we were going over familiar ground but we weren't. The way things usually played out in training was segmented and compartmentalised, so the combination of all disciplines – approach, entry, task and exfil, as in exfiltration – rarely flowed in one large uninterrupted scenario.

*

Hitting the sand, I smashed my face into the seabed and was rolled, tossing and turning uncontrollably towards the beach. My face mask had slipped down and was covering my nose and mouth; in vain I tried to raise my head above the waves to grasp a breath of much-needed air. The swell had pushed me ashore and I was almost drowning in knee-deep water. My knife had come out of its sheath and was flailing wildly behind me on its lanyard, the weight of my equipment was making it hard to stand and the thumping waves gave no quarter. As the wash cleared I noticed a figure standing above me. Somehow I regained my footing and managed to stand, choking and spluttering.

'Finished drowning, idiot?' It was Canada, his eyes the only distinguishable part of his camouflaged face. I gave him a look that indicated I was none too impressed with his comment.

Moving slowly, we headed up the dunes, pausing at the top to cache our gear in the scrub and check our equipment, ready for the approach to the house. Our focus was on concealing the noise of our activity. For weeks we'd been working up to this exercise and I wanted to perform well and earn my spot in the Team. I felt my injury had dropped me back a notch and now my Greg Louganis impression in the shallows hadn't helped.

At the form-up point we awaited the final 'Go' to come over the radio. It was a moment of eerie quiet and personal contemplation, an opportunity for each operator to think about the job ahead. Over and over I ran through my mantra in my head: 'Don't fuck up, don't fuck up.'

Radio silence broke as a stern voice intruded into our ears, our hearts: 'Ready, ready.'

'Ready, ready.'

'Standby . . . SLEDGEHAMMER! Now go, go, go!'

Some people ask what does it feel like serving in TAG? Well, the tensions of that day were fairly representative:

Processes flash through your mind: fifty different predetermined responses to a million different scenarios. Adrenaline courses through your body; your feet are shoulder-width apart; you're hunched forwards, searching, hunting; your eyes are straining to take in the kaleidoscope of information travelling at you at the speed of sound; as the instructor's voice booms, muscle memory kicks in, the electrical impulses to carry out the appropriate order fire forth from a tired brain; limbs twirl into motion as the grinding gears of a learnt action release their grasp and you hope, nay pray, you've come up with the right solution to the posed problem – that your decision, your judgement were sound and you've correctly done that which was expected of you, so that the result achieved is the right one.

After the exercise, I flung myself to the ground away from the group, near the edge of a shed. My heart rate now slowed, I put pressure on my knife blade, watching as it slipped below the skin and a sliver of steel rose through the red pool to shine in the false fluorescent light. The small piece of steel was easy to remove and its origin wasn't a mystery – every MOE operator worth his salt had dug these little bastards out of his shin, the result of having stood close to a door charge.

Everything had gone well; it had been a perfect assault with not an element wrong. The weeks of training had culminated in a precise execution of a counterterrorism scenario. The boys had worked their arses off. We had gone without sleep, food and comfort. I too was happy with my performance – a rarity for me. I'd made some good calls, been accurate and fast and believed that if it had it been real, we would have come out on top. I thought that now, maybe now, we would be treated with respect; maybe the powers that be would bestow the smallest of blessings on us and simply let us know we had done a good job. Give us a nod and allow us to feel the honour of being in this unit.

Instead, I sat in stunned silence and listened to our officers deliver a verbal assault that would have made General Patton weak at the knees. Apparently we hadn't done well enough; we hadn't performed up to standard and we were all terrible. Normally I would take this kind of abuse in my stride, as it was often warranted, an integral part of the military machine and a valuable tool to push units to their best. This time though, I saw red: what they were saying was utter nonsense, evidence that those in charge were completely out of touch with the actual performance of the team. Although they were only trying to push us to our best, they knew full well we had excelled but had chosen to berate us because they lacked the means to act differently. For the first time in my military career I felt a swell of dissent and disappointment in those above me. It seemed they couldn't even acknowledge good work anymore. I started to think, 'What's the point, what's so special, why be at this level when you're still treated like a child?'

When I think about it now, it was simply the military way of making us excel, and excel we did. The sometimes 'harsh' treatment, such as that blisteringly negative feedback, is a

necessary evil I guess, and simply one of those military tradi-
tions that, although occasionally hard to stomach, *does* in fact
drive you towards excellence, whether you appreciate it at the
time or not.

In fact the impressive level of competence to which TAG
(East) had risen was no secret in the military community; we
were even starting to receive praise from the trailblazers in
the west, not to mention that we had a few SAS members
working with us and they were able to confirm our ability.

By this stage we had all but taken over the domestic counterterrorism role for the whole of Australia. The boys in the
west were incredibly busy fulfilling Australia's commitments
overseas and I think even they were happy to have us excel in
the domestic role while they took care of the international one.

Over the next few months we continued to expand as a
unit and take on more skills and responsibilities. We worked
with a range of government agencies and sought out many
creative and challenging training scenarios. It was a period of
exponential growth in Australian counterterrorism capability
and scope.

As for me, I had had my fill. I felt my personal life was
suffering and my personality needed some adjusting. It may
have been different if we'd been deployed overseas or had
a few more real-time ops. In the end, above all, I needed
a change and felt the time was right to call it a day.

Twenty-three

EXIT

'The end is nigh.'

— *Anon.*

How long can you pretend to be someone else before you become that person? Counterterrorism is no game to be in once you start doubting your reasons for playing there. Much less when you start doubting yourself. It had been an intense eighteen months online, with over a year of selection before that just to get into TAG. Add to that four years as a clearance diver proper; I can't deny I was a little tired. For some reason I no longer felt the desire to smash myself for the cause, whatever it may be.

When I'd begun, I was able to compartmentalise my work and my life but I'd begun to find the lines increasingly blurred and really needed to explore other things. Not to mention I had recently gotten back together with Alex and I wanted to concentrate on my relationship, something I hadn't done while at TAG. All this was on my mind, along with the fact that I felt I needed something new. I've always been like that: I get bored easily and need to find the next challenge, the next cliff to hurl myself off in a vain attempt to locate something within.

The respect I had for the boys I served with at TAG prevented me from simply pretending and going through the motions with the job. In my opinion, far too many defence force members do this and it's a disservice to them and the unit with which they serve. If you don't believe in it, if you don't give it your best every day, if you wouldn't lay down your life for the unit, then it's time to go.

Once my heart was no longer in it, much as I tried to keep up my performance, I felt like a footballer at the end of his career about to be dropped from the rep side. So rather than tempt fate, and because I respected the honour of serving in such a unit, I decided to leave and return to life as a clearance diver. To my mind I had given Special Forces my all and it was now a case of better to burn out than fade away. My contracted six years with the ADF was almost up anyway. Plus soon I was due to be posted back to my CD team – as two years was considered the optimal duration of going online with TAG – so I simply requested to go a few weeks early. It was no big deal as my Chief knew the effort I gave to the unit and, although he expressed his reluctance to lose me, granted my request.

Before returning to the Team, I had one last diving exercise with the unit. We were getting a new dive set, a flash bit of kit from Divex called 'The Shadow'; cool-sounding, ay? I have to say I remain a massive fan of the LAR V because of its unfathomable ability to have the shit kicked out of it and still be operational. Anyway, we were putting the set through its paces and as usual smashing ourselves in the process. It must have been on our fourth or so night of this when it dawned on the boys that the next dive would in fact be my last with TAG. I'd tried to keep this quiet as the boys weren't known for their sentimentality. Once it was common knowledge, however, it was only a matter of time before the lads tried to pull a prank on me, and I knew it. I was like a meerkat on crack! I was checking my shoes for spiders, my bag for jellyfish and, yes, even my car for explosives (just kidding). Although that might seem a bit paranoid, Canada had a talent for screwing me over when it came to pranks. He once salted my bread and butter at lunch for a month before I worked out why it tasted funny. Bastard!

So on alert for pranks was I that I ended up being a walking zombie and practically forgot all about it being my last dive. Our kit was lying on the wharf ready; we had a quick bite to eat, held a brief and headed back out to kit up. As I'd done a million times before, I started going through the motions, putting on my gear. 'Fuck!' I thought. Something was wrong; I wasn't sure what.

Fuck, this shit's heavy. Must be tired. Shut up, shut up; don't let the boys know you're tired . . .

Even though something niggled me about the odd feel of my kit, I moved to the edge of the wharf and put it out of my mind. I had a mission to do and no time to worry about my tired arse not being able to carry my share of the load. I fired up, bit down hard on the breathing piece and launched into the water.

The squad took off at a frenetic pace, suspiciously so – I now realise – for an end-of-night compass dive. Within minutes, my legs burned and I struggled to stay with the squad – a first for me. To my alarm, I was starting to hold the squad back now, making everybody work harder, dragging them down with me, something unforgivable in our world. My breathing began to labour, my vision closed in and I even considered pulling the plug and telling the Chief Diver next to me to stop the mission, something that would have absolutely killed me on the inside. What was wrong with me? At first I was concerned, then quickly concern turned to frustration and then anger.

Fury gripped me as I reached behind to my pack, then to my pockets, then on my kit, then to my belt – on and on, discovery after discovery: they were all full of lead weights! The boys had loaded me up like the ballast of a warship. I must have been carrying at least an extra fifteen kilograms. I'll never know. I started to dump the useless lumps of lead on the seabed while we moved along at what I later discovered was a pace especially designed to screw me over with all my extra cargo.

Returning to the surface, I let fly with a spray of obscenities that would shame Red Fox. The only thing that dwarfed my voice was the laughter of the boys as we swam back to shore, arm in arm; alone in the dark; cold, wet, hungry and . . . yes . . . happy . . .

After a week or so of leave I reported to HMAS *Waterhen* and the welcoming embrace of Australian Clearance Diving Team One.

Initially, being back with the Team was a wholly positive experience. It was great to reconnect with my first love: diving, simply diving. Plus it felt awesome to catch up with all the lads; inevitably I'd dropped off the radar while I was out with the army. The fact that the Team did not operate at the furious fever pitch of TAG was a welcome and restful change for me. Naturally I still tried to throw in with the lads and wholeheartedly endeavoured to brush up on my clearance diving.

Having come from TAG, the natural progression for me was to slot into MTO, as tactical operations most closely mirrored my role with the army – well, at least with regard to LAR V O_2 swimming. The role suited me, and I had a kind of unofficial leadership position even though my rank did not reflect this. I was happy to teach the new blokes a few tricks and give back to the Team after having been gone for nearly two years.

One of the first tasks that fell to me was to get all the kit up to scratch. This was not a small undertaking as there was a lot of equipment that was about to be brought online for an upcoming exercise. It only took me a day to realise the enormity of the job and also the poor state of the equipment. It wasn't the lads' fault it was in disrepair: they were undermanned and were working all the time. They simply hadn't had enough extra time to do all the repairs, stocktake and upkeep the life-supporting equipment.

With a two-week deadline, I tried my hardest to get the lads together and have all the kit up to scratch. It simply wasn't ever going to happen in that timeframe. After a valiant struggle by all concerned, I realised I had to step up and confess that there was too much equipment being tested and fixed and we were simply not ready.

There was no way I could sign the equipment logs saying we were ready; it was my name and I would be committing to a legal document. If we used untested gear and someone died, it would be my arse in jail.

Although I didn't relish the prospect of telling the boss, what made it seem a little rosier was that the last Chief in charge of the MTO element had recently moved to another element and my old Chief from TAG had just moved in. I had a good rapport with him and was confident he would understand my position. As neither of us had been at the Team more than two weeks, neither of us was to blame and we would simply put a hold on things until the situation could be remedied.

On my way up the stairs to the offices of the head shed, I realised I was a little peeved that the element had been left in such a shambles, not that I felt the need to rub anyone's nose in it. My intention was to let the Chief know that I would handle it, given a little more time, without advertising that there was a problem. I was sure he would grant the request as he was a sensible man, and discreet as well.

I was not two sentences into my whispered conversation with the Chief when a ranking officer nearby let go a terrible blast of obscenities in my direction: 'You fucking so and so, how dare you, blah, blah, what would you fucking know, blah, blah, the unit's not like that, blah blah . . .' and so on and so on. I could not believe it. What the fuck was this bloke on about? Here I was, covering and fixing the issue, and he was broadcasting his cluelessness to the whole office.

'I beg to differ, sir,' I calmly replied. 'I have the paperwork right here; all our equipment is out of date; this unit simply isn't operational.'

That only sparked another tirade of obscenities; it was so vehement that I even questioned my own paperwork. 'Fuck,' I thought, 'maybe I'm wrong,' and I checked it again as I had it in my hands.

No, still right. This guy was so out of touch, he wasn't aware that the unit had been left with life-supporting equipment that was almost two years out of date!

After a few hushed words from my old TAG Chief, basically to the effect of 'Don't worry, Obi; we'll just sort it ourselves and forget that guy', I walked downstairs, dejected.

How could this once proud unit tolerate such stupidity and arrogance? The needs of the unit and its function should come before the ego of some bloke with a chip on his shoulder.

I refused to sign off the dodgy equipment and I put in for my discharge the following day.

I had a bunch of leave up my sleeve so I only had a month or so to serve before I could take holidays and run down the clock on a beach at Byron Bay, where my parents now lived. It had not been the ending to my military career I had foreseen. In some ways I had fallen into the navy and I had almost as haphazardly fallen out of it.

Despite the ugliness of what had happened, I felt no malice toward the Branch and the military as a whole, and I don't think I will ever change my mind about that. Regardless of what the job is, there will always be people who don't warrant the trust that an institution or organisation bestows on them. In my experience, they are always in the minority anyway. The Branch contains some of the most inspirational individuals I have ever met and it has imparted in me a sense of pride and accomplishment that I would not have attained but for the dedication of those who trained me and those I worked with.

It's a pity to have to end the story of my time with the navy on that note, but that's what happened.

After I'd resigned, my last few days were awesome and many of my colleagues expressed dismay at my leaving. Especially Canada, who at my farewell barbecue kindly made me skol two litres of beer through a snorkel, purely to show his respect . . . Fucking Canadians!

Twenty-four

PURGATORY

'These men had one great thing in common, their underwater life. They fought efficiently but without rancour, they were not men to make war, but they were the type who made war when it was inevitable. Courage alone is not enough underwater; it is the essential framework to which is added purpose, determination and cold calculating intelligence.'

— The Frogmen, *T Waldron & J Gleeson,*
Evans Brothers, London, 1950

Crumpled and spent on a windswept Byron Bay beach the day after I left the navy, the relative warmth I'd felt recalling my career ebbed from me like blood from my veins. In qualifying as a CD and making TAG (East), I'd achieved more than I had set out to, but what it had once meant had started to drift away from me, fading fast and soon to be forgotten.

Re-entering civilian life was going to be challenging; my decision to leave the navy had been anything but premeditated.

243

How was I to adjust to my newfound freedom? The only way forward was to seek a challenge, but what? What was available to me? It wasn't as if I had a law degree or a doctorate in theoretical physics. My choices were limited if I wanted to continue living in Sydney with Alex and maintain the lifestyle that we enjoyed.

A lot of ex-clearance divers had slid seamlessly into commercial diving when they left the forces. I knew that the industrial side of commercial diving consisted of a range of activities structured around underwater engineering. It's hard work; one day you can be involved in a subaquatic engineering marvel; other days you are a glorified deep-sea brickie's labourer. It seemed my best option for now.

After a break of several months post military separation, I threw myself into the commercial diving industry. I concentrated on learning as much as I could about the sector's skillset and soaking up all the information the other divers would share with me. It was entirely different to military diving, hence the saying, 'Diving's just how you get to work; it's what you do down there that matters.' Jobs could run for weeks, months or only a couple of days, and I found myself on the couch playing Xbox quite a lot. It probably took me a year or so working for a few different dive companies before I knew fully what I was doing. But I learnt fast and built a reputation in the industry as a hard worker and effective problem-solver.

The work itself wasn't all smooth sailing. For a while I was working for a small dive company run by an ex-clearance diver; we won a contract to work on a reservoir supply dam in Sydney's west. Among other things, I had to install a grate over an overflow inlet valve. It was on a large dam and should have been a simple job, except for one important difference. The valve had an automatic actuation unit on it in case the dam got too full. When there was sufficient pressure of water above it, the automatic function would trip, opening the valve, spilling water out the freefall side of the dam. This created an enormous pressure differential and the issue with the installation was that the blasted thing couldn't be turned off prior to the job, nor halted – heaven forbid – once enacted. Should the valve function during installation, the result for the hapless installer would not be pretty. It'd be like a spaceship getting sucked into a black hole. I believe it's called spaghettification!

There had been heavy rain during the week leading up to the scheduled installation and nobody had any idea whether the resulting increase in dam depth would actuate the valve. No one wanted to be the guinea pig to test it either. As supervisor, theoretically I could have sent in one of the two young guys I had working with me, but if I did that, how could I sleep at night? With my heart in my mouth, I entered the water . . .

My breathing was heavy but I controlled it by humming the slow Latin hymn 'Sub Tuum Praesidium', my old school song. I'm not religious, far from it, but its unhurried, steady cadence always seemed to calm me. I often used it when free diving to slow my heart rate and focus my shaky excuse for courage.

When I sighted the valve I realised it wasn't that deep but I was approaching the event horizon: any closer and its functioning would mean 'pulling back the curtain and joining the choir invisible'. Whipping the grate around in front of me, I gingerly approached the valve, cursing Murphy and his legion of gremlins. As the gap between me and the super-gravity black hole narrowed, metre by metre, my nerves began to untangle. All I could hear was my heart in my chest; I was quite sure the only thing stopping it exiting my chest cavity was the strength of the surrounding wetsuit.

This was it. I didn't want to spend any more time here than was needed so, discarding my usual level of care and precision, I slammed the grate home onto the bolt lugs. Even as I was spinning on the hex nuts as fast as possible, I still wasn't entirely confident the valve couldn't suck me through the grate, creating what I could only imagine to be cartoonish cheese-cube-sized pieces of diver meat.

I called down the comms, asking the lads in the boat to haul me backwards as fast as they could. 'Fuck me, I must be mental,' I thought, as they dragged me into the boat.

It was job complete for the end of the day, back slaps all round and calls for a fricken beer, ay! That was commercial diving! Get the job done, baby; get it done and get paid. Simple.

I worked throughout Australia and for many different diving companies over a couple of years, and the entire time my relationship with diving and the industry as a whole ran hot and cold. On a daily basis I struggled with the implications of the work to my life and health: seeing a ten-tonne I-beam swing past you out of the brown swirling water and hearing the crane operator cry 'Oops!' over the comms is enough to give anyone pause for thought. On the other hand, I loved the ocean, and the comfort I sought beneath its glassy surface wasn't easily replaced. So I continued on, hoping to reach the ease of heart I'd once had in the military.

While I was working for the Botany Bay expansion project in Sydney's southeast, the dangers of the profession became even more front of mind.

Thirty-five metres down; I'd been subsurface for the best part of two hours in the black murk that was Botany Bay. A thin stream of blood drifted past my sightline, defying gravity as if in the vacuum of space. The pain hadn't hit me yet and my determination to complete the task remained resolute.

It was the middle of winter and I'd recently started diving with a large South Sydney-based diving company. Being my first couple of weeks, I was forever trying to prove myself, putting my hand up for every task and doing my best to spend the maximum time underwater. I would come home utterly broken, wishing for a relaxing CDAT. It was quite an unforgiving environment.

My employers had been tasked to install large T-walls – retaining walls made of precast modular T-shaped units – along the Port Botany shoreline. The walls were to be lined and then backfilled with tonnes of earth, reclaiming the land for use as a port. We were working underwater with these massive concrete shapes, sealing the gap between two walls. It was like aligning two pieces of paper and then sticky taping them in the middle. This was done by lowering a large piece of steel or sheet piling on the inside and then using a strongback, or secondary support beam, to draw it tight from the other side.

Thanks to an impending storm, the ocean was pumping wildly, mercilessly smashing the T-bar-shaped piece of steel I was trying to tighten into the concrete wall. The small gap between the concrete slabs acted like a funnel, channelling the water into the sheet piling on the opposite side, creating an incredibly dangerous state of affairs. I should have waited and requested them to shore up the steel and stop it from slamming the strongback into the wall, but I was stubborn and I wanted to complete the task. Visibility was terrible, my position precarious and my resolve to tighten the wing nut on the strongback illogical. Nevertheless I went for one more try. I always did, more is the pity.

A large swell drove me against the wall, smashing my small frame and helmet into the hard face of the towering concrete façade. My hand slipped against the steel strongback as I struggled to move my head from the crush zone; it was then I saw the blood.

I felt a tingling sensation in my hand, but the embarrassment of hurting myself welled up inside me, rivalling any pain I could have felt. *Fuck, not again!* I got on the comms. 'I think I'm ok, just nipped my thumb a little.'

The dive supervisor had had a good view of everything from my hat camera and spoke slowly and clearly to me. 'Mate, I think it's worse than that. Come up and we'll take a look.'

By the time I got to the surface, I was well pissed off with myself. When dressing out of my dive gear, the guys eased off my glove to take a look. The injury was bad but it could have been worse: the top part of my thumb, about halfway down the nail, had been sheared off. I applied pressure and headed for the hospital, apparently still protesting that I could complete the job – what a dickhead.

It would be a long and painful recovery but one that taught me a lesson: cold, fatigue and arrogance underwater can get you hurt or even killed. The ocean makes equals of all men and commercial diving will humble the best aquaman, hence the old commercial diver saying, 'Never stick your fingers anywhere you wouldn't stick your dick.'

Commercial diving was starting to lose its novelty. I craved a more challenging environment, and the fact that my mates were fighting the Axis of Evil made me yearn for the validation that only a non-permissive environment can bring.

I knew there were plenty of Australians working as mercenaries – sorry, 'security contractors' – in faraway lands and began to mull over the possibilities – although it appeared that despite my military history, I was still a little underqualified, that is in terms of 'in country' experience. I decided to find out as much about it as I could.

Post 9/11 the private security industry has ballooned into a vast and pervasive enterprise; its scale rivals that of the immense private armies of ancient times. In an era when almost every facet of the government is privatised, why not the business of war?

To a large extent, the public was uninformed about the clandestine activities of the 'merc.com' generation. That is until in March 2004, when some contractors from the American firm Blackwater got lost, became victims of mob violence and then had their bodies desecrated and hung from a bridge in downtown Fallujah.

Much has been written now about this multibillion-dollar industry and we all know that, like any entity, it has its heroes and its villains. For the most part, contractors are in the business of doing what our armed forces were previously engaged to accomplish. They seem to many to be modern-day ronin – masterless samurai searching for a cause without the guise of patriotism or politics.

It wasn't like I took the decision to enter the fray lightly. It was tricky to build upon my rudimentary knowledge of the 'gun for hire' world from Sydney. I had several friends in the industry and picked their brains. On top of that, I did as much other research as I could, but that doesn't amount to much, does it? To have any real comprehension of a subject, there is nothing quite so educational as full immersion.

As to the more philosophic questions of what it would mean to undertake such a role, after thinking long and hard about the moral and ethical consequences of entering what is known as 'the circuit', I came to one fundamental conclusion: it was beyond me to control the actions of others; I could only really control *my own*. Provided I chose the companies I worked for wisely and acted honourably, then my career choice could remain reconcilable with my internal code. I'd only ever done what I thought was right before; why should this be any different? Besides I was getting restless and even though it would mean being apart from Alex and my family, they all knew I needed another Everest.

Around the time I was making the decision to leave commercial diving, I thought Canada was still in Iraq, where he had been working for a while. He had left the military shortly after me but got some early runs on the board teaching community policing and security in Iraq, a fortuitous opportunity sourced through our commando connections. However, I discovered he had left there and was teeing up a gig to provide armed security on a vessel moving through the Red Sea. The sneaky bastard was always up to something!

Piracy was becoming an increasingly hot topic in the Gulf of Aden and off the coast of Somalia. Shipping companies had resorted to protecting their valuable investments by hiring private security firms to organise armed escorts for their maritime assets. Keen for some adventure, I wangled an invitation to join Canada working for a maritime division of a large international security firm. To be frank, many aspects of the operation seemed a bit half-arsed. I did wonder what I was letting myself in for. But in the end the prospect of working with my mate Canada and the need to get some practical experience won over my initial hesitation.

Canada and I met up in a small out-of-the-way villa in Sana'a, Yemen. From this small outpost, the security company ran its anti-piracy operation. My understanding was that the company had a 'perfectly above board' deal with the Yemeni Ministry of the Interior. There were to be two Yemeni coast-guard personnel seconded to come with us on the ship. They would be supplied with a box of AK-47s and a couple of heavy machine-guns – 7.62mm PKMs. This way, according to the law, the weapons belonged to the government and we were simply borrowing them; a good deal, really.

The plan was that some guys from our company would accompany us on our long overland journey to a port town called Hodeida, where we would join the vessel that we would be escorting. Already Canada and I weren't impressed with the guys from the company; they didn't seem to have much of an idea what they were doing, but we went along with it, for now.

Confirming our suspicions that things weren't entirely up to scratch, only one Land Rover arrived to pick us up, and it was reserved for the boss and his buddy. We were told to get in one of the local bongo vans, a kind of Yemeni taxi that smelt like a camel, and the less said about the driver the better. The weapons were waiting for us at the port, so at this stage Canada and I weren't strapped. We felt vulnerable as we loaded our gear into this dodgy transport and headed into the hilly bandit country.

The security situation in Yemen is not what you'd call stable. It's a cradle of terrorism and anti-Western sentiment. A mass uprising, mere months away, was to see the country descend into even more chaos, if that were possible. Meanwhile, every time we stopped for fuel or a whiz we got the 'Fuck you, infidel' look. I wasn't that concerned, until I realised that Canada was!

I started taking stock of a few other things too. Considering we were in a piece-of-shit bongo van, we were travelling at breakneck speed through the twists and turns of the mountain pass. Sheer cliffs rose up on either side of the road, and it was totally crazy how the local drivers passed each other on blind corners, with blatant disregard for all sense of self-preservation. It was a case of *inshallah*, or God willing. This little phrase allows for the most god-forsaken acts of stupidity I have ever witnessed.

All Canada and I could do was laugh. We were dumbfounded as well as powerless in our situation so there wasn't much we could do but kick back with that familiar diver fatalism and enjoy the ride.

We passed dozens of road accidents and saw more than a few dead bodies mangled in the wrecks, but once again there was nothing we could do: *inshallah* indeed. As night fell and the mad Bathurst 1000 continued, we noticed the driver was chewing on something, which turned out to be a kind of root called 'gat', and apparently it acts as a stimulant not unlike cocaine. The guy was high as a kite and he was putting the bongo van through its paces in order to keep up with the company men's Land Rover out in front. He could drive, I'll give him that. Maybe Allah was on his side after all.

Trying not to look out the front window had become a self-preservation mechanism by this stage, but as we descended into the valley I caught sight of a hair-pin turn ahead and three semitrailers coming in the opposite direction blocking our path. 'Ahhh, Canada . . . Is this bloke going to stop?' Flagrantly defying all common sense and logic, our driver appeared to be accelerating!

I leant forward to express concern, for all the good it would do, but was violently thrown across the cab and right into a sleeping Canadian. As the small van turned into the chicane I was pinned by the sheer G-force of the driver's right hand-brake turn. The back of our vehicle lost traction and we slid around the corner, narrowly missing the semis and centimetres short of a death drop off the front face of a sheer cliff.

I believe fans of *Fast & Furious* refer to this manoeuvre as drifting; to me it seemed like near suicide. The driver turned around and said, 'Is good, is good!'

I collapsed back in my seat and looked for some support from my travelling companion. 'Wake me when we get there, ay' is all he said.

When we arrived at the port, the scene brought to mind that description of Mos Eisley spaceport in one of the

'Star Wars' movies – 'You'll never find a more wretched hive of scum and villainy.' After much confusion we boarded a large survey vessel – a gargantuan workhorse from Southeast Asia. I was grateful to set foot on it as Canada had dared me to walk to the local 7-Eleven and buy him some chips! I'd had to pass a gang of unsavoury-looking characters who'd eyed me off with disdain. It was clear that my presence on their turf was none too appreciated.

Following some initial kit inspection on our part, amounting to little more than radio tests and magazine loading, we immediately began our security checks and crew briefings. Interestingly, this involved instructing our fellow team members how to use an AK!

The seafaring beast creaked and growled, begrudgingly answering the foreign voices that yelled and screamed to cast off her lines and ropes, freeing her from the imprisonment of the dock and allowing passageway into the ceaseless night. Away we went. I stood on the bow overlooking the boundless reflective pond outstretched to the horizon, holding the promise of adventures unseen, the prospect of a new environment and fledgling career enough to keep me awake in what should have been a restful pre-mission slumber.

Canada and I proceeded to run the job as the boss and his mate, though we soon discovered we weren't really equipped to supervise so much as a kid's birthday party, and our local liaisons spent most of their time asleep in their cabin. The long days and nights wore on me quickly and the promise of an exciting life pirate-hunting at sea faded like so many sunsets.

After a week on the open sea, the boredom of the eight-hour shifts on deck was starting to drive me crazy. I was eating seasickness tablets like they were Tic Tacs – I'd been troubled by seasickness occasionally in the past, which though ironic for someone of my career, isn't uncommon. There wasn't a pirate to be seen for miles. But then one afternoon a small skiff was spotted heading directly for us. It wasn't responding to requests to identify itself and our radar identification system was unable to ID the vessel either. Through my binoculars I saw that the individuals were a motley crew dressed in a mismatch of jungle fatigues. On closer inspection I could make out the silhouette of assault rifles and then, the clincher: the boat moved slightly sideways and I spotted the unmistakable outline of a rocket-propelled grenade (RPG).

Canada was on the bridge seconds after I alerted him by radio. Calmly, he began trying to establish comms with the vessel, in order to get them to change direction or identify themselves. I was standing on the top deck of the survey ship next to the communications equipment. I had the drop on the skiff as I raised my AK and placed my finger on the trigger. I had expected my heart to race and my mind to be filled with questions, but neither occurred; I felt calm, ready, relaxed even.

When they were twenty metres away, I took up the first pressure on the trigger. I had decided to take aim at the guy with the RPG, as I felt he posed the greatest threat, when suddenly a voice came over the radio: 'DON'T SHOOT, OBI! They're Yemeni coastguard.'

Lowering my rifle, I'm not sure if I felt joy or disappointment; it was a strange feeling. Had I wanted to take their lives? The duality of that moment is one that echoes in my mind today. The desire to go up against an enemy merely to see who wins is an emotion I will never fully understand. Those fuckers will never know how close they came to getting brassed up either.

I got on the comms to Canada: 'What the fuck, mate?'

The coastguard hadn't identified themselves until they were right next to our vessel and even then the captain of our ship told them to bugger off. They had no right to board us and were probably looking for some shakedown money. But they hadn't counted on a couple of seasick clearance divers being on board, I can tell you that.

After seeing what the maritime security industry had to offer, Canada went back to work for his former security company and I went back to commercial diving in Sydney. But it wouldn't be long before I received a phone call from my old friend: 'Want to come to Afghanistan, you weak prick?'

'Hmmmmmm, let me think.'

Twenty-five

NEVER BEEN SHOT AT

'No need for immortal verse, those that live by honourable means, defend the bad, against the worse...'

— Poet unknown

The pistol was larger than I'd expected and looked even bigger in my small hands. It was heavy too, heavier than I'd anticipated. It was a Beretta, the same gun Mel Gibson uses in the 'Lethal Weapon' movies. Well, that's how I recognised it anyway. My frame of reference is always Hollywood movies or the inimitable *Simpsons*!

Canada had handed me the Beretta as soon as I'd stepped off the plane from Dubai; the gesture made for a memorable arrival in the dusty shanty metropolis of Kabul city. I looked around for a holster, body armour and some military equipment to gear up with; there was none.

'What am I meant to do with this then?'

'Stick it down the back of your pants, fuckhead!' Canada wasn't known for long explanations.

As I complied with his directive, I reflected that I wasn't in Kansas anymore, and shit was a little different over here.

'What's next? Is there a briefing? Some mission orders? Where are the lads?'

Naïvely, I was looking around for what I expected to be a military-like set-up with whiteboards, PowerPoints and teams of lads and armoured vehicles, equipment of all shapes and sizes. But that's not what I saw. Instead there was only a run-down mud-brick villa and an old Toyota 4×4 . . . And Canada, in T-shirt and jeans, with a smile on his face as if to say, 'What did ya expect, ay?'

Canada started to walk out the gate onto the dusty urban street. 'Let's go,' he said.

'Where we going, mate?'

'Got a mission.'

Not much of a bloody explanation.

'We have to pick up one of our clients from the whore-house a few streets down.'

You can't be fucking serious! My first real wartime mission was to be carried out with a Beretta down the back of my jocks, extracting a drunk American businessman from an Afghan whore-house . . .

Walking behind Canada I was nervous, although I doubt that this was obvious. Still, after looking ahead, I decided to move quicker and catch up to my mate. 'Arrrhh, bro, we're a little exposed out here, aren't we? What do we do if we see a bloody insurgent?' I asked as I adjusted the cool steel wedged in my waistband.

'Shoot the cunt, ay!' was the curt reply, and Canada probably thought that response was generous.

Canada appeared to know exactly what he was doing; it was if he were strolling down to the shops for a chocolate milk and a Paddle Pop. It was this calm yet confident approach that I would need to master if I was to become an effective contractor. This was a completely different scenario to anything in my military experience and I didn't have time to acclimatise. There was no set classroom instruction or four-week induction with lesson plans included; it was the Wild West out here and I had better get my shit sorted or mine would be a short career as a mercenary.

Not two months into work in Kabul, I was starting to pick it all up. One of my fellow contractors was ex-Irish Special Forces and he was shit hot. The phrase 'as flash as a rat with a gold tooth' was invented for this boyo. He was a bona fide door-kicker and had killed more terrorists than I'd shot paper ones. *Note to self: stick close to this bloke and learn what you can. Oh, and don't piss him off!*

Between Canada and the Irish lad, I was learning the trade of PSD (personal security detail). Our brief was to protect a bunch of clients from an American business firm, and although I had bugger all experience as a bodyguard, my easygoing nature and desire to educate myself helped me fit in without too many dramas.

My new company was a medium-sized one, though small compared to the likes of Blackwater or DynCorp. It was well run, with plenty of experience up top as well as on the ground; the guys in charge had been around a while and it showed.

Late one evening, one of the clients working at our villa needed to go to the UN compound, a gated community some two streets away. The other lads were still out on a job and

I was the only one in the office. Wanting to be helpful, I told the bloke that I would walk him over there. It wasn't far and the guy was toying with the idea of walking by himself, so I thought I'd do the rightie and escort him. Chucking on my dusty Altama desert boots, I opened my desk drawer, grabbed my Taurus pistol and we headed out the door.

The trip over was swift and without incident but as I turned back from the UN gate and started walking back down the street, I noticed a black four-wheel drive with tinted windows slow to a crawl and take what I believed to be a little too much interest in what I was doing. I could see through the windscreen that there were some shady-looking characters inside and straight away I became concerned. It was common for Afghanis and even Westerners to be abducted off the street by insurgents or opportunistic gangs seeking ransom or perhaps a quick political beheading: take your pick.

Changing direction I entered my street, maintaining composure as there was now a mere 200 metres to go before the relative safety of my compound. We employed Afghan locals with AK-47s so once inside I would be contained within a reasonably secure perimeter. Checking the reflection in the rear window of a parked 4×4, I noted that behind me at the T-intersection, the vehicle had slowed, turned off its lights then followed me into my street. Remember: in the jungle, always a sound; in the city, always a reflection.

I picked up my pace; my gate — and safety — were only ten metres away. When the sinister black vehicle abruptly accelerated and was almost alongside me, it clicked: a) they'd seen me exit the UN, and b) I was dressed like a Western journalist. Our intention is not to look too military and scary when escorting clients. I realised that this attire was presently making me seem like an attractive snatch-and-grab target as media outlets typically paid ransoms for any staff kidnapped while pursuing stories.

Time for analysis had long since passed; I heard the electric window descend as the vehicle drew parallel with me. Luckily, I had reached the secure gate of my villa. I spun around and in the same motion drew my pistol from my rear waistband, pointed it at the passenger-side window and took my stance. In that exact instant, the gate behind me opened and I looked the bastards in the eye as I stepped backwards and the gate shut in front of me. Our Afghan guards observed my Clint Eastwood impersonation with mild amusement.

My heart rate slowed and, to my surprise, I realised it had not been all that high during the incident. In fact I felt calm, even vaguely amused. I sort of laughed to myself as I climbed the stairs to our office. Looking back, I couldn't remember planning my actions; they were simply *reactions*. I had responded to the situation without even thinking. 'Hmmmmmmm,' I thought, 'that's interesting. I kind of expected I would be more scared.'

Strange. It's not that I was especially brave or even skilled for that matter; it's a simple case of training. A rugby player doesn't think about the tackle when someone runs at him, he just tackles the guy.

The days were long and hot. The heat – fuck, the heat – you've never seen such a dusty, oppressive place, but I was starting to enjoy it. Canada would spell out the jobs for the day over a morning coffee then we would break, grab our local Afghan security guys and take the clients to their myriad nefarious business dealings. Come nightfall we would meet up for a further brief, then take the clients to a local restaurant for dinner. It was surreal: here I was walking around the city in my trusty Converse One Stars, AK-47 slung by my side and people walking past us like it was normal.

The company I worked for was expanding and development got underway on a life support area (LSA) – effectively a base incorporating accommodation, dining and ablution facilities and so on – on the outskirts of Kabul on Old Bagram Road. We would travel out there on a daily basis escorting the clients involved in its construction, further to which it was my job to organise security for the new base and facilitate all manner of tasks relating to perimeter hardening, guard force and emergency procedures. Often I would have to go out with just my Afghan offsider to get shit organised. It was fun really, kicking around in that wide brown land, driving speedily across mountain passes, arranging my own missions. Sometimes I felt like Michael Caine in the movie *The Man Who Would Be King*.

My diminutive Afghan helper was an absolute legend; I couldn't have done it without him and I'll be forever grateful for his friendship and advice in what was often a difficult environment. I tried to teach him a few of our ways as well, especially the Australian sense of humour and the laconic attitude of the Aussie military. A lot can be lost in translation as I would discover.

One day, while at the construction site, I witnessed an incident that brought home the differences between the

Afghan culture and the Australian culture. I was checking on the security at the front gate, making sure the procedures were up to scratch, when one of the local workmen near me started having some type of seizure. Having had only a small amount of basic field-care training, I didn't know how much I could do but I rushed over, saw that the guy was in serious trouble and radioed for assistance. Instantly, his fellow workers surrounded him and wouldn't let anybody get close. Trying to reason with them was next to impossible but once I got across that I wanted to help, one of his friends 'explained' to me that the man had demons and that they would leave him alone until the worst was over, then get him to his holy man/personal priest! Summoning all my tact, I tried to explain my perspective and persuade them that I needed to get him to a hospital; however, they were having none of it.

There wasn't much I could do. They loaded the bloke onto a small truck and then took him to the mosque to see his religious leader. I never saw him again and could only hope that luck, and not religion, found him that day.

That incident really made it clear to me the situation Westerners often face in countries like Afghanistan, where the people have their own values and beliefs and don't always want outside help or intervention. Does that mean we shouldn't try to assist them when there are crushing humanitarian problems? Well, I don't know; that's something maybe only time can answer.

I started to feel an affinity with the Afghan people. I had a lot of respect for the guys I worked with as they were true warriors in every sense. That's not to say they were all hunky-dory – I ran into my fair share of 'throat-slitters', that's for sure – but the lads I worked with were incredibly loyal, hard-working and brave. Learning Afghan customs and day-to-day etiquette was difficult, however. I once offered a local warlord/businessman US$100 to hurry through some paperwork; he laughed at me and walked away. Later I found out he was a millionaire many times over, and from then on, working with him became extremely difficult. Oh well, live and learn I guess.

Kabul was a city divided. There were areas of tremendous wealth, and some of the most debilitating poverty you have ever seen. Bustling street markets would be held right next to roads lined with metre-deep culverts of raw sewage, and only two streets away there'd be three-storey villas with private gardens, servants and luxury cars. It was a duality that could be hard to get used to and one made all the more real every time I travelled home and was shocked anew by what we took for granted in the First World.

It surprises many people to know that it's not political or religious lines that divide the Afghanis; the divisions are tribal. Affinity to one's tribe appeared to be the governing principle of the locals' lives and it was an allegiance worth understanding.

In considering how to secure the safety of the new LSA, it struck me that no matter how many physical measures were put in place – be they guard towers, sandbags or weapons – the safety of the occupants would come down to one thing and one thing only: our relationship with the tribal warlords of the surrounding area. The company I worked for had never factored this aspect into their thinking, let alone – God forbid – their planning.

My Afghan offsider suggested I meet with one of these tribal chiefs – whom we would call community leaders. Although I was open to the idea, initially I was resistant to the specifics involved: driving to some unsecured meeting to mediate a metaphorical peace. Eventually, I agreed to the meeting, figuring it paid to be culturally sensitive. Although I didn't have a clue what to expect, some level of cooperation with the Afghanis was the best course of action, especially when we employed an all-Afghan guard force and we were only a couple of Westerners without any military support.

It was the late afternoon. We'd been waiting for the call all day. This bloke's people were going to call my colleague, who had tribal ties with the head honcho, and then we'd have to go and meet him in a certain timeframe in the affluent part of town.

The two of us drove as fast as possible through the crazy peak-hour traffic – dodging speeding motorbikes going in the wrong direction, past the groups of young men conducting business, avoiding the cart-slung donkeys with their loads of LPG gas tanks – then headed uphill, away from the worst of the open sewers. The change in environment was dramatic: the higher we went, the bigger the houses, the clearer the streets and the thicker the security. I looked across the cab and asked, 'Who lives around here?'

The answer surprised even me: 'The drug dealers, all the drug dealers.' I was aware of the large influence the opium poppy trade had in Afghanistan; now I was witnessing some of the direct results of all that money.

At the entrance to a large estate we pulled up, my colleague waved and the heavily armed guards let us in. I stepped out of the vehicle and did my best to follow the lead of my little mate. There were big signs of affection between him and the tribal leader; I tried to be as respectful as possible. It had been my experience so far that when conducting Afghan business deals, one has to expect two things:

1) To drink a shitload of chai
2) Virtually no discussion about the real subject of the meeting.

Everyone asked about each other's families, so I employed the tactic I always used for these situations: I explained my father was a farmer and that I came from a rural background and worked with the soil. That seemed to go down well; talk of one another's father was a popular topic of discussion, and the farming angle was solid gold.

The meeting ended abruptly but amicably, as far as I could tell. It was dark when we drove away and I was unaware of exactly what had been achieved, if anything. A day later, my offsider received a phone call informing him that we would have no trouble out at the base building site and that we were to contact them directly if anyone gave us any.

Perhaps it was a coincidence but not one incident occurred during the construction of the LSA. Like my father often said, 'Better to have them inside the tent pissing out, than outside the tent pissing in.'

The new base was a good hour's drive from our compound, past the government and military headquarters in the centre of town. To get to the LSA, we'd head along J-Bad Road doing our best not to hit the beggars in the middle of it. Mostly they were outcast females; I felt terrible for them – covered top to toe in a light blue sheet that was simply draped from their head, with a sort of grille at eye level for them to look out at the world from. Often they had kids with them, and even though it was a slight breach of our security, I would sometimes pass them some water or spare power bars that I had with me.

The drive was madness: daily pushing through the horrendous Kabul traffic, narrowly avoiding catastrophe at every interval. We would duck and weave as best we could, the skill of my local driver on show. I would be sitting in the passenger seat, AK at the ready.

This particular day was no different from any other until . . . The sound of the explosion was deafening. Instantaneously, a plume of smoke rose in the air behind us and debris flew through the air. My instruction to the driver to 'floor it!' was as redundant as my hoping he would hear me. Already he had accelerated and quickly we were well away from the area.

Later I heard that, rattled by some military activity in his proximity, a would-be bomber had been moving his IED, which was in the boot of his car, to a separate location. Not one minute after we had passed through the same intersection, the insurgent had driven over a bump in the road and, without meaning to, sent himself straight to paradise! Well, as near to paradise as the explosion propelled him in the air anyway.

This incident is indicative of my time in Afghanistan: all the action seemed to happen either shortly before I arrived or shortly after I left. I guess I was lucky and the enemy not so. I mean, it wasn't like the lads and I were sitting at home reading. Typically, our regular visits to the InterContinental Hotel on the hill overlooking the city were punctuated with mortars and rockets passing safely overhead; they didn't hit the fucken place once while I was there. On a daily basis something somewhere would blow up and all the soldiers and police within a three-kilometre radius would start shooting wildly into the ensuing dusty haze. What that was supposed to accomplish, I'll never know.

Unlike some of the other contractors – actually, most of them were more well-'ta'-do than ours – our little operation was modest. We ran out of a local villa in a suburb called Shahre Now, which was right in the centre of town. The villa was only protected by a basic perimeter of besser brick walls edged with a liberal sprinkling of broken glass and with a tangle of rusty barbed wire on top. Our local guards were pretty good but they often fell asleep and they were no defence against anybody who genuinely wanted to take it to a few Westerners. In view of this, we all slept with loaded AKs right next to our beds and had in place a standard evacuation drill and defensive procedures in case of a situation.

On more than one occasion a large bang or gunfire that was a shade too close would have Canada and the Irish lad up and coordinating a stand-to. They would yell across the room, 'Hey, Obi, hurry up and take the north face.' I'd run upstairs with my gat to a predetermined location and take up point within my area of responsibility – usually it was the arch facing the main road.

It was quite comical sometimes seeing the various security teams from the surrounding villas scramble around. It quickly became hard to tell who was who as the dust and smoke from the explosion – never that far away – would drift readily in the cool Kabul night, hindering visibility. Occasionally I would spot some gangsta with an AK and the only way to work out if he was a 'goodie' or a 'baddie' was to wave and see if he'd wave back – a tad basic, I know, but what do ya want! Then you'd spend the rest of the night watching and listening for anything of a proximity worth worrying about.

Dealing with clients was probably the least fun part of my job; sometimes it felt like I was a glorified babysitter. Nine times out of ten, their complete lack of situational awareness was staggering, to say nothing of their inability to understand basic instructions. One night we took a few of the Yanks to a well-known restaurant and bar called the Gandamak, in the more cosmopolitan area of Kabul. The atmosphere there was not unlike a 1920s speakeasy: they regularly had illegal alcohol and it was an infamous ex-pat haunt that attracted an interesting cross-section of Euro trash, NGOs and Afghan mobsters.

Well into the evening, by which time our clients were drunk as skunks, some South African mercenaries started some shit in the beer garden – it was always a Saffa. Before long, glasses were being thrown and a mêlée broke out. Canada radioed me and we started to round up our clients, who were none too pleased to be going. I was fairly composed until I heard above the noise that members of the Afghan National Directorate of Security, the feared NDS, were on their way.

These cats were not to be messed with. I knew of them mostly by reputation but had seen them about and knew well enough they were serious players. According to the rumour mill, they weren't averse to throwing individuals under interrogation off the ten-metre diving platform of a local swimming pool – sans water. Closer to home, an NDS officer who came to check our company's registration felt that one of our perimeter guards was disrespectful towards him. The officer came back the next night dressed in black and 'asked' us to hand him over – for what, I can only imagine. Luckily, the lad had had the good sense to hoof it out of town.

With the NDS inbound, my sense of urgency increased. I began grabbing these dudes we were escorting by the scruff of the neck and forcing them out the front and into the waiting 4×4. The last thing I wanted was some smart-arsed client yelling at an Afghan spy, 'Don't you know who the fuck I am? I'm an American!' You didn't have to be Nostradamus to see how that would play out, PSD or no PSD. In the end we got all our clients out, but not before smashing through a soccer-type riot escalating on the street; at one point I had Canada looking at me from the passenger seat, cool as a cucumber, yelling, 'Hurry up, fatty! What's taking ya so long?'

I could see the roadblock now, some thirty metres ahead of us; it wasn't unusual. We had taken a mountain track, bypassing Old Bagram Road in order to avoid its many stoppages as we were in a hurry. It was just another day really and I was fairly blasé – until I noticed the uniforms, that is. It was the NDS manning the roadblock and they looked pissed. Rolling down my window I gave them a friendly hello in some broken Arabic I'd picked up. This tactic usually elicited a smile from your average checkpoint and I was taken aback to see the guard's face contort into a scowl and that unmistakable face of contempt for the infidel. Me being me, I saw this only as a further opportunity to win him over with my sparkling personality, so I reached into my pocket and took out some cigarettes I held for just such an occasion. It was then I took notice of my Afghan offsider's demeanour – something I should have done earlier – he looked scared . . . really scared.

'It's okay, it's okay. All good, bro,' I said, in my customary clearance diver vernacular.

'No, Mr Obi, please. No smile, no smile.'

'Fuck me,' I thought: I'd never seen him like that.

My senses kicked fully into gear and I felt a rush of adrenaline as they ripped us from our vehicle at gunpoint, positioned us off to the side and started to comb through our car.

They were checking our equipment, pocketing what they could and thumbing our paperwork. All our registrations and licences checked out, which was a fucking miracle as that was the first week I think we managed to have all of it in order. They made their way to the rear of the vehicle and it was then I had a moment of panic. We were banned from carrying grenades or flash bangs of any sort, but it was a contractor rule of thumb that you always had a few around for a rainy day. I saw them grab a bag from the back, the same bag I usually kept such contraband in.

My mind spun and I looked at my options. Could I grab my AK fast enough? Where could I run to? In what direction? Who was my best target? . . . The possibilities flew through my brain like a shotgun blast. Then a moment of calm. What the fuck was I going to do? It wasn't the movies; these guys had two tripod PKMs (general-purpose machine-guns) set up; there was a mountain face on one side and a thirty-metre drop on the other. Unless I planned to unfurl my parachute and base jump to freedom, I was shit out of luck. Just then NDS guy emptied the bag to reveal a couple of smoke grenades, completely harmless and more importantly completely legal. We got pushed around a bit more, then they let us pass.

'For fuck's sake,' I thought, 'that was close.'

I laughed as we drove off into the desert evening, me cracking up and my Afghan friend smiling a little, but shaking and pleading for me to slow down: 'Is not funny, Mr Obi, is not funny!'

The contract ended shortly after this incident and once again I found myself at home in Sydney playing Xbox on the couch. But it wasn't long before I answered a call from Canada: 'Hey, bro, you want to hunt some pirates, ay?'

An international security company Canada had begun working for had won a contract to go into Nigeria and help set up anti-piracy operations. They had recruited Canada to sort out the details, organise manpower and so on. He had arranged for two support vessels and enlisted the cooperation of the Nigerian Navy, in theory to secure their AO (area of operations) containing oil platforms and transport ships.

The last time Canada and I had tried the maritime security game, it hadn't been much chop, but he promised me that this would be different, accused me of being a pussy, then hung up the phone; somehow my acceptance was assumed.

I arrived in Lagos, Nigeria, and felt the sweet-smelling humidity cling to my nostrils. From the outset I had had fairly low expectations and so far nothing was encouraging me to revise them. The place struck me as chaotic, to say the least. With nothing more than a backpack in my hand, I felt quite exposed as I waited for Canada to pick me up from the rudimentary airport, which wasn't unlike the Temple of Doom's foyer in that Indiana Jones movie.

A 4×4 pulled up and, looking like the quintessential white African hunter, Canada jumped out, brimming with his usual exuberance, and shook my hand. I knew he needed me to help make the job work and I had agreed to the gig mainly out of loyalty to him rather than the promise of any riches or grand desire to go back to sea.

On the trip to the hotel Canada gave me the low-down. Essentially, we would work as a subsidiary to the security firm who had done the hiring, but we would be fairly autonomous in our operation. My job would be to manage a bunch of Nigerian Navy personnel who manned the two support vessels. I would oversee the whole operation from a central position on the oil rig. Although it seemed a bit ad hoc, I could see Canada had done a lot of work to put everything together and I didn't want to let him down.

Our first task was to organise the local naval personnel. I had done this in other countries; it was not at all unusual for local military to work under the stewardship of a Western professional. It had been relatively easy in the past; how wrong I was in assuming history would repeat itself.

After procuring a small speedboat, we meandered around the corner from the oil company's port to the navy barracks. The sailors – if you could call them that – were supposed to be waiting at the pier for our inspection and introduction brief. The unmistakable thud of the sound barrier breaking snapped us from our morning complacency. *What the fuck!*

'Are they shooting at us?' Canada said.

I raced up to the bow past the small cabin and witnessed the sailors testing their weapons and jovially blasting off rounds in our general direction!

Seeing us waving at them to stop, they graciously put their 'attack' on hold while we tied up the boat and went to see who was in charge.

The only way to describe the situation is that it was an absolute cluster fuck; it was anarchy. This motley lot must have been plucked from their day jobs, given a bunch of weapons and told to report for duty at the shoreline. They had no idea what the task was or what they were even required to do.

Trying to talk to the guy in charge was a nightmare. He wouldn't listen to me and seemed to think it was all a big joke that a couple of 'white boys', as he kept calling us, were going to in any way tell him what to do.

Basically, the security company had paid some high-ranking naval officer a big chunk of money. The officer had simply waited until the day before the mission, then strolled around the base, gathered together whoever had been standing around and told them to go with us. It was a complete shambles.

Canada had not been involved in this part of the organisation; that had been left to a longtime Australian ex-pat who was as drunk as he was lazy, and consequently the entire mission seemed to be in jeopardy.

After witnessing a couple of these guys try and fire their PKM machine-gun and seeing it violently kick in the air out of control, I was concerned for our safety as well as the safety of the local fishermen not 200 metres away!

I walked down the wharf, intending to talk things over with Canada and try to come up with a plan. On my way, I passed one of the sailors; he was playing with a Sten gun – a submachine gun! – as if it were a toy. Bang! Bang! Bang! A burst of automatic fire rang out. Narrowly missing me, the rounds smashed into the water next to the moored boats. My ears ringing, and absolutely fuming, I continued down the wharf. That conversaton with Canada was going to be interesting.

'This is HQ to Support Vessel One. Do *not*, under any circumstances, marry up with V2. That's an order.'

We were barely three days into the expected month out at sea. Canada was busy at the oil company's port, organising supplies and so on. 'The Lieutenant', one of the Nigerian naval personnel, had decided he'd had enough and was attempting to take control of the vessel he was supposed to be guarding. Luckily for me he was on Vessel Two (V2) and all the weapons were on Vessel One (V1)! Trying to control a mutiny with nothing but a radio and a stern tone is incredibly difficult; I wouldn't recommend it.

Everything had got underway, with the naval personnel – who were supposed to remain on whichever of the two vessels they'd been allocated to – patrolling their designated area. Then this bloke had wanted more room so had transferred himself – under the guise of being sick – onto V2, the larger of the support boats. Unbelievably, the dumb ass had decided to start his mutiny, without all his men or any of his weapons!

From my vantage point high up in the control room of the oil rig, I could see the now pirated boat steaming towards V1. I was in communication with the captain of the captured vessel and had just instructed him that under no circumstances was he to meet up with the other craft. No way did I want to give The Lieutenant the opportunity to retrieve his AK-47 and PKM, for if that happened, we were all in the shit!

Next I established comms with V1 and informed the captain of the situation. Immediately, he began to speed away from V2, and then ensued a comical cat-and-mouse game in what seemed like a bathtub from my elevated position. At the same time as all this was going on, I was talking with Canada on Skype, keeping him abreast of the bizarre yet dangerous events that were transpiring. Fuck me, what a job.

Fortunately, between the two captains and me, we kept the ships apart long enough for the crew to subdue the rogue lieutenant and end the siege. Why they hadn't done so in the first place was beyond me, given that he'd had nothing to threaten them with other than the promise of a weapon on another boat!

Weeks passed and with them some of the dramas with the naval crew. We settled into a mild truce and just tried to get through our duties with minimal offence to both parties. The threat externalised reasonably quickly when pirates hit one of our supply boats as it was heading back to port through the Niger Delta. I was nowhere near there. Against our advice, Addax Petroleum, our employers, were only paying us to protect the AO; the fee did not cover their assets while they were in transit. I heard about the incident via a phone call from Canada; he told me a mayday call had come through from the

Swire transport vessel. Several hours later, he went to meet the vessel when it docked. Wisely, the crew had barricaded themselves in the engine room. The pirates easily boarded, stole anything that wasn't nailed down and shot up the wheel-house pretty badly. Miraculously, no one was injured.

None of this happened in a political vacuum: the pirates were in a long-running dispute with the government over the perceived rape of their country's natural resources. In particular, they accused the nation's leaders of selling out to big oil. If you ask me they had a point; nevertheless, the rule of the sea is sacrosanct, and you don't try to solve your problems with the government by harming innocent civilian sailors and damaging their livelihood.

When I think about all the different conflicts I've had some sort of engagement with and gained some on-the-ground knowledge of, it's generally been hard to determine who is on the side of right and who is wrong. Mostly, issues are messy and full of grey; it's rare to see black and white; there are no absolutes. Personally, I draw my line in the sand with regard to choice: you either choose to be a combatant or you do not. The corollary is that anyone who wishes to stay out of the game should remain unmolested. If I'm out on the playing field, then I'm fair game and vice versa; if the enemy pick up a weapon to solve their problems and harm innocents, then the enemy are fair game. Those are the rules we play by: anyone seeking to bring civilian non-combatants into things is breaking that code – it's just not cricket, as they say!

Corruption and crime were rife in Lagos and Port Harcourt, the latter being our forward operating area. Trying to arrange logistics was a bit of a nightmare at the best of times; the system of greasing of palms put the brakes on and was a pain. Canada and I were amazed that even an oil company could not organise their own support structure. On more than one occasion we stepped in, staggered at the ineptitude around us, and arranged fuel, food and water for a large part of their operation.

While Canada was on one of these fuel acquisition runs, he encountered a major problem. He had arranged delivery of the fuel to the port through a third party on the proviso that the company would pay for it. As it turned out the company wouldn't pay for the fuel until they themselves had been remunerated from the contract the fuel was supporting! So it was catch-22. Furthermore, Canada now found himself on the run from the local constabulary – he was wanted on the erroneous charge of grand larceny! The fuel had already been delivered and the proprietor who supplied the fuel hadn't received his hundred grand.

Canada and I spoke by sat phone and agreed he should move hotels, to be on the safe side. We even set about planning our E&E (escape and evasion) in the event we needed to hoof it out of the country.

The imbroglio with the fuel took a good deal of manoeuvring and some back and forth conversations but eventually the young Canadian managed to sort it out – though both of us had more than a few sleepless nights while awaiting a resolution.

Towards the end of the contract, I had to arrange my transport home, and even that was fraught with danger. It was taking forever to get a seat on the helo off the oil rig. Eventually I took myself up to the heli-pad and, with more than a bit of jostling, simply pushed my way onto the helicopter. I couldn't get away fast enough.

Another drama took place when I arrived at the airport from the rig. All oil workers were supposed to clear customs when returning from the rigs; somehow I encountered more obstructionist nightmares and was detained at the customs gate; I was facing the prospect of ending up in a foreign jail. With my phone running out of both batteries and my pockets empty of money, I sat in the sweltering holding cell hoping like hell that Canada would pick up the call on its first ring. If not, it was going to be a long night.

'You there, mate? They've thrown me in the clink! Something about a re-entry visa.'

Canada sounded calm but tired. All week he had been dealing with his own complications while trying to avoid the authorities. I'm sure the last thing he needed was a phone call from a Nigerian security facility.

'Yer, bro, give me a sec. I'll be there soon. Don't drop the soap!'

Fucking Canadians! I'm sure it was really funny to him.

Luckily, Canada arrived a short time later with a substantial bribe for the customs guy and we were on our way again, with a heartfelt thankyou from the Nigerian customs department.

I came home to spend Christmas with my long-suffering girlfriend, Alex, who had supported my decision to go on the contract as she knew we needed the money in order to set ourselves up. Deep down, I knew how much she hated me being away, yet it was only about to get worse. I hadn't been back for more than a week when an old client who I had done bodyguard work for emailed and asked if I'd like to go back to Afghanistan and run a secret operation for him. The details were sketchy but it had something to do with the US State Department, the US Marine Corps (USMC) and running trucks to Kabul's Ministry of Interior (MOI).

Well, the call had come again, and for me it was simple. I asked myself only one question in these situations: 'Will it be an adventure?' You're damn right it would! Count me in. Let's do it! Convincing Alex would be another matter . . .

This is the way it is with contract security work but it doesn't make for an easy home life. Alex and I had been together for eight years or so by this stage, and she knew who I was and what drove me to take such risks. And she was also aware that this was the only way for us to get to where we wanted to be in life. In the event, it was a case of 'Let the die be cast.'

So it was back to Afghanistan again.

Arriving at Kabul airport, I was excited at the prospect of running my own show, if a little nervous about the business side of things. I tried as best I could to get intel from the crazy American who had hired me, but it was kind of like talking to the Tasmanian devil: the guy just spun in a circle and I interpreted what I could from his ramblings.

'Ozzy, we need those trucks here ASAP.' The phone call ended, but that was all the information I required. I'd spent the day in a soft-skin (unarmoured) Toyota, trying to procure for myself some black-market body armour and a pistol; successful on both counts, baby! My driver, who I'd hired through a local Afghan company, had proved to be quite a resourceful lad, with friends in high and low places. He managed to arrange my entry into one of the most secure ministries in Afghanistan *and* scrounge some black-market weaponry the same day. Talented!

What the crazy American had requested of me was to get two truckloads of crates to the MOI for installation. They were full of secret squirrel communications equipment designed to enable the generals to talk with each other and do concurrent mission planning. The deadline for installation was the following day but I'd received the crates late from Bagram Airbase. That left me with one option: to drive them through the city at night – how hard could that be?

Everything turned out to be trickier than I imagined it would be. For starters, there was a ban on trucks entering the city limits after dark as historically, those vehicles had a tendency to explode. My trusty local colleague pointed out this small but significant fact to me during a hurried conversation as we neared the city's inner ring road. It was known as the ring of steel, supposedly for its ability to keep out IEDs; the irony wasn't lost on me.

Next thing, the Afghan police surrounded us; how long would it be before the two of us were sharing a prison cell?

My offsider got out to talk to them while I paced up and down the footpath, fighting feelings of dread about spending the next twenty years in a Kabul dungeon.

The lad returned and uttered four short words of broken English: 'Big trouble, Mr Obi.'

I asked him if anything could be done and he just shook his head. I reached into my pocket and pulled out my emergency roll of US dollars. 'Will they take a donation?' I said.

'Ohhhhhhh, Mr Obi, you have money? No problem, no problem!'

He paid off the police as I walked back to the 4×4 checking my shorts with one hand and pocketing what remained of the 'administration fee' with the other.

It only took about a week to wrap up the MOI job and I was enjoying being back in Afghanistan. I found that I liked working around the streets of Kabul. Living in the American civilian LSA, called Green Village, was kind of like being in an old western town complete with gunslingers of all shapes and sizes; it had a real atmosphere of the last frontier.

My next task was to be conducted down south in the infamous Helmand Province. The deal was that I was to meet up with the USMC and arrange the transport of communications equipment from Camp Leatherneck to the outlying Forward Operating Bases (FOBs) – Camp Delaram and Camp Dwyer. I was excited to be working with military guys again as my recent experience with civilian contractors had not been flash.

The Marines welcomed me with open arms even before they found out about my military past. They were exceptional lads and I didn't think it would be hard to arrange the logistics. I had to get my equipment quota to the camps, which urgently needed them.

'First things first,' I thought, 'I'll see if I can get this shit sent by C130 plane or even by chopper at a stretch.' This proved to be impossible, so I sat in the dusty storage yard racking my brain as to how to achieve this intricate task. The navy had taught me that giving up wasn't an option and I should do whatever I could to accomplish the mission.

As it happened, I was good friends with the DHL delivery manager at the base, a large South African lad. They had an outlet on base at Leatherneck to deliver the soldiers' mail so I hit him up, asking if he could get his hands on some Cuban cigars. 'No dramas,' he said, as I handed him the bottle of vodka I had recently procured from one of the less law-abiding areas of the base.

Next I arranged a meeting with the major in charge of transportation and slid the Cubans across the table when his secretary had left the room. He looked up from his desk and, with a broad smile and a thick Texan accent, said, 'Where'd y'all want ta go?'

My employers had told me in no uncertain terms that I was to send the equipment out to the FOBs but I was *not* to accompany them on any road moves. In their eyes, it was simply too dangerous. This was hard to argue against as Helmand Province was one of the nastier pockets of a bad land and the chances to meet your maker out there were manifold.

I met the Marines as they transferred my equipment into large connexes (shipping containers) and then loaded them onto a couple of massive trucks. The convoy would include two of their Cougar MRAP armoured vehicles front and back armed with .50cal machine-guns and MK-19 40mm grenade launchers. Good luck to anybody who wishes to play with these guys! Travelling with each colossal vehicle were four heavily armed Marines, each with years of combat experience under their belt.

As I finished the load and started chatting to the guys, my military experience happened to come up in discussion;

funny that. Then the trucks started to pull away; at my behest, they were about to undertake a perilous journey into enemy territory. On impulse, I began running as fast as I could after the trucks and I saw the back door of the Marine vehicle open up. I jumped for the platform below the door and a young Marine called 'Bushy' stuck out his hand. Grasping his forearm, I was pulled on board as the trucks picked up pace and approached the exit of the base, our last safe haven for the next two days.

'You coming now, Ozzy?'

'Yeah, bro! Can't let you guys have all the fun.'

Sitting in the back with these young American warriors, I was struck by their humility. They were doing amazing work out there for little thanks or financial reward.

A well-built sergeant looked over his shoulder at us from the passenger side, where he was navigating the mission, and asked if I was armed. I had to admit I wasn't, as I hadn't been able to bring my weapon when I flew into this particular American base. After rummaging around in his kit, he turned back to our position and tossed me his Beretta 9mm pistol. 'There you go, bro, and there's a big gat there that belongs to the gunner if things get really sticky.'

'Thanks, mate,' I said as I stuck the pistol in my leg pocket and positioned the M4 assault rifle next to my right leg, where I could grab it in a hurry. Fucking how good was this! No paperwork or OH&S bullshit here, just a bunch of blokes getting it done. *Semper fi*, baby! Always faithful!

We dropped off the equipment that afternoon and I spent one hellishly cold night on a stretcher in the army lines; in my haste to jump unsanctioned on the mission, I hadn't brought a sleeping bag or any kit. You wouldn't think it, but it gets mad cold in the desert at night and I didn't get much sleep.

Next morning, we loaded up and tore off back to the USMC home local base, Camp Leatherneck. The speed of these armoured vehicles was amazing; they flew over the dunes. We weren't using the main roads but were sort of going cross-country, as the crow flies, to the base.

Although trying not to choke on the dust kept me occupied, as did keeping my head from hitting the roof, I managed to hear the comms guy call the convoy to a stop. The front mine-sweeper contraption on one of the vehicles had broken, and the lads had to repair it before we could continue.

Stepping out into the hot sun, I was momentarily blinded. Like I said, I had no kit and that included any sunnies. I strolled over to where the guys were finishing the repairs, grabbed a ratchet strap and tried to help them jerry-rig the busted axle of their forward mine-sweeper. They were grateful and started giving shit to the guy I helped: 'Hey, looks like the Ozzy knows more than you, Tex.'

I tried to apologise for jumping in but they all had a good laugh and the repairs resumed.

When I was walking back to my vehicle, I noticed I was the only one not keeping to the tracks the trucks had made in the thick dusty sand. Why was that? Fuck! The realisation hit me: land mines.

Land mines are a big problem in Afghanistan. The Russians had spread them around like birdseed; they were everywhere, especially in these large areas between American bases. As lightly as I could, and doing my best Olympic hop, skip and jump, I positioned myself back in the wheel tracks.

'What the fuck were you doing out there, Ozzy? You crazy or sump'en?'

'All good, bro,' I said with a little embarrassment and I hastily made my way back to the safety of my ten-ton armoured truck.

OVERHEARD RADIO TRANSMISSION:

'Delta One, Delta One, this is HQ, over. Watch.'

'This is Delta One; go ahead, HQ.'

'Delta One, could you change your direction five degrees to the east?'

'Roger that, HQ; why is that?'

'Delta One, you are firmly in the centre of our mortar range and command frowns upon blowing up Americans.'

'Roger that, HQ; will do!'

In our rush to get back to base before nightfall, the lead driver had approached the entry gate from the wrong direction and we were driving through the primary target area! Fuck me!

'How close were those mortars landing?' I asked.

'Not too close; 100 yards or so.'

'No dramas,' I said, with a smile.

While I was residing at Camp Leatherneck, some major international news broke: the Americans had killed Osama bin Laden, the world's most wanted man. I was sitting in the meal room when it was announced on the news. I would have expected cheers to ring out and hats to fly into the air in triumph, but I saw none of that. It was a simple case of people's eyes rising to look at the ceiling-height TV monitors, giving a small nod and then getting back to their meals.

That impressed me: these men and women knew the score; they knew the war continued regardless, and the death of one man, however significant, would not affect the day-to-day fight they were engaged in. They were quiet professionals. I respected them for that.

I ended my Afghan days after doing several four-month trips. The toll on my relationship was mounting and I needed to spend more time at home to consolidate things for a while.

Shortly before I left Afghanistan, I received an interesting email from a friend of my brother's – a former 3RAR paratrooper now working in the private sector. It read:

'Hey, dickhead, still keen to work in Iraq?'

Twenty-six

ARABIAN NIGHTS

'It is not the critic who counts; not the man who
points out how the strong man stumbles, or where
the doer of deeds could have done them better. The
credit belongs to the man who is actually in the arena,
whose face is marred by dust and sweat and blood;
who strives valiantly; who errs, comes short again
and again . . . who knows great enthusiasms, the great
devotions; who spends himself in a worthy cause;
who at the best knows in the end the triumph of high
achievement, and who, at the worst, if he fails, at least
fails while daring greatly, so that his place shall never
be with those cold and timid souls who neither know
victory nor defeat.'

— *Theodore Roosevelt*

Iraq, ay! How was Alex going to feel about this contract? It
was a difficult and emotional discussion, but she had long
known it was my dream to go there and play with the big

boys. I had always seen Iraq as the ultimate challenge; the skills and qualifications needed to work there were always of a high standard and the war was still very much alive.

I loved Alex dearly, and the fact I would yet again be leaving her behind in Australia gave me pause for thought. Ultimately, she understood that wanting to do these trips was a huge aspect of who I am. If I were to deny that part of myself, I would no longer be the person she fell in love with in the first place. Our relationship of almost a decade has always been a negotiation between two fiercely independent and driven individuals who respect each other and the commitment we each make to our careers. As far as I could see, Alex's work, at a Sydney-based advertising firm, took every bit as much commitment and guts as looking down the barrel of an AK. Anyway, with her continued support, it was 'Once more unto the breach, dear friends.'

I was shitting myself. This was 'Welcome to First Grade, baby!' My crushing self-doubt was winning over my internal dialogue to 'harden the fuck up!'

I'd done a bit of contracting, yes, but I'd hardly call myself a seasoned mercenary. I'd landed the job partly through general respect for the ability of TAG members and partly for my minor Afghan adventures but mainly because the bloke knew my brother Phil! As they say, it's not what you know . . .

My heart was racing when the plane came in to land at Baghdad International Airport. As ever, I had just jumped off the cliff and now, halfway to the water, I was questioning my ability to land safely. But as has always been the case,

I put that to the back of my mind: think of Mr Orange in *Reservoir Dogs*, talking himself up prior to the mission: 'They don't know a goddamn thing; you're super-fucking cool.'

I'd say it took me at least a month to get my shit together, work out the intricate driving drills and master the specific set of PSD doctrine the team employed. You see, this wasn't any run-of-the-mill contract, it was an embassy contract, and for better or worse I was placed on the ambassador's team.

Working directly under the paratrooper who hired me, I was subjected to old-school 3RAR 'instruction'. He had to smash me into shape and fast. The para was a good bloke deep down, even if he didn't show it at this stage. He was a hell of a marksman, and I would continue to learn from him on a daily basis. What I wasn't prepared for was the idiosyncratic nature of Tier One, or diplomat-level, contracting. Where I'd come from it had been T-shirt and jeans, rusty AK and attitude. Here it was suit and tie, 'yes, sir, no, sir' and proper military ethos with all the trimmings. It felt good to be operating at such a level and I took to it like a duck to water. My shooting background earnt me some credits on the firing range, where my lightning-fast drills and pinpoint accuracy alleviated some of the pressure I was feeling because of gaping voids in my competency in other areas.

The ambassador was quite an adventurer, so we went on numerous trips and into places most American teams wouldn't dream of entering. But this also meant more exposure in the Red Zone, the area not secured by the military, and the ever-increasing chance of being in the wrong place at the wrong time . . .

*

When I pulled on my body armour, the weight felt good, familiar, but more than that, it made me feel like I was made of Teflon, as though nothing could touch me. I'd missed it – missed the feeling I got from voluntarily stepping into harm's way. I checked my equipment again – not for the first time today, and it wouldn't be the last time either. No doubt I was obsessive, but focusing on my kit helped take my mind off the things I couldn't control, the things that went boom in the night.

Tikrit is the home town of the dearly departed Saddam Hussein and it wouldn't be stretching the truth to say that there are still quite a few bad guys kicking around there. Our mission for the day was to escort the ambassador to a meeting with the governor of Tikrit at a government building known as the Investment Commission. Situated not far from the centre of town, the building could best be described in Aussie terms as akin to a country town scout building or Rotary Club hall.

It wasn't a bad drive. We hooned up the northern road out of Baghdad at Mach 10, instituting our customary vehicle-blocking drill, which has the characteristics of an NFL football team's modus operandi: players scramble in all directions blocking threats and ensure the fullback gets a clear run. Now we were approaching the meeting point. I was in the rear car with the paratrooper, who as per usual was giving me shit about my lack-lustre driving. Being in armoured cars was a bonus – compared to my Afghanistan days, that is – plus we had a full complement of weapons, including our SIG 552 long guns and trusty Glock 9mms. If need be, I felt we could look after ourselves.

With the ambassador safely dispatched, we settled in to wait, expecting it would take about an hour until the talks were completed. When the meeting started to drag on, I leant back in my driver's chair and popped some Guns N' Roses on the old iPod. I hadn't got three songs into *Appetite for Destruction* when I heard two large explosions, or that's what I assumed they were; the sound had been muffled by Axl Rose's dulcet tones.

To my right, the paratrooper had a worried look on his face. 'What the fuck was that!' he asked.

'Was that a fucking mortar round?' I yelled.

Both of us cautiously stepped out of the car. Not 100 metres away, in an empty lot to the rear of the commission building, two plumes of smoke were rising gracefully into the afternoon air.

Quickly getting on the comms, we alerted the Team Leader (TL), a former recon lad who was hard as nails and tough as the day is long. Chances were he had already heard the sound.

Essentially, there isn't much you can do when confronted with this sort of scenario. It's called indirect fire: it's random, not very accurate and generally not targeted at anybody. But we were the only 'good guys' in the area so we assumed those angry birds had had our name on them. This was later confirmed by our Iraq fixers. The try-hard terrorists knew we were there and were most assuredly sending their calling card.

The TL got on the comms and informed us the governor wanted to take our ambassador to his office building, about three kilometres down the road into the main city. It was an odd request; originally, we had specified that the meeting take place in situ at the commission building, as the area had been secured. However, the governor was insistent, so we prepped to move; it wasn't that difficult really.

On approach to the governor's offices, we noticed a commotion out the front: basically, the Iraqi Special Forces had the place surrounded. After some tense talks we drove through the perimeter, and the governor, with his honourable ambassadorial guest, proceeded into the building and up to his office for a chai. All of us were of the same mind: what the fuck was going on here?

With Spiderman-like senses tingling, our TL quizzed the SF commander, whom he knew from previous dealings, luckily for us. The story that emerged broke down like this: Said governor of Tikrit was wanted for corruption, as well as other Machiavellian dealings. Knowing full well the authorities were coming for him, he was using our ambassador as a kind of human shield to avoid being arrested; while he had the ambassador in tow, his building wasn't going to be searched. Another thing the wily governor had banked on was that the SF guys would back down when he rolled in accompanied by a bunch of hard-hitting contractors in embassy-plated vehicles.

In the end, we managed to defuse the situation and head home with the ambassador – no doubt with the thanks of the governor. His would-be interrogators would have to wait for another day, one without a bunch of good-natured Westerners getting in the way.

Much has been said about the infamous Iraqi roads; it is well documented how dangerous it is getting around the country, no matter by which route. By the time I arrived, the number of explosively formed projectiles had dropped off, since Barack Obama had pulled out most of the US forces, but that's not to say the roads were safe by any stretch of the imagination. The simple fact is that many contractors lost their lives in road traffic accidents. The sheer speed and danger of driving in these areas was enough to get my heart racing, I'll tell ya. Whether it was zooming along 'Route Irish' to do an airport pick-up, heading up north on the aptly nicknamed 'Route Cheyenne', or a quick trip down south to Basra just for kicks, the probability of coming unstuck was only mitigated by your driving prowess. This didn't bode well for me as I was still a ways off from perfecting the art of driving at 160 kilometres an hour.

My concentration was tested big time on a trip to Kurdistan. The mountain ranges of the disputed area of Kurdistan regional governance are some of the most treacherous in the region for driving, and the fact it was winter only made it worse. Snow had built up on the side of the road so I found myself in the surreal situation of navigating perilous icy conditions in a desert!

The objective of the trip was for the ambassador to meet several regional governors and foster future relations.

Kurdistan was interesting; its infrastructure and generally high level of civil order stood in stark contrast to that of its Iraqi neighbours to the south. The main city of Erbil was fascinating to visit. It's constructed in concentric circles, with a giant walled citadel at its centre. The citadel is the longest continuously inhabited city on the planet. It is an amazingly ancient city surrounded by a huge wall that wouldn't look out of place in an Indiana Jones movie. We contractors got a tour of the whole joint; it felt strange to essentially be a tourist for the day, taking happy snaps, then in the evening dress again in body armour, rack our weapons and cruise away in armoured cars, but that's just how it was: weird.

I cannot talk about my time in Iraq without making mention of the archaeological and historical significance of some of the locations we visited. It was a privilege to see the sites I saw – an unexpected bonus.

Under the same sun that shone on ancient Mesopotamia, I looked down at where my feet were in direct contact with the stones. I'd casually stepped up from the dusty ground and now stood on the parade road where in 331 BC Alexander the Great had triumphantly ridden into town, having conquered Babylon. As a former student of Ancient History, I was truly moved to be in that spot; few Westerners could hope to do so in this day and age, for Babylon lies squarely in the middle of Hillah Province, which remains one of the more dangerous areas of Iraq.

The history of the site highlights some of the conflicting ideologies at play in the Arab world. Various teams of archae-ologists have combed through the area and, latterly, most have tried to preserve what they've found there. But in 1983 old Saddam Hussein decided to build over the area and make it into a kind of Euro Disney! Using misappropriated foreign aid, he literally built new structures over the top of the old ones, then constructed a sprawling summer palace for himself overlooking the site.

Walking into the palace was simultaneously eye-opening and creepy. Saddam had studded the ceilings with mosaics of himself, and there were massive frescos everywhere in which he was depicted as the former ruler Nebuchadnezzar. On the outside of the palace were profiled reliefs of the dictator in heroic repose! Oh, did I mention this was all built atop an enormous man-made hill with a view across all of ancient Mesopotamia? . . . Psycho!

Although it was going to be a hell of a drive to get there, when I heard of an upcoming trip to the holy city of Karbala, I began looking forward to it immediately. It was a part of the country rarely visited by security companies. Our mission – to visit one of the holiest Shia areas in the world – was one of huge importance to the ambassador, and rumour had it we would even be allowed to tour Masjid al-Hussein, the tomb of Hussein ibn Ali, slaughtered grandson of Muhammad. I'm not big on religion, but the historical significance of such a place was not lost on me and I was appreciative of the opportunity to visit somewhere few Westerners were permitted. I'm not sure whether or not my fellow contractors gave a shit about anthropology, to tell you the truth; that is except for the TL, who was a keen student of history himself.

Made famous by the battle of Karbala in AD 680, the location had twin shrines – one dedicated to ibn Ali Hussein and one to his brother Al Abbas. When the client's PSD team, including myself, headed to the entrance of the main shrine under the guidance of the governor's people, I became somewhat nervous. One of our Iraqi interpreters was visibly emotional at the prospect of seeing the shrine. So reverent was the atmosphere that I couldn't help feeling like I was Goldi-locks entering the three bears' house, a reflection more on me than on my companions, I'm sure. I removed my footwear and was about to head towards the doorway when I glanced down and noticed my boots. They were from an American manufacturer and had two large American flags printed on the inside of the tongue flaps – blazingly obvious to all the passing pilgrims! I stepped sideways and pushed them both down with the tip of an extended toe. Hmm; not sure what might have happened there otherwise.

To say I was treading lightly was an understatement. A woman had been stoned to death here only a day or two earlier for conducting herself inappropriately and, although I am a collector of experiences, that was not one I wished to have knowledge of. After an hour of queuing, we reached the tomb itself. It was moving to see the impact it had on the worship-pers. The outpouring of emotion was something to behold; they truly believed that to touch the shrine would be to absorb some supernatural intervention into their lives. I had to respect their commitment, even if I didn't share their belief.

At the conclusion to the mosque visit, another lad and I were assigned to ready the vehicles for departure so we went ahead. The rest of our group was escorted by no less than the governor of the province himself and his security team, so odds on they would remain relatively unharmed should there be any trouble. For the two of us, it was another matter alto-gether. Moving the cars proved tricky as there were thousands upon thousands of pilgrims milling around and it wasn't hard to see we were strangers in a strange land. The crowd swelled, along with my anxiety.

I got on the comms and spoke to the bloke in the other car. He was from Sydney's Northern Beaches and responded in a broad Australian drawl: 'Yer, she'll be right, Obi. No wucken furries!' His humorous yet reductionist view of the situation did nothing to allay my concerns, but I trusted him, as he seemed to know what was up.

Next I tried to assess what is commonly referred to as atmospherics – really just a quick, subjective temperature appraisal of the situation – and I didn't think ours was getting any cooler. Again I radioed the lad in the other car and we decided to exit the vehicle and try and see what was up. Although an armoured car is warm and fuzzy to be inside, it offers limited visibility and awareness, creating a kind of false bubble around you. The worry was that because we had no identifying marks on our vehicles, as far as the crowd was concerned we could have been British or, even worse, American!

That thought was running through my head when I looked over and saw that the other Aussie operator was talking to one of the locals who had approached him. 'Here we go,' I thought. 'I'm sure my mate is filling him in on his encyclopaedic knowledge of Islam and prophet-like hold on the Arabic language.' But to my surprise the local turned around and addressed the crowd, then very matter-of-factly, they dispersed immediately and with good cheer. What the fuck! I asked what he had said.

'No worries, mate; that local was from Marrickville, Sydney. He just told the crowd we were Australians.'

Yep! No wucken furries for sure.

A major factor in this respect for Australians, which wasn't uncommon, was the soccer matches the two countries engaged in. Once I went through a checkpoint where the soldiers held up three fingers as we drove by. At the next checkpoint, three fingers again; same symbol. By the third checkpoint, after some hasty interpretation, we realised they were indicating the Under-19 Australia versus Iraq soccer score: three nil Iraq's way! If all it took to gain good will with the Iraqis was a few soccer losses, then I was all for it. Besides, I played rugby!

Working in a professional team was everything I hoped it would be, but that's not to say it was all beer and skittles. Most days were as boring as hell and consequently I became a subject matter expert on American sitcoms. What made the tedium more bearable was joking with the lads and taking the piss out of each other. I copped a lot over my 'lowly' naval origins. That little part of my history was the source of a neverending stream of insults, and a stubborn habit of referring to me as 'Scuba Steve' – real funny!

After I'd worked for the company for eight months or so, I started seeking to expand my horizons. My military experience had taught me to look for the best guys in the room and aspire to their station, rather than be content to settle with one's own. It was obvious, to me at least, that the place to be was the Forward Recon team. This was a bunch of lads hand-picked from each of the three PSD teams. Their job was to run the mission profile prior to clients being taken out. This was crucial, especially on the longer runs to outlying destinations such as Basra, Najaf, Kirkuk and the like. The recon guys were more senior and experienced – a specialised group within a group – and came to represent what I hoped to achieve while in Iraq. Hmmmmmm, you guessed it; I wanted a piece, baby. I wanted in.

The Recon Team wasn't always together because when things were running as normal, each member rolled with his usual team. It was only prior to a long run that the call-up went out and a list of appointees was emailed to those concerned.

This menagerie was loosely referred to as the Nomad Team, and if I wanted in, I would need to work hard and hope to get noticed. It wasn't like you approached the Team Leader and asked for inclusion; that was a good way to get noticed for the wrong reasons. With all this clear in my mind, I put my head down over the next couple of months and tried to do everything to the best of my ability. It was taxing: I was still learning really, and pretty far from where I would need to be if I wanted to step up on recon duty.

One day one of the Nomad guys asked me for some help with his GPS mapping and planning for an upcoming recon trip to Basra. I had developed a reputation for knowledge of Garmin GPS devices and computer mapping programs and so on. In truth, it wasn't a subject I had known all that much about but it seemed like an area that few others were keen on, so for some time I had been staying up late every night after work and studying my ass off, poring over instruction manuals and practising my coordinate plotting and route planning. The net result is that I managed to sort out the bloke's GPS for him, and to his credit he told the TL about my assistance.

The TL was the most knowledgeable operator I have ever met in or out of Iraq. Like I mentioned earlier, he had come from an army recon unit so he knew his shit. His extensive knowledge of the country and how to manoeuvre his way through its official and unofficial dealings was legendary;

not to mention his savant-like understanding of the terrain and the enemy, which was also quite staggering. The TL had already started to notice my keenness to join the team; my sought-after skill with the GPS stuff now added to the guy's positive view of me. Only days later I was shocked to receive an email stating my inclusion in the next Nomad recon team to be sent out on task.

Nervous as hell but excited all the same, I prepped my shit for the mission, checking my mags, my weapons and my grab bag, plus a few too many knives – I was a diver, remember. I was to drive the third vehicle in the convoy, the sweep vehicle responsible for all the blocking and general security for the trip.

While striking up a conversation pre-mission, I mentioned my surprise about inclusion in the team. The TL's answer was as curt as it was complimentary: 'You can shoot, and you want to learn; what else do ya need?'

'Fuck,' I thought. 'Happy with that!'

The mission was a whirlwind of learning and eye-opening opportunities. The drills were slicker, the driving faster and the expectations high, but that's what I was there for. I've always felt it's better to be a little fish in a big pond; that's the only way you get better at your job and it's a sure-fire way to keep your ego in check as well. I got smashed and embarrassed more than a few times before I was up to scratch.

After a few more runs in the ensuing weeks, I felt I was coming up to speed. I still had a lot to learn but my aspirations were manageable. When playing with the big kids in the desert, really all I wanted was to be competent. Just to be trusted to be part of one of these teams was all the success I could hope for.

The violence in Iraq was increasing on a daily basis, with up to 700 dead in any given month. The embassy was more than a little concerned. It wasn't a place that would tolerate mediocrity in its protectors. Many a sleepless night I would lie awake worrying about my ability. That is when the questions would come: did I have what it took? Would I step up when required? Was I good enough?

I don't believe I've been in Iraq long enough to comment on what is transpiring here. Suffice to say, I see it as a beautiful country marred by religious hatred and sectarian violence. Witnessing two kids playing in the rubble one day, using broken bricks as toy cars, I couldn't help but form the fervent hope that someday things might change . . . *Inshallah*.

I can say little more about my experiences in Iraq, as the people, places and companies I work for are still on operations and discussing it further could well compromise security.

On an ongoing basis I try to reconcile the part of me that loves being at home with my friends and family and which craves the contentment of a regular life with Alex, with the part that wants to ride across the desert plains tempting fate.

Twenty-seven

LAST DRINKS

'It belongs to the few...'

– HR

I hate bullies. I always have. I hate those who hold their perceived advantage over others like it was earnt, like it was their right. Throughout my life I've encountered such people and it seems to me that they only ever position themselves over people who are weaker than them. If my life in training has taught me anything, it's the power of perception and that no matter what form adversity takes, it can be beaten down with one's ability to endure.

When I think back to those times in my youth I may have felt fear, I am comforted by a simple mantra spoken to a metaphorical adversary:

Feel strong do you? Feel tough, confident and unbeatable? Now hold your breath for thirty seconds. What's changed? Maybe just a little; you're not as assured. Keep holding it for another thirty ... what's that like? How's your strength? Still there? No problem, hold it for another minute. Still able to throw that punch, score that try, sprint that 100 metres? What are you up to now – two minutes? Hold it for another minute; that's three in total. Where's your courage now? How's that confidence in your abilities going for you? Don't panic, hold on for another thirty. Still able to throw that upper cut? Still strong, are we? I have an idea: just for kicks, hold that shit for another thirty, still riding that bull, flipping that motorbike. How's that side-step going to look now? Still king of the octagon? Don't breathe for another minute . . . you're only just starting to know how it feels to be a clearance diver.

If nothing else, when confronted with adversity, when standing in front of that bully at work or school, ask yourself this: would he/she be able to endure what they are inflicting? True courage comes from the mastering of oneself, not another.

In the course of my relatively perilous pursuits in life, I believe I've acquired a unique perspective; well, I've at least been in a position to ask myself the heavy questions on the precipice of impending doom, and the answer is always stunningly clear. When confronted with the possibility of not seeing another sunset, the clarity with which I'm presented is staggering.

I just want to be with her . . . I just want to be with my girl, Alex.

My world is one of constant flux, continual environmental change and unpredictable situational occurrence – be it forty metres down in the ocean's dark embrace or standing alone, in pensive anticipation, in the desert heat. Miles from home and 'miles to go before I sleep' . . . but I'm always trying to get home, forever looking at the distant horizon, continually trying to swim back to the shore, back to where my girl is.

Ultimately, what am I to say as I end this book – of what happened, of what I've lived and of whom I've lived alongside? I've done good selfless things; I've done bad selfish things; I've never left a mate hanging; no one is the worse off for having known me; I never backed down and I've tried to make more with less. What do I want you to know?

Well, that it's doable, and that to believe what you are told is your lot in life – that it is finite – is as much a falsity as the corrupt visages of those who peddle such a message.

Don't crucify yourself on the spectre of unseen failure; remember that the glory belongs to those who tried, those who strove for more when they had no right to expect any better . . . and whisper these words: *Go on, hit me again, it matters not . . . I might not win, but neither will you, for strength lies not in what you can inflict on others but what you can endure yourself . . .*

EPILOGUE

'There is nothing to fear, but fear itself.'

— *Theodore Roosevelt*

Having just regaled you with a story of unending struggle, it might seem odd to say that the military was the greatest thing ever to happen to me, and that I have no regrets whatsoever. I enjoyed every bloody second of it and I define myself by the impact it had on my life.

Call it macabre or fatalistic, but to put oneself in harm's way for a cause or, better yet, for no apparent reason, places me in a unique position to comment on what I perceive to matter in life. And that, my friends, is love – love of life, love of family, of friends and, most importantly, love of the one you're with. The one who you wake up to, the one you come home to, and more than anything else, the one you hope you make it to the end of the fricken day just to see. That's what matters, that's what's real and that's certainly what I observed when surrounded by chaos and indifference.

Nothing in my existence will probably come close to the experiences I had in the forces. The bonds I formed exist in a vacuum, untouched, unchanged, frozen in time. I've tried to give an honest account of what it was like for me to join this elite club – despite having no discernible talent, no significant athletic ability and, what *must* be clear by now, no real clue what the hell I was doing.

The end (for now)

Addendum: The author continues to work in Iraq as a private security contractor and is looking forward to spending time with his now wife, Alex Baker, without whom this would not have been possible.

LIST OF ABBREVIATIONS

ADF	Australian Defence Force
ADG	Airfield Defence Guard
AO	area of operations
BCD	Basic Clearance Diver Course
BIP	blow in place
CD	clearance diver
CDAT	Clearance Diver Acceptance Test
CDSEC	Clearance Diver Skills Enhancement Course
COMSURV	Combat Survival Course
CPO	chief petty officer
CQB	close-quarter battle
CQF	close-quarter fighting
CT	counterterrorism
DP	dry practice
DPCU	disruptive pattern camouflage uniform
EA	emergency action
EOD	explosives ordnance disposal
FOB	forward operating base
GP	general-purpose [Australian Army clothing supplies]

GPS	global positioning system
IED	improvised explosive device
LPG	liquefied petroleum gas
LSA	life support area
MCM	mine countermeasures
MOE	method of entry
MOI	Minister of the Interior [of Afghanistan]
MTO	maritime tactical operations
NCO	non-commissioned officer
NDS	National Directorate of Security [of Afghanistan]
NGO	non-government [aid] organisation
OH&S	occupational health and safety
PO	petty officer
PSD	personal security detail
PT	physical training
PTI	physical training instructor
RAR	Royal Australian Regiment [of the Australian Army]
REO	reinforcement training
RFCR	room floor combat range (aka 'kill house')
RPG	rocket-propelled grenade
SAS	Special Air Service
SEAL	sea, air, land team (special operations force)
SF	Special Forces
SFET	Special Forces Entry Test
TAG	Tactical Assault Group; TAG (East) is based in Sydney and TAG (West) is based in Perth.
TL	team leader
UN	United Nations
VAL	validation shoot
WO	warrant officer

ABOUT THE AUTHOR

The second of Amanda and Gerard O'Brien's four sons, Hugh 'Obi' Robert O'Brien was born in 1979 and grew up on the family sheep and wheat farm, near Young in New South Wales. Obi attended Sydney boarding school St Joseph's College, a rugby academy, where old-school English customs and Dickensian group living honed his fast-developing survival skills. His lacklustre performance in both sporting and academic endeavours ingrained a sense of underachievement that would fuel Obi's later success in the Special Forces.

After high school, Obi attended university somewhat aimlessly. On the advice of his younger brother Phil, a member of the armed forces, Obi applied for the navy as a clearance diving candidate, and against all odds he found success and acceptance with these subaquatic supermen.

With an unquenched thirst for adversity, Obi applied for Special Forces with the army's counterterrorism unit, TAG (East), a secretive team of divers and commandos tasked with defending the domestic population from harm post 9/11. Admittance to this unit – their failure rate is in the eightieth percentile – was the defining moment of his life, the chance to serve where angels fear to tread and maybe, just maybe, feel worthy of the path less travelled . . .

In 2007, Hugh left the Special Forces and has since pursued a career in private security. Currently he is stationed in Iraq and recently married his childhood sweetheart, Alex.

Hugh continues to seek adventure wherever it may lie, be it pirate-hunting in the Red Sea or mentoring soldiers in Afghanistan. He believes you will only ever regret the things you do not do, and nobody wants to die without any scars.

ACKNOWLEDGEMENTS

Special thanks go to Philippa Donovan and Anne Reilly, my editors; Curtis Brown, my agents; Penguin Random House, my publisher; and my mother, Amanda, for all her tireless editorial work. To all the lads and NCOs I worked with at the School, in the Teams and at TAG, you have taught me a great many things. To my brothers, Andrew, Phil and Matt, for always being there. To Troy White and Peter Medich, my good friends, for all their support. To the members of BCD 53 'The Hellfish': you are my brothers in arms, and to Dixie Ford, for helping me realise a dream.

PICTURE CREDITS

The author and publisher are grateful to the following for permission to reproduce their images:

O'Brien family (page 1), Jason Pepper (page 2 bottom, page 3 middle and bottom, page 4 top, page 14 top), RAN Clearance Divers Association (page 2 top and middle; page 3 top; page 4 bottom; pages 5, 7 and 8; page 9 top), Chris Smith (page 6 top), Troy White (page 13).

All other photos, courtesy the author.

INDEX

Loved the book?